THE BOOK OF VOICES

ALSO BY JOSEPH ZITT:

Surprise Me With Beauty:
The Music of Human Systems

The Rounds *

Shekhinah: The Presence *

Five-Minute Friendships:
Making Human Connections in the
Landscape of Commerce
(originally published as *19th Nervous Breakdown*)

* Published by the Apocryphile Press

THE BOOK OF VOICES

Joseph Zitt

the apocryphile press
BERKELEY, CA
www.apocryphile.org

Apocryphile Press
1700 Shattuck Ave #81
Berkeley, CA 94709
www.apocryphile.org

Printed in the United States of America
ISBN 978-1-937002-92-3

Bible translations are drawn from the New International Version,
with addtional translations from the Hebrew text by the author.

Front cover design by Lauren Curtis <www.LaurenCurtisArt.com>
adapted from the first edition's cover by Travis Dixon <www.ultravisceral.com>

Book interior and back cover layout by Joseph Zitt.
The text was set in Adobe InDesign using the Minion Pro and Myriad
typefaces, with some titles in Theano Didot and Smudger LET.
Hebrew text is set in the Habakkuk typeface from the Culmus Project.

DEDICATION

*For Tom Bickley and Nancy Beckman
and for
Katherine Setar and Brad Fischer*

and

In memory of Jack Kanefsky (1910-2013)

CONTENTS

The Book of Dwelling

The Book of Singing

The Book of Struggling

The Book of Dissolving

The Book of Returning

Afterword

Translator's Preface

by Ariel Atid
Dept. of Linguistics
Frankfurter University
Boston, MA
20 September 2013

To my beloved stepchildren Justin and Emily (and all others who might read this):

Now that you are no longer children and are heading out into the world, I am sending this book out with you. It was the work of more than a lifetime for its original author. It has taken years for me to bring it to this state.

At its core, it is a book of brief stories. Each comes from a moment in the life of a person from the Hebrew Bible. I hope that you will recognize some of the names within it, though even I did not recognize all of them. Each speaks to us from a moment when that person's own life changed.

I first encountered this book a little under ten years ago, back before I met you. You may take my story of discovering it as truth, hallucination, metaphor, fiction, or "Oh, that's just Ariel." Any of these is OK.

The day was Yom Kippur, the most sacred moment of the Jewish year. I was living in San Francisco at the time. I had no interest in going to synagogue, but wanted to note the day on my own. Heading out early, I took the N-Judah train to the end of the line, a small beach where the city meets the Pacific Ocean. I settled into the nook of a hill facing the sea and turned the pages of the traditional liturgy. I read and contemplated the passages that spoke strongly to me, and avoided those that did not.

At some points, everything seemed as clear and present to me as the best experiences of being "in the moment." At others, I dozed,

1

letting the realities of the waking and sleeping worlds merge until I no longer knew, or particularly cared, which was which.

Late in the afternoon, after I had drifted away for a time, I was apparently awakened by a sense of feathers brushing against my arm. As I opened my eyes, I saw a man sitting next to me on the hill. He was tall, pale, and beautiful, with piercing eyes that seemed to continually change color and white feathers on his head where I would have expected hair. What I thought in the first moment that was a feathered shawl revealed itself to be folded wings.

I was not afraid or particularly surprised, even when he called my name. "Ariel," he said, or his voice in my mind said, since his lips did not move.

"I am here," I replied.

"I have come to bring you a gift," the voice of the angel said. "You may choose to accept it, or you may choose to decline it without fear of having done wrong. May I show it to you?"

I nodded. The angel and I turned to each other. Leaning down, he kissed me.

The kiss lasted longer than an instant but less than a moment. The touch of his lips was as gentle as any that I had ever felt. His scent bore hints of musk, of cloves, and of cinnamon.

Then he looked deeply in my eyes once again. "Do you see the gift?" he asked. "Look within your memory."

I did. There, within my memory, were the words of this book. They were in the languages in which they were originally spoken, ancient Hebrew, Persian, and Aramaic. I could recall each word perfectly clearly as I listened to them within my mind.

"You have heard legends of angels," he said, "of forgotten times. The legends are true, sometimes as metaphor, sometimes as literal fact. The kiss of an angel, after death and before birth, seals and reveals memory.

"Each of our souls is a tapestry, formed from threads of the souls of others who have lived or will live. Your soul shares aspects of the soul of the prophet Elisheva. She had the power to speak in voices drawn from others' lives. These voices can now live within you.

"Your mother brought you to this specific land, to this particular time, without ever knowing why. Here, now, with the studies that you have pursued and with the technologies that have been brought into existence, you can bring these voices back to the people of the present world, in the languages that people speak today.

"If you accept this gift and this responsibility, you will be able to bring this book into this world. If you decline, the memory of the words, and the memory of this meeting, will disappear. The decision is your choice alone."

"I will do it," I said. "I will listen to the voices and translate them for today."

The angel leaned forward and kissed me again. I closed my eyes, surrendering to his touch, his scent, drifting once again from being conscious of my surroundings.

When I awoke again, he was gone. I sat alone by the hill on the beach, watching as the sun began its descent into the ocean. After a few minutes' silence, I remembered what the angel had told me, and tried to remember the voices of which he had spoken.

There were all there in my memory, perfectly, as clearly as if the person speaking stood before me. Even now, the memory still remains.

I came home and began to translate the voices, beginning with the voice of Elisheva herself, and continuing through the fifty other voices that Elisheva brought forth and that the angel brought to me.

Justin and Emily, I know that you never met my mother, Drorit (or my father, whom I never knew). She was a wonderful, odd woman. Many thought her insane, but she never was a bother to anyone. She rarely spoke. When she did, it was in spare phrases, often aphorisms. She only learned the phrases that she needed in English very slowly, after observing other people using them. For the most part, she mostly spoke in what I gradually realized were ancient tongues. Her eyes were blind, but she always seemed to be perceiving things that none of the rest of us could see. A group of unusual women who surrounded her helped her to survive and helped her to raise me. Since her passing, I have not seen them, and miss them as the only family that I knew.

As I grew up, I never knew exactly who I was or where or even when I was born. These stories have shown me the reasons for all of this. The answer is as implausible as my encounter with the angel. You may choose to believe them or not. I find my memory, my belief, and my understanding to be a comfort, and I hold them gently within my heart.

These transcripts, these stories, show deep emotions, as they show the most difficult times within the speakers' lives. Since I met you, and met and married your father, I have meant to give this book to you. I realized, however, that I needed to wait until you had stepped away from childhood and were ready to enter the adult world.

I also realize that as you grew up, you did not learn the stories that surround these stories. Your father brought you up without religion. I have honored that, and have not imposed my religion upon you.

I have added introductions and annotations to each of these stories to help you see their context and their world more vividly. If they inspire you to investigate the texts in the Bible and the related legends, I will be pleased and eager to help you look further. But I hope that the book itself, as you hold it in your hands, will seem complete and clear.

Here is the book. Here are the memories: my memories of the voice of Elisheva, Elisheva's memories of the Biblical voices, and the memories shared by the voices themselves.

I look forward to your reading them, and to what you might learn of the many worlds in which we live, as shown within the pages of this Book of Voices.

Fondly,

Ariel

ELISHEVA (PROLOGUE)

אלישׁבע

This angel sits here, silent, forever by my side. His head is bowed, but his eyes look up toward me, here as I lie on this soft stone bed of comfort. His wings, his feathers whisper without words in the gentle breeze that flows through this sealed room.

He says nothing. I can say nothing to him, cannot speak in my own voice. But his words emerge from the silence of his heart and hover in the air, at the archway of the doors between our souls:

Speak to me.

Who are you?

Where are you now?

The glimmers of myself that remain within my mind try to retain this little knowledge of myself: My name was, is Elisheva. I am the last of these prophets, of these women, the last of my kind.

I once knew other stories of myself, but they have drifted away, lost like a song hummed by a child in a meadow in the gentle rain. Now I only know my name, what people called me, in the time long ago when there were other people here to call my name.

But now my voice is silent. Only voices of others speak from me, voices of those whose souls have touched mine, have been parts of other souls that had included parts of mine. When I open my mouth to speak, I hear these other voices, speak with these other voices.

This angel sits here silent, listening, recording, remembering. Again he prompts me, and again: Speak to me.

I hold my voice in stillness until I cannot keep from speaking, until the voice of a life from another time, another world, forces itself through my lungs, my throat, my lips.

The angel nods in silence. Let the voice flow, his soul says to mine. You speak in safety when you speak to me.

I shudder, breathe more deeply, start to emit the sounds of speech after seemingly eternal silence, with a cough, a moan, a sigh. Speak to me, the angel says. Who are you? Where are you now?

I breathe in the angel's silence, close my eyes, and breathe forth the voices of ancient souls.

THE BOOK OF BEGINNING
ספר הראשונות

Adam

אָדָם

Adam was the first human on Earth,

At the beginning of the world, God created everything that is. On the Earth, he created a garden known as Eden. (Yes, the Bible calls God "he," I don't think of God being particularly male or female, but to avoid confusion, so will I.)

The Bible tells us:

> The Lord God took the man and put him in the Garden of Eden to work it and take care of it. And the Lord God commanded the man, "You are free to eat from any tree in the garden; but you must not eat from the tree of the knowledge of good and evil, for when you eat from it you will certainly die.'"
>
> The Lord God said, "It is not good for the man to be alone. I will make a helper suitable for him.
>
> *(Genesis 2:15-18)*

So God created the first woman, Eve.

The Snake, who in those days could stand tall, walk, and communicate with humans, convinced them to taste the fruit of that tree.

God was not pleased:

> And the Lord God said, "The man has now become like one of us, knowing good and evil. He must not be allowed to reach out his hand and take also from the tree of life and eat, and live forever." So the Lord God banished him from the Garden of Eden to work the ground from which he had been taken.
>
> *(Genesis 3:23-24)*

Adam speaks as he stands in his last moment in the garden, as he watches it disappear.

Snake stands tall beside me. His bronze scales reflect the steady sun as they glisten in this constant misting rain. My left hand rests on his strong shoulder, as his hand rests on mine. "So this is the end," my thoughts say to him.

"The end of this existence," his thoughts reply. "The beginning of the next."

Around us, the garden is shrinking. All my life, it had extended throughout all that we could see, off beyond the horizon where everything grew vague. Now the garden has edges, and they are rushing toward us.

Beyond them, I can see dusty ground with infrequent, stunted shrubs. Clouds, at once both pale and dark, hide the sun and sky. Shards of lightning flash between them, as if sparks of heaven are shattering, exploding above the land. An endless curtain of heavy rain pounds down. The shrubs, defeated, are crushed even closer to the earth. The dust becomes mud, smears, runs, into gullies and puddles that make the ground look even more treacherous, even more grim.

"What happens now?" I think to myself.

"Do you really want to know?" Snake replies.

I turn my head to look at him. "Do you know?" I ask. "You know the future?"

Snake does not turn his head. He stares more fixedly at the garden's edge. "Some. Not enough."

"Did you know what would happen—"

"When I did what I did? When I... gave you that fruit?" His mind becomes clouded with pain, with memory, with flashes of guilt and anger at our God.

I shift my hand from his near shoulder, sliding it gently along the scales of his back, until it embraces his far shoulder, drawing him closer to me.

His mind clears, the pain replaced by sadness, heavier, dense. "No." He sighs. "I thought I knew, thought that the fruit, the knowledge would bring you joy, instead of... this. God told us that it contained the knowledge of good and evil. But all that we have come to know now is how much we do not know. Everything—the garden, the world, the future—with just that one taste of that enticing fruit, everything has changed."

"I had—I thought I had loved God," I think. "How could he have done this to us?"

Snake's mind darkens again with another inverse flash of anger, of pain. His tongue lashes out into the air in front of him, slashing through and disrupting the misting rain. "This God fooled you, tricked you, though when those who come after you tell the story they will call me the Trickster. They will come to hate me, to fear my children."

"I could never hate you, could never fear you, my wisest friend," I think.

"No, but only you will ever have shared my thoughts, shared my heart, you and Eve. The others, your children, will only know second-hand whom I have been. They will only know the thing that I will become, the mute, hissing, slithering serpent that will haunt their dreams. They will only know that once we could communicate, that once I was this God's pawn, his instrument, as he forced you out of this garden into the harsh world that rushes in toward us. They will hate me for the pain of being pushed into that world. Some will even blame me for the pain with which your children will be born into that world, pushed through blood and screams and tears from the warmth of their first home into the harshness of the world of the rest of their lives.

"And I will never be able to speak to them again, not even to explain, not even to apologize. My kiss will kill them, and they will crush my head beneath their heels. I will be forever on the move, forever on the run, forever leaving my skin behind and starting out anew. But I will never be able to escape the hatred that they will feel, the guilt and the regret whose embodiment I will forever have become."

The storm, the sodden desert, are closer now. Standing in silence in Snake's embrace, I can feel drops of colder rain, wisps of harsher wind biting through the barrier, slicing into the garden, lashing us with hints of what lies outside.

I look up at Snake and wonder whether the streaks of denser water on his face are rain from the impending world or are tears. "Must all my children hate you?" I ask.

"Some may come to worship me," he replies, "to build icons of me that glisten in the sun as I do now. But that worship will come from fear, not love. Some will dance with my children, or will play music that forces my children to dance. But they will do so out of daring, of bravado, to try to convince themselves that they do not fear me.

"Some will come to handle my children in worship of this trickster God, believing that their faith in him will protect them from my children's kiss. And as my children whisper in their ears, mix their sound with the music that your children find holy, new languages will break forth that our children will not understand, will completely understand. Together, they will break out past words and return to this communion that we now share."

"And, one by one, our children will join together, toward a world we can share in love?"

"No." He sighs and his head, his scales brushing against my skin. "That moment will end, and they swiftly will forget. They will return to their battle, return to their hatred."

"Forever?"

"I do not know. The future that I can see ends sometime, though I do not know when, and I cannot see what lies beyond it. Perhaps all is destroyed, all is for naught. But perhaps..." He pauses, closes his eyes.

"Perhaps all will be healed someday." He speaks slowly, tentatively. "Perhaps your children, perhaps mine, perhaps this God will find some way to put things back together, to put things right. Perhaps what we have come to know from eating that fruit is not the end of knowledge but its beginning. Perhaps we are being sent out of the garden to learn, and when we have learned what we must, we might return to the garden. The garden might return to us."

I look down, then look up at Snake, and see that he is, indeed, crying. I turn and embrace him fully. He holds me in his arms, as I hold him in mine.

Then I hear a massive, terrifying, rushing sound. I look down and see the edges of the garden a long stride away, an arm's length away, a step—

And then the ground drops from below me, one, two hands' breadths, and I fall into a puddle of mud where green grass had been. I hold Snake more tightly within my arms, but feel his skin collapse, hollowed. I roll to my knees and kneel. The harsh rain pounds my head without mercy. Flashes of lightning and explosions of thunder surround me as I kneel, helpless. The clothes that we had fashioned from the leaves of the garden are thrashed by the rain, shredded, peeled away, until I am again as naked as I had been for most of my life.

I kneel in silence, not knowing what to do. Then I feel something writhing against my arm. I open my eyes. It looks like Snake—it is Snake—but small, crippled and diminished. He has no limbs, no arms, shoulders, legs, just a long body that moves in an ever-changing line against the ground, against my arms.

"What can we do now?" I think to him. And I realize that he can no longer hear my thoughts, that I can no longer hear his. My mouth opens and tries to speak aloud, but I have no language, no words.

The small Snake slides up my arm, faces me, strokes my lips with his hissing tongue, and I understand what he means: I will need words now to speak.

Snake slides down to the ground, to his former skin, now inert beside me. With his fangs, he grasps the underside of where his head had been and pulls down, slicing an opening past his arms, his belly, his legs.

I know what he means me to do. I stand and slide my arms into the skin of his arms, my legs into his legs, pull the skin of his head over mine. I look out, protected from the rain, and see Snake slithering away from me.

At the nearest shrub, he slides upward, wraps himself around a limb, and shakes it. Fruit, hidden by the spare leaves while on the tree, drops to the ground. I look at the fruit, wonder if it is forbidden or not, then shrug. I am already in the harsh world. I will eat what I can, what I want.

Looking farther from where I stand, I see that there are breaks in the clouds, spots of drier land, places where the sun shines down. And in one of the drier spots, not far away, I see another person seated beneath a tree, the only other person, the one that God had named Eve. She is safe, unharmed from when she ran screaming from me, from Snake, from the knowledge of good and evil, from the knowledge of what we had done.

I know that that knowledge has followed us now, that it did not die when the garden disappeared, and I know that we have much more to learn. I will have to communicate with her, to let her know that all may be well.

For that I will need words, will have to build language. I reach back in memory and find an idyllic moment:

Snake and I sit on the ground beneath that fateful tree, in the timeless time before Eve arrived. He and I have discovered that I can use my breath, throat, and mouth to create sounds, more subtle than those made by any other animal. At first I only use my voice in song, sounds with no meaning other than the joy of the singing itself.

But Snake challenges me to create brief images in sound to depict the other animals. Enjoying this game, I create words, create names: a great beast, lying beside us, his mane ruffling in the breeze, becomes "ari"; a smaller, woolly creature that it nuzzles, that it cradles gently with its broad paws become "seh"; a tiny bird, lithe and fragile, becomes "drorit."

I recall these words, and remember those that God used in building these worlds.

I test my breath, my lips, my tongue against these words, give them sound. I speak these words, at once sacred and mundane, and know that with these words my new life begins:

Light.

Day.

Night.

Heaven.

Earth.

Ocean.

Life!

For comments and discussion about the tale of Adam
and to hear the audio version, please visit
http://www.thebookofvoices.com/Adam

THE WIFE OF CAIN

אִשָּׁת-קַיִן

The Wife of Cain is a paradox. Logically speaking, she shouldn't have existed.

Not long after they were banished from the Garden of Eden, Adam and Eve bore two sons, Cain and Abel.

When the two sons were grown, each offered a sacrifice to God. God appeared to prefer Abel's sacrifice. Cain was angry and killed Abel. God then banished Cain from his home.

The Bible says:

> So Cain went out from the Lord's presence and lived in the land of Nod, east of Eden. Cain made love to his wife, and she became pregnant and gave birth to Enoch.
>
> *(Genesis 4:16-17)*

If there were no other people, then Cain couldn't have found a wife. (There are, however, theories that he simply married one of his sisters whose birth hadn't been mentioned yet. That happened rather often in the earliest days, and God apparently considered that OK back then,)

The Wife of Cain speaks here in the moment when she first appeared to Cain, in an origin both earthy and mystical.

I slide down from atop the man, feeling the damp earth for the first time, remembering how it will feel when I feel it again. The man and I are also damp, damp with sweat. I remember that his name is Cain. He is breathing heavily, eyes now open, smelling the way that I remember that men who sweat will smell.

After a while, his breathing slows. He turns his head to look at me. "Who are you?" he asks.

"I am your wife."

"Yes. But who are you? Do you have a name?"

I think. "The stories don't tell me of one."

"Where did you come from?"

"I come into being in your embrace. I am here at least until Enoch is born." He frowns. "Enoch?"

"Our son. We have a son."

"We have a son now?"

I frown, too, then remember that he has a different sense of time. "Our son has begun his process of existing. He will be born soon."

"Born?"

I rest my head on his outstretched arm. I place my hand on his breast, so flat and hairy where mine are round and smooth. "You learn these things in time. And you do have time."

"Yes," he says. "Though I have little else."

"You need little else," I say. "You find plenty of food, water, shelter, here in this land of wandering. What do you lack?"

"I am alone. Since Abel, my brother... since my family..." He turns his head abruptly. "But you are here. Am I no longer alone? Do you remain with me?"

"For a while," I say. "You will no longer be alone. And when I am gone, there will be Enoch."

"A son," he says. I nod. "The son will be... born? To you? As my... my brother was born to my mother?"

"Yes. And as you, two, were born to Eve."

He closes his eyes, thinks. "So this is how it works? Women appear in men's embrace, and boys are born to them?"

I laugh. He wrinkles his brow, starts to say something, stops, starts to smile, frowns instead, and closes his eyes. "This is not how it works?"

"I see why you could think that to be so," I say. "Your mother did appear in Adam's embrace, as I appeared in yours. But girls—that's what women are called before they grow up—are also born to women. You have sisters now (that's what women born to your own parents are called) as well as another brother, though you never get to meet them."

"Then you were not made from my rib, as my mother was made from my father's?"

"Let's see," I say. I touch my finger to his belly, just below his rib cage, and run it over each of his ribs, up the left side and down the right, as if I were playing a zither. "They all seem to still be there."

"So did God create you so I would not be lonely? I thought that God was angry with me, and had punished me by making me alone."

"Yes, God was angry with you, and he did punish you. But the punishment is to help you learn that you can never again do to another person what you did to your brother. And, maybe more important than that, he wants you to learn that you can learn, and that other people can learn, too."

"Yes." He nods. "But why?"

"When you raise Enoch, you have to help him learn. And there are times when you are angry with him, and you have to punish him—but not too much, just enough to help him learn."

He nods again, then lays his head back and looks at the sky. The few clouds pass slowly, revealing the nearly full moon.

"These things that you remember," he says, "these things that have not yet happened... had they happened already in your past?"

"I have no past," I say. "I begin—I began here. Now."

"So how do you remember?"

"There are stories. They are my memory. I don't know how I know them."

"Stories? Told by whom?"

"In future generations—"

"Generations?"

"In future times, just as your parents bore you and I bear Enoch, Enoch has children who have children who have children. Those people tell stories to each other, and they believe that these stories are true. And sometimes, when you have so many people believing a story, strange things happen. The past can change—that is, things that didn't happen can turn out to have happened after all. And where the stories don't make sense, things happen to make them work correctly."

He nods. "And you came from the stories?"

"People tell stories about you, Cain. They tell the story that you had a child. For you to have had a child, you have to have had a wife, or a woman of some sort around."

"Why?"

I rest my hand on his chest again. "This is another thing that you have to learn. Actually, I'm surprised that your parents didn't teach you, though, come to think of it, they may not yet be clear on the connection themselves."

He smiles. "I have a feeling that I may enjoy learning about this."

I smile, too. "Yes, you will. But that you have a child in the story presents a problem: since you are alone, off in the land of wandering, there is no woman there, here, to be Enoch's mother. So I appeared."

He turns his head and looks deeply into my eyes, trying to understand more than even I understand. I return his look, and we remain there, silent, for a long time.

Finally, he breaks the gaze and looks off to the east, where the sun is rising. "So what do we do now?" he asks.

"What do you want to do?"

"What we were doing when you appeared?"

I laugh. "There will be plenty of time for that. But there are many things that you have to learn so that you can be a good father to our son. You need to have food for him—"

"I find food here in the fields. I can find more for him."

"Yes, eventually. But at first he is not able to eat as you do. He needs milk."

"Where will I harvest that?"

"Do you see those goats there on the mountain? They create milk for their young ones. I will teach you to befriend the goats and how you might get them to give you their milk. And you will need to make clothing for the cold and to build shelter from sun and rain."

"How do you know all this? Is it in the stories?"

I try to remember, but find a blankness between knowledge and memory. "This body that I wear seems to have memory of its own."

"Your body is not you?"

I open my mouth to reply, but can't find an answer that precisely fits that question. I close my mouth, close my eyes, and answer, more roughly than I intend, "It is me now. I don't know how it fits elsewhere in time."

He nods. "I have a lot to learn. We have a lot to learn."

"Yes," I say. "It is time that we begin."

And time passes from there. Memory accelerates, and not all is clear, not all is memorable. But I do teach him these things, ways of taming goats and collecting their milk, ways of weaving together branches so that he can shelter himself from the sun and rain. And most importantly, I show him the way of sharing his world with another, to speak and listen, to feel and to know what others feel, and, when his anger flashes as it did toward his brother, to know what he is feeling and what he must not do. And he marvels at how his world changes with time as wisdom grows within him, much as my body changes as Enoch grows within me.

Then, as if an eternity has passed, as if no time has passed at all, as the world has grown cold and warm again, as the rains have come and gone, as the days, which were long and hot when we met, have shrunk then returned to being at least as long as the nights, I awaken in the long moment before sunrise to see him sitting, already awake, his long hair illuminated by the once again full moon.

"Are you thinking?" I ask.

He looks back at me, then turns around to face me, away from the cliff that looks down on the meeting of the rivers. "Yes. Of you." He smiles, more easily than he had when I first appeared, but with hints of fear and sadness in his eyes.

"What are you thinking?"

"That, as you will say, you will be gone soon, and I will be alone, alone with Enoch to raise. And I fear that I will not be able to remember you clearly, that you will fade, appearing, like my brother, only in dreams."

"How can I help you remember me? What helps you remember other things?"

"When I was young and I had to remember things," he says, "my father would bless those things with words, would create words for them, would give them names. I wish you had a name. But I am not good at creating them."

"And the stories have no name for me." I sigh and try to create an answer, try to remember how I best remember things myself. "Could you connect me in your memory with something else that has a name?"

He looks around himself. "With what would I connect you?"

I pause, thinking of a response. "When you picture me in your mind, what do you see? Where am I?"

He closes his eyes, frowns, waits, and smiles. "It is the morning after you appeared. I awaken and see you clearly for the first time. You are standing, looking over the cliff, one arm embracing that tree. When I see you in my mind, I see that tree alongside you, as if you and its spirit are somehow one."

I close my own eyes, easily picturing what he sees. "And that tree, or trees like it—did your father give it a name?"

He looks back at the tree, then up at the sky. "My father never liked trees much. But he named this type, if I recall. He saw that I loved playing under the tree and gathering its fruit, and he named it the Tree of Happiness: 'Asherah.'"

And I laugh, long and loud, surprising him, worrying him. "Is that a bad thing?" he says. "Is the name laughable?"

"No, no," I say. "It's just... yes, I now know how an old story now begins. Yes, call it Asherah, and remember me, too, as Asherah, so whenever you see that tree or others like it, you will remember me."

I creep over to him and put my arms around him. He buries his face in my hair and whispers "Asherah... you are my magical, my beloved Asherah."

Then, after another moment, long enough to allow the sun to cast shadows of us onto the ground, I look up suddenly, gasp, and wince. Cain looks at me, frightened. "Is something wrong?" he says.

"No, all is right. But Enoch will be here very soon."

And we proceed in a blur of activity, getting everything ready, reciting what needs to be done. When the time comes, everything happens more quickly than I had feared. Enoch joins us, emerging from me, then crying out with a sound that pierces the evening, that summons the ravens to join in his calls.

Then it is night, and Cain and I sleep side by side on a goatskin on the ground, our baby nestled between us. As the moon rises, I feel that I am fading. I see that I have become translucent. I can see Enoch clearly through my hand where it rests on him.

I awaken completely, though Enoch and Cain still sleep, the baby comforted by the sound of his father's breath. I think of awakening him to tell him that I am going, but I have never taught him how to say goodbye.

So I quietly rise and go to stand by my tree, the tree that bears what has become my name. I rest my back against it, place my hands on its branches. I can see its roots through my feet, its leaves through my arms. I feel myself falling, fading backward, upward, downward, inward, into the tree, and out, out through its roots into the water, into the ground, out through its leaves and flowers into the air, the mist, the night.

And I feel the stories calling me again, and I dissolve into the matter beyond matter from which myths and gods are forged. I wait, always ready to return, remembering or not, to the world of appearances, whenever truth or necessary fiction once more need to be given life, to be given flesh, to be given form.

For comments and discussion about
the tale of the Wife of Cain
and to hear the audio version, please visit
http://www.thebookofvoices.com/WifeOfCain

JAPHETH

יפת

Japheth was a descendant of Adam and Eve, some eleven generations later.

Adam and Eve eventually had many more children after Cain and Abel, as did the children of Cain.

In the years that followed, angels frequently walked the Earth. Some bore children with humans. Many of those children grew to be giants.

After ten generations, God saw that the people of Earth had become evil. He decided to destroy most of the animals then alive and to start over.

God warned one person, Noah, of the destruction to come. Noah, his family, and the animals that he was able to save boarded a huge boat, known as the Ark. When God unleashed a massive flood that covered the entire Earth and drowned everything that lived on it, only the people and animals on the Ark survived.

The Bible says that:

> The sons of Noah who came out of the ark were Shem, Ham and Japheth... and from them came the people who were scattered over the whole earth.
>
> *(Genesis 9:18-19)*

After the flood, Noah's youngest son, Japheth, set out to recover and rebuild what was left on the once-drowned land.

Japheth speaks as he travels the Earth on this mission.

Reaching out, reaching high into the night to touch the sky, to touch your stars, I fall again to earth. Here, in the mud, the dust, the ash, I cry, cry out your name. Nothing echoes, here on this sodden plain that we once knew as desert. My voice fades into emptiness, heard only, if at all, by this angel and by the moon.

Each ray of light cast through the dark brush here paints shadows of your form, spells with images of branches the letters of your name. I close my eyes and see in my internal sky the grace of your dance, hear within whispers of wind the streams of your song, feel in the tracings of the rain your hands as you once touched my face, my tears as I heard you leave, the waters as they swept away what I dreamed would be our home.

But when my eyes open, all I see are bones, bones upon bones.

The bones are my life, my destiny, my never-ending job. These fragments of things, of people, litter the landscape, take the place of all that had once lived (a year ago, an eternity ago), take up the space of all that must now live again. I try to keep them abstract, to think of them as simply trash that must be burned. But some are unmistakably human (a skull, a jaw, a hand), and each of these has paralyzed me with momentary grief, with overpowering terror, that they might have been what my heart seeks, that they might have been part of you.

But now, then, this morning, as I made my way over these hills and down toward the meeting of the rivers, I heard what I had never heard before in my wandering: a human voice (a voice that I thought was human) coming from beneath the bones of the giants that lived here before the catastrophe. And as I grew closer, I grew more sure that it was real, more sure that it could not be real, that my mind had truly been taken. For the voice was calling out the name that echoes forever in my heart, was calling out your sacred name: "Istahar!" the voice called, rasped, whispered, sang, cried, "Istahar!" over and over, not breathing, not ceasing, "Istahar!"

I ran to the bone pile and began to pull it down, straining with the weight of the bones (each not only longer than those of a man but far broader and more dense), pushing them off the pile one by one until the morning light revealed a face.

"You are alive!" I cried.

"No," it said, then "well, yes. Alive… if I am to be as you are than I am alive. It appears that I cannot die. So yes, I am alive. Are you alive? Are you from the ark?"

"Yes, I am alive," I said. "And yes, from the ark. But how did you know of it?"

"Back when I could fly, I traveled over your land, and saw Noah building the ark. Are you Noah? No, too young, you must be... a son?"

I nodded. "Yes, a son. They call me Japheth. I haven't heard anyone call my name in a long time. But I still am Japheth. And you?"

"I am—I was Shemhazai," the face said, "Though I have not heard my name in an even longer time. I have been lost in another's name."

I did not respond, did not want to acknowledge (to myself, to him) that I knew the name that he had been calling. I continued pushing the bones off the pile, watching them roll down, hearing their dull, hollow ring as they caught the wind and struck the ground.

As I got to the bottom of the pile, down to where he lay, I saw feathers stretched out to either side. As more bones rolled away, I saw that the feathers were connected to the man (not exactly a man) pinned to the ground. I laughed aloud as I saw the wings, then quickly felt guilty for the laughter. "I'm sorry," I said. "But yes, I do understand how you survived. You are an angel. You lay under the waters not needing to breathe."

As I rolled the last of the bones away, the angel shrugged the dirt from his wings. Scraps of linen draped over him from what had been his robes. These fell away as he rolled to one side, pressed first his hand then his knees against the ground, and stood. He was tall, not as tall as the giants, but far taller than me. And all aspects of his form were impressive.

The angel noticed me staring at him, and shifted his wings so that they covered him, shoulders to knees. He smiled. "I am used to this. Few humans ever see angels, especially without our robes, and yes, we are (I say objectively) beautiful." He looked around, then up at the sky. Seeing the last of the stars fading in the morning light, he flinched in apparent pain, in recognition, and again whispered, almost in a moan, "Istahar!"

"Istahar!" I echoed, not meaning to do so, not able to keep from doing so.

The angel looked at me, understanding me, as I understood him, more deeply than we could acknowledge. "You, too?" he asked.

"You?" I replied.

He nodded. "How? When?" he asked.

I sat down heavily on a stack of the larger bones. "Nine years? No, now ten—we met just before sunset on the third day after the full moon of the month after the summer solstice—yes, I precisely remember the date.

"I had seen her before, drawing water from the well, her long lovely hair (the deep purple-blue that blessed the hair of all the children of Cain) shimmering in the breeze. I had seen her before, and we may even have spoken.

"But at that moment I heard her sing, a quiet song, a song that she had made up herself, that she sang to herself. And that song pierced my depths, exposed the workings of my heart as a blade exposes the seeds of a pomegranate, showed to me in joy, in agony, all that was missing from my life. And being near her, my life seemed suddenly complete, and I could no more be without her than I could be without my own blood, my own skin.

"I ran to her, told her that I loved her. She was taken aback, said that she could not love me, reminded me that the children of Cain could not love the children of Seth, could not marry them. But I told her that I would be devoted to her for the rest of my life. She smiled, laughed gently (the bells of her laughter singing out as if to sketch in outline the vastness of this love), and went back to singing."

The angel had sat down, too, his elbows resting on his knees, his wings retracted behind him. He touched his hands to his face. They drifted to his temples, to his ears. I could tell that he, too, was remembering your song. "How long were you... were you and she..."

"Together?" I said. "We never were together. Though I devoted myself to her, would drop everything in my life to run to her if I heard her voice, the closer I grew to her, the farther she pulled away.

"We never... we touched only once, once when we were by the well. She had dropped one of her buckets (though her image dances wondrously in our minds, she was not completely graceful in real life). I had bent to pick it up for her, and my hat fell into the bucket. She picked it up from there and placed it on my head. As she adjusted it, her hands brushed across my face. I dropped the bucket myself (I was never graceful, either), and reaching up, held her hands in mine, told her that I loved her, told her that I could not live in her presence without being with her, told her that I could not live without her, told her that I knew that she could love me, asked her to accept being loved.

"She pulled back, said that she had to get home, filled her buckets and departed. I didn't... I never saw her again. And some days later, word reached me that her father had sent her to the city at the meeting of the rivers, though nobody knew why."

The angel nodded and smiled. "And you did manage to live without her."

"Yes, I did, though more from the sheer habit of living than from any effort to do so. That, and from remembering that she had made me swear to her, one time when my passion and despair had worried her, that this love would never cause me to harm myself. I lived, and my father found me a wife, and we have had sons and daughters. But my wife always knew that my heart was never fully hers, and when I went off on this mission to gather and burn the bones, I could tell that her sadness was tinged with relief."

"And now you are here..." the angel said.

"And now I am here, and I do my work, and I continue to dream that I might meet her again, though my heart knows even better than my mind that she must have... that she must be..."

The angel reached out and touched his hand to my shoulder. "And now I, too, am here. Have you heard the legend that one never meets an angel by accident? The legend is true."

"How did you know her?" I asked. "How did you come to love her?"

He leaned back, rested his hands on the ground behind him, closed his eyes, and sighed. His wings spread then closed again, fluttering behind him, their tips, seemingly without his knowledge, tracing your name in the dust.

"It was here, by the meeting of the rivers. She had been here for some years when I came to earth, sent to deliver a message to the king of this city that God wanted him to change his ways. (It didn't work. It rarely does.)

"I was walking among the people, my wings concealed, when I, too, heard the magic of her voice. And I went to her, told her that I was an angel, and that her song was greater than any that I heard in our choirs.

"She was flattered, but aloof, unclear (as humans so often are) of how to respond to an angel. I told her that I could love her every bit as much as a human would, that I could show her joys like heaven.

"She ran off, but I encountered her again and again here by the rivers. I told her that one never meets an angel by accident, that we must have been destined to meet.

"I lost my heart to her, though my mind could not tell why. When I sat with the chiefs of the angels, with Gabriel, with Metatron, to seek their counsel, I tried to see her through more objective eyes. And I saw that she was not the most beautiful, not the most gracious, not the most compassionate of people, that her voice was not the most lovely, that she could be terse, could be petulant, and that it seemed that, no matter how many angels or men were captured by her song, she would not let herself be open to them, would not let herself be loved. And they told me to follow my heart, but not to forget my mind, and to remember that with love comes blindness, that with yearning comes fear.

"Then one night, I came to her, threw myself to the ground, brushed her feet with the tips of my wings, and asked her what I might do to show her that the heart of an angel was hers, to convince her that I might show her heaven.

"She backed away, then stopped, as if hovering, thinking. Then she stepped forward, knelt on the ground next to me, and asked quietly, 'You can take me far from here, from this ugly city? You can take me to heaven?'

"'I can travel between heaven and earth,' I said. 'With the right word, I believe that anyone can.'

"'What is that word?' she said.

"'It is a secret name of God,' I replied. 'But we are forbidden to tell it to anybody.'

"She looked at me for a long time, then shrugged. 'If that rule is stronger than your love for me,' she said, 'then you do not really need to be with me. I should have known that,' she said, then laughed, as if in derision, the shards of her laughter slicing through my heart.

"'Wait!' I called out. 'I will tell you!'

"She came back, and I sketched the thirteen letters in the dust. She looked at them carefully. 'I say these out loud?' she asked.

"'Yes,' I said. 'But quietly, so that no one else may hear.'

"She looked at them, then looked up and gingerly, quietly, whispered the secret name. And a small whirlwind appeared, formed around her, obscured her. It roared in my ears, scrambled my vision, spun out the scent of ten thousand sacred spices, then swiftly calmed, faded, disappeared. She was gone.

"My heart leapt in the knowledge that she was now in heaven, waiting for me. I opened my mouth to call out the secret name—and no words came. My memory of the name was gone. I looked down on the ground where I had written it, but the whirlwind had erased my letters, smoothed the dust down to form an unreadable glassy sheen.

"I frantically tried variants of what I could remember, dredged my memory for scraps of the sacred name. But all was forgotten, all was gone. In that moment, I knew that the number of beings who could know the name was finite. In giving it to Istahar, I no longer had it for myself.

"And so I remain here on earth, trapped, immortal, walking the earth in mourning, trying to find how I might survive eternity without Istahar."

He fell silent, his head bowed, his wings trailing limply behind him. I put my hand on his shoulder, as he had put his on mine. "So she is in heaven now? She is not... she is an angel?"

He smiled faintly, looking again to the sky. "In heaven, yes, but not an angel. When the other angels found me, they told me that yes, she had ascended, was no longer on the earth. But once in heaven, she could work no magic on the angels, and never did fit in. Her laughter grated on their ears, and her songs, sung in her human modes, clashed with the songs of angels. She could not stay in heaven, but, being a human who had seen heaven's secrets, could not return to earth.

"So they found a solution, found a way to keep her in the heavens, happy, looking down on the earth. She became a set of stars, a constellation. See, that one, close to the horizon, its stars winking at the rest of the sky. That, now, is my—is our Istahar."

The angel fell silent. We sat and looked at your stars, at the horizon. When a cloud drifted before us, breaking the line from our gaze to the stars, he spoke again. "So when the floods came, everyone, everything else died, everything except the fish and what your father saved on the ark. But she, alone, escaped.

"For months, I walked then swam around this land, still an angel, not needing to breathe, not able to die. Eventually, a sudden current swept the bones of these giants on top of me. I lay here until you appeared to rescue me. But lying here, I realized that I was in exactly the right place, since I could see Istahar, the stars that had been Istahar, in their place in the sky, winking at me in what I have to believe is loving thanks, the shimmering of the stars echoing the rhythm of her sacred laughter."

"So she is immortal!" I said. "The stars will be here forever!"

"In time," the angel said, "even the stars must fade. But that may not be until the end of days, when all names will be revealed, when all will know God's secret name, when all souls will be reunited into one supreme soul, when all the pieces of souls that inhabit men, inhabit angels, inhabit, yes, the stars, will return to being a perfect whole."

I looked up at the sky, at your blessed stars, strove to say something, but only one word came to my lips. In perfect unison, the angel and I called out, "Istahar!"

I lay back on the ground, staring at your stars for hours. The angel and I exchanged few words. Eventually we slept.

And now I lie awake again. In the night, in the cold, the angel has moved closer to me, engulfed me in his wings to keep me warm. His breast rises and falls in the rhythm of sleep, though, close as his face is to mine, I feel no breath from him.

I look at your stars, thinking of you, remembering, rejoicing that you are not—yes, I can say it, that you are not dead. And I know that for the rest of my life, I will be able to look into the sky and know that, even by day, even beyond the cruelty of the sun and the taunting translucence of the clouds, you will be there, always, there in my heart, always, there to comfort me, to save me, to protect me, to join with my voice as I try to sing what I can remember of your songs.

I am not alone. For not only are you with me, but you have brought the angel to me. Indeed, meeting the angel was no accident, and my love for you, his love for you, must have been preordained, must have been real. I now have a partner, a friend. He will travel with me along these ruined hills and plains, working with me to build a new world from the fragments of the old.

I look around me, and all I see are bones, bones upon bones. But with the help of God, with your grace, with your magic and the memory of your music, these bones again can live, as I now know, in joy, in excitement, in love, that I, too, now, once again can live.

For comments and discussion about the tale of Japheth and to hear the audio version, please visit http://www.thebookofvoices.com/Japheth

ELISHEVA (INTERLUDE 1)
אלישׁבע

I come to consciousness here in this sealed cave each time (each day? I can no longer tell how much time a day contains, or whether day has turned to night outside). There is always air to breathe, water from the small stream that flows through my chamber, just enough of the simple mysterious food in this cabinet beneath my bed to keep me alive (by the angel's magic, perhaps, or perhaps the manna has returned), enough to let me continue here, silent as I always have been, alone with the visions in my mind, with the voices that I hear reflected off these smooth rock walls.

I remain here, remembering, dreaming, imagining. I am not upset that I cannot leave. I cherish the comfort, the safety of this prison, this womb. Each day, I stand and walk around this space. At times, I remember music and I dance, now that no one can see me, now that I can move, unembarrassed by my ungainliness. I even almost sing, but still find that I cannot bring myself to be heard, even by my own ears.

My voice still functions. I can hear it in my groans as I stand, as I move. (Have the groans become louder, more frequent over time? I can recall that there have been times when they have been softer, but not the sequence of the times.) Although I still hear myself murmuring prayers as I awaken, as I fall asleep, before and after I eat, the prayers are so soft that they fail to engage my voice at all, emerging as whispers.

I return from speaking the voices as if returning from a dream. Wisps of what my tongue and breath had said remain with me for a fraction of a moment, then dissipate as steam drifts away from a cauldron. I retain nothing except, perhaps, a single still image that the voices have described, a single phrase or fragment of melody that they have spoken or sung, or, most rarely, a sense memory of a flavor, a scent, or a touch. These last dwell not within my mind but in the independent memories of my tongue, my breath, my flesh.

What remains most often, if anything remains at all, is an echo of emotion. It is so now, as I return to my own being. (Did I speak of trees, of bones, of rain?) My heart feels whispers of memories of loss, of love, of the loss of love.

Have I known love in my life? I have a sense that I once had a family. I must have loved them. Others must have lived in this place with me, though I cannot reach the memory of who they were. And I feel love flow to and from this angel, though the sense of this love is both more embodied and more abstract than whatever love I might have felt for any living person.

Have I known loss? I certainly must have felt it for my family, now gone. Perhaps I felt it for the others in this place, now also, I assume, gone. When I look at the face of this angel, I sense a memory of loss, projected both forward and backward in time, loss that I must have known, loss that I again may know. That memory is flavored with notes of guilt, of regret, much as notes of sharper hidden flavors tune the taste of rich, complex wine.

My eyes slowly open, and what little memory there was dissolves. (Did I dream of weather, or what may lie outdoors?) I look to my side, into the eyes of the angel. Peace returns, though not completely. A memory of a memory of love, of loss, remains.

THE BOOK OF BECOMING
ספר חיוות

TERACH

‏הרת‎

Terach, a descendant of Japheth's brother Shem, made idols, small statues of the gods that people worshiped in his day. He grew up in the city of Ur, which was known for its astronomers.

The Bible says:

> Terach became the father of Abram, Nachor and Haran. And Haran became the father of Lot. While his father Terach was still alive, Haran died in Ur of the Chaldeans, in the land of his birth. Abram and Nachor both married. The name of Abram's wife was Sarai... Terach took his son Abram, his grandson Lot son of Haran, and his daughter-in-law Sarai, the wife of his son Abram, and together they set out from Ur of the Chaldeans to go to Canaan. But when they came to Kharan, they settled there.
> *(Genesis 11:27-31)*

Abram and much of the rest of the family continued on to the land of Canaan, which would later be known as Israel. Abram later changed his name to Abraham and spread the belief in a single God.

Terach speaks from a moment late in his life as he sits alone with his idols in Kharan.

Too much time has passed since we last saw each other, too much time since we last talked. But now, after so long, we are alone together. The house is quiet now. My son and what remains of my family have gone. They are finishing the journey that I abandoned so many years ago.

Yes, we must talk again now, face to face. Here: if I hammer this thin brass nail down through your hair, along the fine wood's grain, your head should stay on your shoulders for at least a while more.

You were always my favorite of the idols, Marumat, ever since I first met you when I was small. Do you remember—yes, of course, you remember when I took you from your honored place on my mother's altar and brought you to my playroom. Quite a party we had there, with my dogs, with the toys that my mother had fashioned for me out of leftover linen, wool, and beans. You stood regally as always at the center of the room. I bustled about, making sure all the party guests were happy, making sure that all the imagined guests were well fed. I had taken the plate of grain that sat at your altar as an offering and placed it before you there. I wasn't sure how you would eat it, but I was certain that you would.

Of course, the grain spilled along the way. That was how my mother found you and found me. She slapped me and snatched you up from the floor. "This is not a toy!" she yelled. "We treat gods with love, with fear, with respect."

"But I do love this god," I cried. "That's why I made a party for him."

My mother picked up the plate of grain and stomped out of the room, looking back at me with an expression that was not quite a glare. I think now that she was trying not to smile.

She always did have that streak in her, that fierce brilliance of penetrating doubt that burned through the stories that we told each other, burned through to the truths that the stories both concealed and revealed.

There, outside of our house in the city of astronomers, we would sit on our blanket on a warm night and look up at the stars. "What do you see up there?" she would ask me.

I would lie back and look for the stars, the gods that I would recognize, in the sky, as one would look for friends in a crowd. "There is Nergal," I would say, "red and low to the ground." Or "There is Marduk," or "Is that Ishtar? Hello, Ishtar!"

Sometimes I would ask, "Where is Nephila? His belt should be shining in the sky."

My mother would tell me, "Perhaps he had to visit his children, the giants fallen to earth. Or maybe he was sent on a mission. Or maybe it's just not time for him to be in the sky."

"But why are gods sent on missions? Don't they set their own times?"

"We don't know why they are there when they are there, and why they are missing when they are missing. They come and go. But when they are not in the sky, we have their idols at home."

"Why don't we have an idol for my father? He was once here, and now is gone."

She held me closer. "That is good thinking. But we do not have idols for people. They are only for gods."

"Maybe we should have them," I said.

"Maybe we should," she repeated. Though, when we remembered this conversation when I was older, she muttered, "but not for him."

I never knew my father. I knew that his name was Nachor, and that he, too, crafted idols, as I did, as did my sons. He sculpted you, after all, making this form to please you so that your breath would come down and inhabit it.

He died, or went away, too young. I named my first child for him. Nachor, my son, was the eldest of three, though the middle one, Haran, died too young, in the fire that destroyed our home. Nachor brought Haran's daughter, Milcah, into his home and married her. My youngest son, Abram, ran into the fire and rescued the younger daughter, Iscah, whom he married, and their brother, Lot, who so often seems to need to be rescued. I rescued you.

I couldn't bear to stay in our city of Ur, after my home was gone, after all my work was gone. All the other idols had sacrificed themselves to the flames, the wood burning, the iron melting, the stone crumbling, the breath of their lives returning to their greater selves.

Nachor had his own home, his own friends, business and responsibilities. He stayed behind in Ur. But we picked up what little we had and traveled toward Canaan, to the city of Kharan (no, not spelled or pronounced like my son's name, though I liked to dream that it was the city of his memory). We were a tiny caravan: you, me, Lot, Abram, Iscah, and, as always, Eliezer, Abram's servant, his constant friend.

You were broken by then. Abram had broken you years ago, though he never admitted it. I remember coming into the room where you always stood so proudly, there next to the iron idol of Nakhin. You were lying on the floor, your head snapped coarsely from your neck. (Perhaps my father should have taken more care in creating your body, should have crafted a more sturdy neck for you. Perhaps this fresh brass nail will fix that failure of design.) Grain was scattered across the floor. A small ax rested in Nakhin's strong arms.

"What happened here?" I said aloud.

"They had a fight." Abram's small voice came from behind me. I turned and saw him sitting in the far corner. "I had put the grain out for them. Na-khin wanted more than Marumat. So he took the ax and broke Marumat's head off."

I sighed and looked more closely. Your neck clearly hadn't broken from an ax blow. It looked like you had fallen onto the ground, head first. And I could see Abram's small footprints in the fallen grain, where he must have kicked it around to make it look like the result of a fight.

"Now, Abram," I said. "You know that that doesn't happen. Idols don't break each other."

"But they can do so," he whined. "They are gods. They can do whatever they want."

"They can do so, of course," I said. "But they don't. Idols remain strong, remain silent, for us to worship."

"Does the neck of a strong god break?" Abram asked.

"The neck of an idol can break. It is our job to make them strong, to help them be strong."

"Why do gods need our help?"

"Gods don't need our help. But they want our help. Just like they want our grain, to feed them, to worship them."

"But they don't eat the grain," Abram said. "When we put it out for them, we just end up picking it up later and throwing it out."

"They don't eat it like people do," I said. "I suppose that their magic takes from it what they need, like we separate the grain itself from the chaff. They can see the difference, even if we can't."

"Why do the gods take things?" Abram asked. "Why did they take my friend Farah? I was playing with him a few days ago, but now they say that a god has taken him. They say that they are proud, but I saw his mother crying when she was burning something at the temple."

I stood silently for a longer time than I had intended. Then I reached down and took him in my arms. "The gods do what the gods do," I said. I tried to say more, to explain how you worked, but could not put it into words that a child could understand, could barely have put it into words that I could have understood myself. "The gods do what the gods do," I said again. "We cannot understand."

Abram, too, was silent. I saw that he was crying. I kissed him, and he rested his head on my shoulder. And I thought that, beneath his tears, I caught an echo of my mother's smile.

After he was asleep, I went back to the room that you shared with the other idols. I took the ax from Nakhin and swept up the grain. Then, gently carrying your head and body almost as carefully as I had held Abram, I took you to my workroom, wrapped you in linen, and placed you in a box to be repaired soon.

How many years ago was that? Certainly you know. Though this physical instance of you has been sitting in the box, listening, silent, for all this time, I know that I have been connected to your soul, as you have been in my heart. All my life, I have felt your presence, your love. All my life, I have told myself that I would repair you someday. But the time has never been right.

Now I am alone. We are alone. Nachor passed away some seven years ago. I have not heard from Milcah since then, nor from anyone else that I knew back in Ur.

And my family here all have moved on. Abram never was good at making idols, could never put his heart into it. But he proved good at business, at government, at making deals and treaties. In the way that so many children eventually must, he has become his own man, moved to a new territory.

He has even changed his name in the new country. I don't understand why—perhaps it is the numerology—but he is now calling himself Abraham. What was once his pet name for his wife, Iscah—Sarai, "my princess"—has now become her official name, Sarah.

And he does not care for the gods. His search is elsewhere. His brilliance in his business has gone into his everyday philosophy. "The world that you live in is needlessly complex," he says. "When I look at what people want in a transaction, what people want in their life, it always comes down to one thing, though the one thing that they want can rarely be defined. There must be one desire, one principle, underlying everything in the universe. And someday soon we will understand what that is."

Perhaps. I do not understand my world, do not understand my gods. But I do understand what gives me joy, what gives me comfort.

So here we are, you and me. And as I secure you here within this vise for the moment, as I drive this nail through your head so that you can be whole, I know that you are here with me, in your fragile wooden body, in your place within the stars, in the eternal world beyond the worlds. Laying my hands upon my tools, I know that this is what I do well: I make bodies for the gods. This is what I do well. This is what I do.

And for this knowledge, my idol, my comfort, for this, my god among the gods, I bow before you. I give you thanks.

For comments and discussion about the tale of Terach
and to hear the audio version, please visit
http://www.thebookofvoices.com/Terach

LOT

לוֹט

Lot was Terach's grandson and Abraham's nephew. He traveled with Abraham to the land of Canaan and settled in the city of Sodom.

God destroyed the city, which was full of evil people.

The Bible says:

> With the coming of dawn, the angels urged Lot, saying, "Hurry! Take your wife and your two daughters who are here, or you will be swept away when the city is punished..." Then the Lord rained down burning sulfur on Sodom and Gomorrah—from the Lord out of the heavens. Thus he overthrew those cities and the entire plain, destroying all those living in the cities—and also the vegetation in the land. But Lot's wife looked back, and she became a pillar of salt.
>
> *(Genesis 19:15, 24-26)*

Orpheus was a Greek singer.

After his wife died, he pursued her into the land of the dead and brought her back to our world. But when he looked back at her as they emerged, she disappeared, returning to the fires of the underworld.

Lot speaks as he escapes the fires of Sodom, after losing his wife.

He tells me that his name is Orpheus. He sits before me as I, too, sit, here at the base of this mountain, on this plain that is cursed by fire, ringed with fire. As I sit, my back rests against mossy rock. His back rests against nothing, supported only by his firm resolve never to look to the south again.

41

I was alone, became alone on my path from the north across this plain, before I met this man, before our voices found each other, before we came to sit here with one another. He, too, was alone, became alone on his way across this plain. But when the sound of my mourning, of my wailing, rose from my voice and reverberated from the surrounding hills, it met the sound of his song, flowing with the same rhythm, the same feeling, the same wordless howl as mine, not quite in harmony but with a perfect dissonance that complemented and contrasted with my sound. The pain exploding from each of us made the cries of the other stand out, more stark, more clear, than either would have sounded on its own.

The echoes of our mourning drew us near to one another. Each of us saw the other at first as a specter emerging from the smoke, the haze, then as a shadow. Only when we were almost within an arm's reach of each other did we see each other as distinct shapes, as faces that we could recognize as people. Only then did we know that we did not know one another.

We stood in silence. In the time before one of us spoke, each of us heard the sound of his own labored breath, of the breath of the other, heard the sound of his own pulse within his ears, within his veins.

"You came from the fire?"

"And you?"

"Yes. And you, too, lost—"

"My wife. My love. My soul. I have lost—"

"Everything."

Another silence hung there in the smoke. One of us sighed. One of us coughed. When a moment's breeze showed us that we were on a spot of uncluttered ground, we each sank down into the charred grass.

"You were in the city?" That voice must have come from me.

"No, not the city," Orpheus said. "We lived on the water. We lived quietly, lived well, until death took my beloved from me."

"Yes, we too lived quietly, lived well, though my home became less a blessing than a fortress, defending us against those who lived around me. Then the flames came to the city, and destroyed it all."

Another silence. Again, memory can not tell me which of us spoke.

"You lost her to the flames?"

"No, not directly. I thought that I had lost her, but she reemerged. Then I lost her once again."

"Lost to the looking back."

"To the looking back."

"If I could only relive that final moment, if only I could try again—"

"We can not try again. We can no longer look back, even to the moment of looking back."

And another silence, the paths of its passing time sketched on our faces by our tears, by the tears through the ashes on his face, by the salt of the tears on mine.

"She had died, was as dead as she had ever been alive," he said. (It must have been Orpheus who spoke.) "But my gods, the gods of my fathers, showed what I thought was mercy. They allowed me down to the place where the dead gather, before their souls drift down to the river of fire, before they become the river that flows outside of life. They let me sing my song to her one last time. And as I sang, I felt her soul emerging from the flow, collecting around the strands of my song, as salt—"

"As salt?" I cried.

"—as salt gathers around a reed in a drying sea bed. Then I walked away, drew her away from the river of souls."

"And she lived?"

"For me, for the moment, she lived."

"My love lived also," I said. "She was dead, seemed dead, as the fire from above took our city. We waited perhaps too long to listen to the travelers' warnings, to understand that their god had run out of mercy and that the city would burn. She was asleep when the flames erupted, asleep when the flames burst into our home. I saw her there among the flames and ran back after her. Her robes had already begun to smolder as I lifted her from our bed and ran toward the pool of water that we kept near our house. I immersed her and awakened her. She screamed in panic, in pain, but I told her that we must be quiet, that we must run, that there was no time. And so we ran from the city."

"And she lived?"

"For the moment, she lived."

Another array of breezes blew past us, first clear, but then carrying the grit, the scents, of ash, then salt air, then ash again.

"And then..." one of us, or maybe both of us said. For a long time, neither wanted to respond.

Then the silence became more oppressive than the telling, and I spoke again. "We got outside the city, and kept running, pursued by the rumbling of earth and the rushing of winds. Then we heard an explosion, as if Babel herself were collapsing again. I put my head down, and screamed for her not to look. But she stood, and turned. And then there was the flash, like a sun god dropping to earth, And the searing heat, and the wind—"

"—and she was gone," Orpheus said. It was a statement, not a question.

"Her soul was gone. Her body—where her body had been was a pillar, white as cloud, hard as her body had been so soft. I embraced the pillar, kissed it, but all that was left was the taste of tears, the taste of salt. I fell back—and I saw what I could swear was her soul spiraling upward from where her body had been, dissolving into the wind, melting into the flames of the sky, without warning, without a farewell."

"Without a farewell..." Orpheus said. "Thus, too, my love came away with me from the fire, from the river of flame that roared below. I could not see her, but could feel her breath, her touch behind me. 'I am with you,' she whispered to me, and her presence was as comforting as the scent of spices, as maddening as the brush of angel's feathers hovering just within reach. 'I am with you,' she said, 'but do not look at me.'"

"And she stayed with you?" I said.

"She stayed, for as long as it took for us to travel almost this far. My love for her grew even stronger as the echoes of her breath ignited my songs. But as my love grew stronger, so did my desire, and as a flash burst from your burning city, I thought it was an explosion of my passion. I could not keep at last from turning, to see her, to touch her, to be with her."

"And she was gone," I said.

"If only she had instantly been gone," he cried. "I did get to see her, to touch her—but only long enough to feel her shadow-body dissolve. She decayed in my hands as one does over time in the grave, but swiftly, over the course of a single breath, long enough to see her beauty melt away to sinew, muscle, bone. I saw that what I had loved was now indeed as mortal as any other person. In my greed to be with her forever, I had not been able to let her go, gradually, as each of us must let the ones that we had loved cease to be flesh and dissipate into memory. And now she was gone, without a farewell..."

We both fell to silence. Were there new breezes? We did not notice the gusts of the wind against our faces, feeling only the gusts within us of terror, of regret.

Again, one of us spoke. "And we are here."

"And we are here."

"What are we now? What do we do?"

"We are the lost ones now, those who loved the lost. We continue. We continue. I sense that the gods will not yet let us die—there is more for us to do, more for us to regret. We must fade into stories. When we die, after we die, others will learn the stories of our pain. Perhaps they will learn from them. I fear that they will not."

And then, now, we sat here in greater silence, in a silence that summed together the absences of all that had come before, each thinking of the other's words, each drowning in his own despair.

But now the shadows are lengthening and growing less distinct. We know that it is time to move on. At the same moment, we each stand.

"I must continue, back toward the sea," Orpheus says. "Will you come with me?"

"I cannot," I say. "I know that my daughters escaped the fire before me. We have arranged, if disaster strikes us, to meet in a cave just up the mountain from here. We keep there clean water, warm blankets, jars of preserved food, and wine. There would be room for you."

"I cannot," he says. "We must continue, each on his own path. Perhaps we will remember each other, sing of each other."

"Perhaps." We look into each other's eyes for a brief moment, but neither of us can stand seeing the pain for long, seeing the pain of loss in each other's eyes, each seeing the pain in the other's eyes reflected from his own. Each of us steps aside then forward, past the other, losing the other swiftly in the darkness, in the acrid mist. Neither of us dares to look back.

For comments and discussion about the tale of Lot
and to hear the audio version, please visit
http://www.thebookofvoices.com/Lot

MOAB

מוֹאָב

Moab was both the son and grandson of Lot.

Lot's daughters escaped from Sodom ahead of their father and waited for him in a safe place nearby. They knew that their mother had been turned to salt. They believed that the rest of the world had also been destroyed, and that they and their father were the last people on Earth.

The Bible says:

> That night they got their father to drink wine, and the older daughter went in and slept with him. He was not aware of it when she lay down or when she got up... They got their father to drink wine [the next] night also, and the younger daughter went in and slept with him. Again he was not aware of it when she lay down or when she got up.
> So both of Lot's daughters became pregnant by their father.
> *(Genesis 19:33-36)*

Each of the daughters bore a son whose descendants became a nearby tribe: Moab was the ancestor of the Moabites, and Ben-Ammi was the ancestor of the Ammonites.

Moab speaks as a child, near the place where he was conceived.

By day, my grandfather sits at his cave, watching men watch the sheep who graze above the ruins. By night, he sits in the field and drinks, as his head rests against the pillar of salt, as he wraps his arms around it and tries to dance.

I cannot read the shape that the salt once had, worn smooth now by the summer rains. But my grandfather's tears have worn new paths, their water carving texts of memory as their pools join their salt with the pillar's salt to state that here no life can ever grow again.

My mother drinks and cries with her sister, standing by the pillar (which they call their mother), though only by day, when my grandfather cannot be there. They watch me climb there in the trees, playing with my cousin (whom they sometimes call my brother).

I do not know my father. I do not have a father. And I no longer ask my mother who my father was, since the question sends her from the room, away from me, to the place by the pillar where she drinks and cries.

The men in the field point at me and laugh. And they laugh at my mother as she cries with my sister, and tell tales of my grandfather when they think we cannot hear. They say that he would have given them up to save the pair of strangers, the strangers who then saved them from the men of the city, from the death of the city, from the quakes and fires that turned the city into dust. They whisper that when all was gone to salt and dust, my grandfather and our mothers all began to drink, then went to sleep.

I do not understand the rest of the tales, the whispering and mocking laughter. But I do know that they speak of shame as they point to me, that my name, my presence, are emblems of shame. My family and I will bear this shame for longer than memory can say.

I cannot place a name to what I feel. But I see my grandfather there at night, always far away from me but wanting to be near. As his heart fails slowly, I hear him crying in the night Though he never speaks my name, I feel his cries call out to me. But my heart can never answer, as I hide deep in my cradle of fire, sorrow, whispers, salt, and shame.

For comments and discussion about the tale of Lot and to hear the audio version, please visit http://www.thebookofvoices.com/Lot

ABRAHAM

אברהם

Abraham, the son of Terach, traveled to the land of Canaan with his wife Sarah and his nephew Lot. Abraham was the first person to believe in one God.

God promised Abraham that he would be the father of a great nation, but by the time that he was quite old, he had no children. With Sarah's approval, a servant bore him a son. When Sarah herself finally bore a son, Isaac, she convinced Abraham to banish the servant and child from their home.

God then told Abraham that he must sacrifice Isaac. Abraham and Isaac climbed to Mount Moriah to perform the sacrifice.

The Bible says:

> When they reached the place God had told him about, Abraham built an altar there and arranged the wood on it. He bound his son Isaac and laid him on the altar, on top of the wood. Then he reached out his hand and took the knife to slay his son.
>
> *(Genesis 22:9-10)*

Abraham speaks just after the moment of the sacrifice.

My son is alive. This ram is dead, but my son is alive. I cry and laugh (as promised at the naming of my son) with joy stained by bright terror at the knowledge of what I cannot understand, of the greatness of this god that I have found.

I have never heard the voice of this god, save in hearing how birds and insects far from one another sing the same rhythms at the same time, or how the patterns of distant thunder are echoed in the crackling of the fire in the hearth by my door. But its messages come through in sudden silence, in the certainty that I must do that which is right, despite the belief of others that it cannot be true, despite the knowledge that the sense that it makes defies all sense, that it breaks the logic of our outer world to hint at light that shines from deeper streams.

But I have recognized its presence when I have felt my inner voice resonating with a vibration from beyond. When it told me to smash the idols of the other gods, I obeyed. When it told me to leave my father, I obeyed. When it told me that the shaking of the earth was preceding the destruction of sinning cities, I argued, but I obeyed.

Then I was summoned to sacrifice my son to this god. So many fathers lose so many children to so many gods, some with weeping, some with celebration. We do not know what happens to the soul on the other side of death. But we have told our children and ourselves that those who are called and taken by the gods endure in joy forever.

Yet this call was not entirely one of joy. This god had promised that my line would continue and multiply through this son. I had had another son, yes, but had banished him, sacrificing him to the ravenous desert. And the prompting within my soul and the soul of my beloved Sarah hinted at a history stretching far before us, a world transformed by the children of the child whom I now considered my only son.

But then this future changed. I felt the call, as so many fathers have here, for the death of my son. So it so often is with the gods of this land: these gods demand flesh, demand fire, demand blood.

So I headed up the mountain with my servant and my son. Yes, my son knew where we were going and why we were going there, and his fear was mixed with his excitement that he would join the gods. When we arrived at the top of the mountain, he helped me clear the flat place where I would lay him down, helped me gather the branches that would form his pyre, helped me start the small fire off to one side from which the pyre would be lit after he was slain.

And I laid him on the branches, and I raised my knife to cut his throat, swiftly, with a single stroke, to cause him the least amount of living pain.

But when the knife came down, I felt my hand stop just short of where the blade would touch him. I could not move my hand, neither down nor up, forward nor back, nor to either side. I cried out silently to this god, either to let me do this or stop me from doing it.

Suddenly, to my right, I heard a rushing and galloping, and I saw a mighty ram, head down, horns forward, charging at us, as if challenging our presence on his land. And we were suddenly afraid, more afraid of this ram than we were of this god.

But just before he would have reached us, he stopped short, stumbling and howling, his horns trapped in a low thicket that we had not noticed before. Still frozen in place, I looked into the eyes of the ram, then into the eyes of my son, then into my own heart, and listened for the prompting of this god.

And I suddenly knew that, though I had offered up my son, though my son had offered up his life, this god never would take him as a sacrifice. The offer had not been haughtily refused, but was lovingly declined.

Within my soul, the vision of the imminent death of my son cleared, and the vision of the previous future returned, the vision of a long, beautiful, complex eternity in which the children of my son would survive and thrive. And I knew that this was a different god, one who would not demand the deaths of his people as random sacrifice, a greater god than all the others, a god whom all the others would someday serve.

Abruptly unfrozen, my hand and my knife continued in their previous arc toward my son. But at the last possible moment, they shifted by the tiniest fraction of an angle, and missed his offered throat. The knife swung high into the air as if my hand were moving by an energy other than my own, pulling me off my knees and onto my feet, spinning me around then plunging back down to swiftly, cleanly, slit the throat of the ram.

I took the bowl that had been on the pyre beside my son and placed it by the throat of the ram to gather the blood that flowed from its wound. From the small fire, I took one burning branch and touched it to the thicket. A pillar of flame immediately leaped up and engulfed the ram, echoing its shape in a sculpture of fire, then collapsing in a mist of ash.

I raised the blood bowl above my head, preparing to spill it on the smoldering pyre, to spell out in blood the name of this powerful god—but I did not know how to spell its name. Pouring the blood out onto a single point, in a single stream, I cried out "This sacrifice is for the glory of—" but I realized that I could not pronounce its name.

Then, within the ashes, I saw, gleaming, polished, hollowed but intact, the horns of the ram, now free from its body and from the thicket in which they had been caught. I lifted one horn from the ashes, brought it toward my lips, shouted "This alone is my god! This is the name of my only god!" and blew one long, high note. The sound flowed from the horn, embracing and engulfing all other sound, cascading from this mountain and resounding from the surrounding peaks. Now, in the moments of quiet here, between the returning whispers of breezes, insects, birds, and other life, I can hear it still.

I still sit here now as night falls, lit by the embers of the small fire that we began so many hours ago. My son sits next to me, baffled, terrified, muted, but alive. I embrace him as he shivers, as we wait for our servant to dismantle the pyre. Instead of death, the burning of its branches will bring us living warmth.

And I feel the presence of this living god, and feel the certainty that in its presence, I will never be alone. I sense the whispers of its name written in the wisps of smoke that emerge from the small fire, tracing paths of gentle chaos against the fading colors of the sunset, yet always rising steadily upward; in the scent, the acrid taste of the ashes of the ram as they mingle with the stillness of the air; in the echoes of the horn, still hovering at the edge of silence; and, most fully, in the embrace of my son, of the love between a father and son that no human nor god can ever destroy.

I open all my senses to this presence in this holy place. "This alone is my god," I murmur in silence. And as the gentle silence answers me, I know, finally and forever, that this is a god that I can worship.

This is a god that I can love.

For comments and discussion about the tale of Abraham and to hear the audio version, please visit http://www.thebookofvoices.com/Abraham

SARAH

אשרה

Sarah was the wife of Abraham (who was once known as Abram) and the mother of Isaac. She traveled with him from their childhood home as he spread belief in one God in Canaan. She was said to retain her youthful beauty and health into her old age.

Sarah's travels with Abraham were often difficult. On two occasions, once in Egypt and once in Gerar, Abraham tried to protect himself by telling the people there that Sarah was his sister rather than his wife. God intervened in each case to prevent Sarah from being taken by the places' rulers.

Sarah's only child, Isaac, was born when she was very old. God ordered Abraham to sacrifice Isaac. The Bible says that Sarah died soon after:

> Sarah lived to be a hundred and twenty-seven years old. She died at Kiriath-Arba (that is, Hebron) in the land of Canaan, and Abraham went to mourn for Sarah and to weep over her... Abraham buried his wife Sarah in the cave in the field of Machpelah...
> *(Genesis 23:1,19)*

Sarah speaks as she waits for Abraham to return from sacrificing their son.

"Hello, Grandmother."

So it has come to this: after all these years, in the moment of my deepest grief, of my final betrayal, as my husband has led my only son off to die, a stranger has come to mock me.

"I am no one's grandmother," I say.

"No," she says, "but you will be."

"I have had enough of prophecy." Sitting here on this low bench at the gateway to my home, I pull myself inward, away from those milk-white feet, clutching my knees even more tightly to my chest.

"This is not prophecy," she says. "This is fact. Isaac, your beloved only son, comes back down the mountain with Abraham, quite alive, and fathers sons himself, who father sons and daughters, and so on. I am indeed your granddaughter, seven generations removed. I am Miriam, known as the sister of Moses and—no, my brothers' names will not yet mean anything to you. But I am Miriam."

"I am Sarah," I say automatically.

"Yes, Grandmother," she says. "I know."

"You say this as if this is history. Has the heart of time itself been broken? Has it flung me into the future?"

"We are still in your present time," she says. "But I have stepped back into what, viewed from my lifetime here, is the distant past."

"And why have you come here?" I say. "To confuse and to mock me?"

"I have not come to mock you," she says. "I have come to take you home."

"This is my home," I say, "or as much of a home as I have ever had. Where would you take me? I lost my childhood home in Ur to fire long ago. None of us remain in the next city that we lived in, in Kharan. Abraham has dragged me all over Canaan and beyond, down to Egypt, up to this hilltop in Kiryat-Arba, and throughout all the rest of the lands that we know. His god told him to go forth. He went. I followed. But since I was a child, I have never had a home of my own."

The stranger's feet step closer. "May I sit with you?" she asks.

I point to my right. "The bench is large enough," I say. "Please pardon me, but I do not feel up to being a perfect host."

"I understand." She sits, and all that the corner of my eye sees is white upon white upon white.

I turn my head just enough to get a good look at her. She wears a robe of white linen, its hem faintly dusted and discolored by pale sand. Her skin is as white as the linen, and her hair even whiter than that. But dark eyes like mine peer out from behind pale lashes, and her features are like ours, not like those of the bleached travelers from the North.

"*Tzara'at?*" I ask.

She nods, tenses, waits, then relaxes. "You didn't flinch away from me though you recognize the disease! I assure you, though, that this peculiar joke that God has pulled on me is not contagious."

I shrug. "I am not worried. God's joke on me was to make me young and keep me from aging. I no longer get ill, even from the most trivial or virulent of diseases. I am afraid that I may be forced to live forever."

"Would it be a consolation to learn that you do not?" she asks.

"I suppose that it would."

"Then," she says, "I can tell you that you do, indeed, pass from this life eventually and rejoin the realm of souls."

"When?"

She closes her eyes, tilts her head to the left as if trying to remember, frowns, tilts her head to the right and then upright, then opens her eyes and smiles slightly. "That is a surprisingly difficult question," she says.

"So you are not allowed to tell me."

"No," she says, "I am allowed. But I only know part of the answer. As viewed by people here, you leave your life quite soon. But you should live for many more years elsewhere."

"Where?" I ask.

She seems not to have heard me. "Tell me," she says, "when you picture your life, the way that you wish that it had gone, what do you see?"

"Really? Other than having been dragged about by my husband's missions and his god's whims?"

"Yes. Try to remember who you were, and who you wanted to become."

My eyes close, and I wait for ideas, for images. But all that I hear, all that I see is the jumble of my current life, all that I have endured, all that has exhausted me.

I feel the faintest of touches brush and then rest against my temples. I open my eyes and look into the stranger's. Her voice seems to come not from her lips but from within my own mind. "Speak to me. Who are you? Where are you now?"

My sense of where I am dissolves as steam disappears in the path of a cooling breath. "I am indoors," I say, "in a large room, in what feels like a very old building. This room, its walls, its floor are simple, solid, as are the tables and chairs. Threads of text are inscribed on all the surfaces, intertwining into patterns, symbols, diagrams that reveal more than the words themselves.

"Others sit in the room with me, in a circle. I am teaching them, learning from them, speaking of history, of art, of all the things that join us together, that make us who we are as people. Most of those in the room are my many daughters, and it feels as if all of them are. We all have been here for a very long time, though we are continually learning things that are new. There is a sense of stability, of warmth, of all the things that I have missed in my life."

My breath catches. The image shatters, dissipates, propels me back, to my home, to this dusty gateway, to this low stone bench.

I pull back away from this Miriam, away from her gaze, her touch. "Why have you forced me to see this, to remember this? I had forgotten what my life could have been. I had almost grown happy with who I am."

She smiles, takes my hand in hers, pale flesh surrounding dark. "I show you this because it is true. This is where I came from, where we are going. It is indeed a memory, not of your past, but of your future."

"Where is this place?" I say.

"This is also a surprisingly difficult question. I can say where its entrances are, but the location of the school itself is an ongoing source of debate. We seem to exist in a different space, a different time, connected but not the same as here." She pauses, releases my hands, and rises to her feet. "So shall we go?"

"Why should I believe you?" I say.

"Because your heart knows it to be true."

And as she says this, I look deep into my heart, out beyond the world that I know. Time suddenly spreads out before me, not as a line but as a plane. I see the world through Miriam's eyes, and know that I am to leave here, know that what we see will indeed be my choice, my destiny.

"But what of my future here?" I ask aloud. "How will Abraham and my Isaac continue without me? Will they come to hate me for abandoning them?"

"The stories say that you pass away here, soon, as or just after they come down from the mountain. None of us can step back into this world within the span of our natural lives. But once you pass away, we can return you here. They will find that you had died while they were away, quietly, at rest, at peace."

"And will they continue well?"

"They will," she says, "from what we know. You have set up your household to run well without you. Your friend, your servant Eliezer, will watch over them. Soon, he will find a bride for Isaac from within your clan, and generations will extend through Isaac as far into the future as we can see."

Silence falls. I sit and Miriam stands in the fading light of evening. When my shadow has lengthened to the point that it darkens her pale feet, I, too, rise.

"So shall we go?" Miriam asks. "We have a long walk ahead of us."

"What may I take?" I ask.

"Whatever you wish. Whatever we can carry."

I step back into my house and look around. Though, like all our homes have been, it is a temporary shelter, it is cluttered, strewn with gifts and tokens that have accumulated in our travels and transactions.

Off in a corner, one item stands out, as if a different light shines on it: a doll, intended as an idol, I suppose. My father Haran carved it from the wood of an asherah grove. I had clutched it as my Abram saved me from the fire in my home, and kept it with me throughout all these years.

I walk to the doll, pick it up, and cradle it in my arms. I take a couple of favorite robes and scrolls of stories that I would like to remember and teach.

I turn to the door, then turn back again. Taking a reed and some blank parchment, I write a quick note to Abraham reminding him to complete our purchase of the caves at Machpelah. After what he has experienced and is likely to experience, he is likely to forget. And I do love that piece of land, and would like to be buried there.

I pause at the end of the note. Should I say goodbye to my husband and my son? No, better for them not to know that I left them. Better for them to believe that my passing was sudden, was unexpected.

I cover the ink pot and rest the reed beside it. Looking around for what I know is the last time, I try to engrave the image in my memory. Looking into myself to remember my feelings as I leave, I am surprised that where I expect to find sadness and resignation, I find excitement, anticipation, joy.

I turn again and step out of the house. Miriam reaches out wordlessly and takes some of the scrolls and robes to carry.

"Shall we go?" she asks again.

I nod. We start down the path, down this hill, away from what had been, for awhile, my home.

After we have walked for awhile, I realize that I have been considering a question for a while. "This place where we are going," I ask, "does it have a name?"

"Not one that we know," she replies. "But our group, our school, takes one on." She looks toward me, the glow of her pale smile as warm as that of the horizon's setting sun.

"We have always known that you would be joining us. Even though you have not come to join us until now, we have always spoken of ourselves as the Sacred Sisters of Sarah."

I stop, surprised, then quickly return to walking down the mountain. Yes, I am returning to the life that I was meant to lead. Yes, I finally am coming home.

For comments and discussion about the tale of Sarah and to hear the audio version, please visit http://www.thebookofvoices.com/Sarah

ELISHEVA (INTERLUDE 2)

אלישׁבע

I awaken to find my mind clouded with thoughts, with voices. The echoes speak to me of events forgotten, of chains of memories and stories that confirm and contradict each other, all of them at all times true.

I sit up, pivot on this slab of a bed, and gingerly stand by its side. I catalog my movements and sensations as prayer. (Can I sit upright? Yes. Thank you. Can my wrist push well against the stone as I turn? Yes. Thank you.) The stream whose quiet melody blesses this room is, I know, eight steps away. My feet carry me slowly forward to the water. (Yes, my feet still can carry me. Thank you.)

A large cup rests in the water. I start to bend down to pick it up and discover that I can not. (Thank you for the awareness of my limitations.) I see that a rope leads up from it, loops over a hook in the ceiling, then comes back down to within my reach.

I pull on the rope on my side of the hook, and the cup rises to where I can reach it. I look at the top of it, see an image of my face faintly distorted in the curve of the water. The image shimmers with the faint shaking of my hand, and the whispering of a word echoes in my mind's ear, as if in tune with the vibrations: Aspaklarya, the whispers say. Aspaklarya.

I try to dig within my mind to find the reason for the whispers, but resistance blocks my path. Digging for memory only causes the memory to revolt. I have a moment of frustration, then anger, then acceptance. Recalling what I had learned from people (Whom? When?) from the East, I relax and open my mind, letting the word repeat and expand, as if forming ripples and vibrations within the cup of water, within my thought.

Aspaklarya. The word brings me back to another language. It feels comfortable on my tongue as I whisper it aloud. Is this the language that I once spoke? I speak, think, remember now in the language of our prayers, but it feels even more ancient than I do myself, not quite natural, a language that I must have consciously learned. But this word, this language...

Aspaklarya – yes, a viewing glass, reflecting, refracting the world as the surface of the water reflects and rearranges its echo of my face. A word from this other life, returning through this crack in the walls of memory.

The image in the water shimmers and shows me another face, a face other than my own. I remember another person. A sister? No, though I feel warmth in my heart towards her as I might remember toward a sister. This woman was part of my life for longer than my actual family. (How long was I with my family? When were they or I taken away?) Her image shifts and vibrates, showing her at many different ages: young (though not quite a child), maturing, grown, and aged (though not quite as aged as I am now). Her true name is lost in other whispers. But I know that we (who?) all called her Aspaklarya.

What else do the whispers tell me? That we were as close as sisters could be, closer than twins. We were joined in voicelessness. Neither of us could speak with voices of our own. But she could speak with my voice—not the voice of my own memory, but with the voices that had inhabited my breath.

Aspaklarya was my mirror, my recorder, my memory. When I returned from speaking, I never knew what I had said. I remembered nothing. But Aspaklarya remembered everything, every word, every nuance. She could repeat whatever she had heard, at any time in her life, perfectly, as if the original person was speaking.

I would sit with her (in this room? in another? It must have been nearby, within this same place). She would hold my hands as I returned from speaking the voices, sometimes embracing me as I shook when returning from speaking ugly memories that were not my own. "Do you want to know what your voice said?" her sightless eyes would ask. "Would you like me to repeat it?" Sometimes I would. Sometimes I would not. Sometimes, when I would return filled with fear, when the shaking was too fierce, she would simply hold me and not ask, though her eyes spoke clearly of the horror that she had just heard, that she would never be able to forget.

Did she repeat the voices only to me? I remember hearing her voice, her voices from a distance, as she must have been repeating them. To herself? To others? Yes, others. We must not have been alone. In this place—

A rustling of wings, the brush of bare feet against the stone floor startles me. The angel is here. (Had he ever been gone?) In my surprise, my hands jerk slightly upward, disrupting and spilling the water.

I look down into the cup. The water in it shimmers in complex, chaotic ripples, reflecting nothing. Had I been remembering something? All that remains is a sense of warmth, of a bond with another, of a word that sings to me without context: Aspaklarya. Aspaklarya.

I raise the cup to my lips to drink, to drink to that memory, to drink in offering, in prayer. (Thank you for what blessings I gain from water, from air, from remembering, from forgetting. Thank you for it all. Yes, thank you.)

THE BOOK OF BELONGING
ספר השייכות

ISAAC

רֶֽחְצִי

Isaac was the son of Abraham and Sarah. He married Rebecca, who bore him twin sons, Jacob and Esau.

When Isaac and his family went to Gerar to escape a famine, he followed his father's example and told the king that Rebecca was his sister rather than his wife. The king spotted the ruse the second time, and eventually sent Isaac and his family away.

Isaac grew to be quite old and became blind. When Esau asked Isaac for his blessing, Rebecca and Jacob conspired to deceive Isaac so that Jacob would receive the blessing instead.

The Bible says:

> Rebecca took the best clothes of Esau her older son, which she had in the house, and put them on her younger son Jacob. She also covered his hands and the smooth part of his neck with the goatskins..."
>
> *(Genesis 27:15-16)*

Isaac speaks as he waits to give Esau the blessing.

I sit. I sit and I listen. This is my life. Sometimes I move. Sometimes, rarely, I am moved to action. Frenzies may surround me. Change may erupt around me. Emotions may disrupt my family. I choose to be the still center. I sit.

I breathe the flavors of the air. I listen to the sounds around me. I catalog my perceptions. From the fields: The bleating of goats. The voices of goatherds. The footsteps of goats and goatherds in the wet grass. The scent of newly-grazed grass after afternoon rain. The smell of goats and goatherds, hair still matted from the rain.

From the kitchen: Bread baking. Venison roasting over fire. The fire crackling, sounding so much like Rebecca's lips when she smiles near me. The fire, sounding so much like the rain. The voices of my family: Rebecca and Jacob as they cook the venison that Esau has brought. It is good that my family works together. Jacob lacks the attention to hunt. Esau lacks the patience to cook. Rebecca sees the truth in things. She manages the family. Everything works. I sit.

I listen. I say little. When I speak too much, I get things wrong. So I am silent. I speak when needed. I speak when asked.

Esau has asked for a blessing. He will have a blessing. I have sent him to the fields to hunt. I sit and think as he hunts. I construct a careful blessing.

Jacob rarely asks for anything. Jacob rarely speaks to me. He speaks only to his mother. Esau only speaks to me. He rarely speaks to his mother. But things work well. What needs to be said is said. What needs to be heard is heard.

I had a big brother once. We spoke. We played. We wrestled in the fields. He ran faster than me. He was smarter than me. Then he was gone. My mother said that God wanted him gone. She said that I was saying bad things that my brother taught me. She said that my brother was bad for me. I wondered what I had done wrong. I wondered what I had said that made them send him away. I wondered why people always laughed when they talked about me.

Then my father took me to the mountain. He said that it was time for me to go away. He said that it was time to join God. He tied me up. He raised his knife. I trusted that he knew what he was doing. Then he killed a ram. He untied me and we walked home. When we got home, my mother was dead. My mother was gone. After that, my father rarely spoke to me. He only spoke to God. I never knew why he tied me up. I never knew why he untied me. I never knew what I had done wrong.

His servant went away for a while. He brought Rebecca home. They said she would be my wife. She became my wife.

Then my father died. I found out that my brother was alive. He came home once to help me bury my father. We only spoke a little. He said that I had made them send him away. He wanted to know what I had done. I did not know what I had done wrong. He went away. We never spoke again. I hear that he has died.

My life goes well. Rebecca runs the household. We raise our flocks where we find grass and water. We move when famine comes. We rarely have trouble.

In the last famine, we moved to Gerar. The people there saw that Rebecca is beautiful. They asked me about her. I told them exactly what my father told people about my mother. But I got it wrong. They got angry. We had to go away. And Rebecca got angry. Now she runs things herself. She no longer asks me how to run our business. She no longer asks me how to run our house. She runs things herself. She runs things well. I sit.

I hear the tent flap from the kitchen to this room drawing back. The scent of dinner is growing stronger. I hear my son approaching. I hear the brushing of the skins that Esau wears. I hear the feet shuffle like Jacob's. I only seem to hear one person. As the food is placed before me, I sense a scent that could be both of them. Perhaps they have arrived together. Perhaps Jacob is eager to hear me bless Esau. Perhaps Rebecca has gotten them to work together well.

And perhaps I have gotten things wrong. But I will trust my family. I will listen. I will eat. I will bless my son. And I will continue to sit.

For comments and discussion about the tale of Isaac and to hear the audio version, please visit http://www.thebookofvoices.com/Isaac

JACOB

יעקב

Jacob was the son of Isaac and Rebecca. Early in his life, he conspired with his mother to deceive Isaac, so Isaac gave the blessing intended for Jacob's twin brother Esau to Jacob instead. Isaac discovered the deception after blessing Jacob, but delivered another blessing to Esau.

Jacob feared his brother's anger. He left Isaac's lands and went to the territory owned by his kinsman Laban. After a series of other such double-crosses, done both by and to him, he was able to accrue a lot of wealth and to head off on his own. One of these deals was a complex transaction involving black, white, and mottled goats.

Jacob married Laban's daughter Rachel, as well as several other women. Rachel bore him his two favorite sons, Joseph (who became known for his ability to interpret dreams) and Benjamin. Rachel died when Benjamin was born and was buried in Ramah. Her grave is still a shrine today.

Jacob had several vivid dreams and visions. In one, he saw a ladder on which angels traveled up and down to and from heaven. In another, he wrestled with a man who blessed him and gave him the additional name Israel.

When Jacob returned from Laban's land, he had to pass through Esau's territory.

The Bible says:

> Jacob sent messengers ahead of him to his brother Esau in the land of Seir, the country of Edom... When the messengers returned to Jacob, they said, "We went to your brother Esau, and

now he is coming to meet you, and four hundred men are with him."...

Then Jacob prayed, "Save me, I pray, from the hand of my brother Esau, for I am afraid he will come and attack me, and also the mothers with their children."...

But Esau ran to meet Jacob and embraced him; he threw his arms around his neck and kissed him. And they wept.

(Genesis 32:3, 6, 9, 11, 33:4)

Jacob speaks to us on the night before his reunion with Esau, from within the timeless world of dreams where he dreams of our reality.

Through the years, this landscape has grown familiar. To the north, a ladder rises without visible support. Men with hidden, glowing faces climb and descend, moving past and sometimes through each other as they travel to and from what must be the heavens. In what should be the ladder's shadow, a man without a name waits in a circle of blinding light, in wrestling garb, always prepared for battle. The moon is always three-quarters full, shining through a gap in clouds that never block the stars. Constellations spell new signs each night. A rainbow, full and bright against the darkness, arcs out to the caves beneath the stars. Where the colors meet the sand before the caves, my sons await.

I am always running when I find myself here, running with my flock of mottled goats, running from a darkness behind me that I cannot see, but can feel, can smell. The scent of the skin of slaughtered goats pursues me, threatens to envelop me. I know that if I stop, if I am captured, the skin will bond to me, shape itself to me and me to it, suffocate me, make my blood its blood. I shout out the name that my father gave me, but the echo comes back in the laughter of the man beneath the ladder, with a new name that he says that I must now use.

The weeping fades toward me as I approach the caves, shading from high-pitched peaks of sound down into full-throated sobs. Wisps and gasps of breath become audible as I grow nearer. From the mouth of each of the caves I hear the tears themselves, like the rushing, the rhythm of invisible rain. They are the tears of Rachel, my beloved, the only woman that I have ever loved, crying for being taken too soon, crying for her sons, unable to be consoled about her sons, because she cannot hear them.

She cannot know that her sons are both right here, outside the stone-sealed mouth of the caves. The older son, Joseph, stands in the caves' cool shadow. His blond curls wave in the gentle breeze as he makes up wordless songs in his high, ethereal voice. He rocks the cradle of his younger brother, Benjamin, as he taps one foot in rhythm with the rain of tears, with his song. He does not recognize the sound of the rain as his mother's tears. To him, the rushing, the darkness are simply the weather, the way that things have always been, will always be.

In the shadow of the caves, I reach, lift, embrace, and hold my older son. The running, the panic cease as the scent of the pursuing skins is replaced by the whisper of pure soap, of flowers, of my son's flowing hair. I listen to him breathe until the rhythm of my own breathing matches the pulse of his breath, the cradle, the tears, the rain.

After a long moment (I cannot tell how long—since the moon and shadows never move and the breeze always blows steadily from the west, it is as if time does not move when I am still), I slowly put my son down. I sit on a flat rock next to the cradle. My son sits next to me, tilting onto his side, his head resting on my thigh. I lift an earthen cup that is on the other side of me and drink its warm spiced tea. My free hand gently rubs my son's back as we sit in silence.

I finish the tea and put the cup back down on the rock. My son looks up at me. "You are tired," he says. "What dreams kept you awake?"

I look into his eyes, which seem so much older than the rest of him. Drawn into his gaze, I feel the memory awaken within me.

"I am in that strange, familiar world," I say. "I appear to be successful, with many wives and many sons and many, many goats. I am traveling across a parched landscape, as I have so many times before. This time, I am going to my father's house. He has died. Why am I dreaming this?"

My son closes his eyes, sits silently, then opens them. "You fear for me when you die. You fear that you may be taken from me far too soon. The family and flocks are the wisdom, the skills that you have accumulated here. You fear that even they may not keep us from being separated."

I nod, say nothing, take his small hand in both of mine and hold it tightly.

"Was there more to the dream?" he asks.

"In the dream, I, too, have a brother, a twin. His name is Esau. I have not seen him in many years. I fear and distrust him, and even consider finding an excuse to be late for the funeral so that I will not encounter him."

"This brother," my son asks, "had he hurt you in the past, betrayed you, shown bad faith toward you?"

"No, no, it is more that..." I pause, reach more deeply back into the memory of the dream. "It is more that I have hurt him, that I have repeatedly lied to him and betrayed him. Yet he continually pursues me, wants to connect with me, embraces me when he does encounter me, and does me no harm."

"And what is pursuing you here? Can you see what he represents?"

"The... skin?" I ask. "The scent of the invisible skin?"

My son nods. "What do you know of the skin? Why does it pursue you?"

"It seems like it is rushing to fill a void, to fill some gap in itself. It wants to engulf me, make me part of itself."

"Do you see your brother in the dream? What does he look like?"

"I didn't see him, but I remember having seen him. He looks... he is my twin, and looks exactly like me, only hairier. His skin is rough. In the dream, I remember the sensation of wrestling with him, remember the sense, the scent of his skin, all bristles and acrid sweat..."

"And you are running from him."

"Yes."

"As you are running from the skin."

"I... Yes. But they cannot be the same."

"Why?"

"The skin is pursuing me, always pursuing me. And there will be great danger if it catches me." I shudder audibly.

My son places his free hand on my right hand, so that each of us holds the other's hand in both of his own. "But in the dream," he says "you recall finding welcoming peace each time that your brother has caught up with you."

"Yes. But still I fear him, fear what he might do, what he might say."

"Why?"

"I fear... I fear that he knows me too well. He has seen me take from him what should be his, has seen me betray him, has heard me tell lies when he knows the truth. He knows that he is the good man that I only appear to be, and even though he knows that I—and even my sons—cannot keep ourselves from telling the stories that deride him, he still has..."

I feel my tears begin, gathering in my eyes and flowing in parallel to the sound of the tears from the cave. I lower my head, rest my forehead against my son's soft curls. "Compassion," I whisper. "For all that I am renowned to be strong in the dream, that I am known to be brilliant and successful, he is the bearer of compassion, honor, and truth that I can never know."

"And when he reaches you?"

"When he reaches me, embraces me, I feel the void in my life, then feel it filled, as the halves of a soul that was split in the womb become one. And when he lets go, I feel myself diminished, as if what I need has been taken away. And I resent that, and that turns into fear, fear and hatred of him."

My son looks into my eyes even more deeply, and his own eyes glow and reflect like screens, like mirrors, showing me an image of myself. In a slow transformation, I see myself grow coarser, hairier, yet somehow gentler, see myself change into the image of my dream brother.

Then the image of my brother thins, like steam dissipating from above the kettle. But the mist breathes away only what my brother's image shares with my own form, subtracting and dissolving until all that is left is—

"Yes. The skin," my son says. "Why do you run from it? What danger do you fear if it reaches you?"

"If it reaches me," I say, "it will absorb me, consume me. I will become part of it."

"Or," my son says more quietly, "it will become part of you. The gaps in each of you will be completed, and you will be a whole being."

We sit in silence. Around me, I sense the colors of the landscape becoming richer, stronger. The foot of the rainbow, which had been closer to the mouth of the cave, is now nearer to us, now surrounding us, until all is color, and the rocks and sand and caves have faded away.

"Listen," my son says. "All that you have ever been, all that you have ever seen, all that you have ever dreamed is part of you, and will be part of you forever. What is in your arms is in your soul. What you are running from is running to you. And you, and it, and I will always be here together."

As he speaks, the sound of the rain of tears grows louder, until it is a rushing of waves on a beach, until it is the roar, the hiss of a stationary storm that obscures all other sound. I hold my son tightly, but I feel him being taken from me by a torrent of history that crashes across realms. I cannot hear my voice when I cry his name, can no longer feel his pulse, his breath, his warmth against me. My arms fold in against me, collapsing across my chest. I open my eyes and see that I hold only his cloak, a cloak made from the rainbow. I howl in pain, in loss, and start to run, in no direction but away.

When again I look around me, I see that I am running through the usual landscape, with the ladder, the wrestler, the moon, the caves all in their usual positions.

A voice comes to me from beyond the caves, its echoes preceding it, as if the words have been flung backward from a distant future: "Do not fear, my servant Jacob, for I am with you." I have never heard the voice before, have always known that voice, which rings with memories of my son's voice, of my brother's voice, of my own.

I hear a silence following me, a gap in the landscape of sound, almost tangible in its presence of absence. Then my senses are overwhelmed by the scent of the skin, the memory of dreams of slaughtered goats, the hole in this world, in this life, that I know will fill me, that I know that I must fill.

Fighting my own momentum, I slow my running, stumbling as I walk, as I stop, as I turn. The presence of the skin hurtles toward me. I whisper my son's name, then look up, close my eyes, and open my arms.

For comments and discussion about the tale of Jacob and to hear the audio version, please visit http://www.thebookofvoices.com/Jacob

JUDAH

𐤉𐤄𐤅𐤃𐤄

Judah was one of Jacob's older sons. His mother Leah was the older sister of Rachel, the mother of Joseph and Benjamin.

Jacob favored Joseph over his other children and gave him a coat of many colors. Jacob gossiped to his father of things that his brothers had done wrong, and proudly spoke of dreams in which his brothers bowed to him. The brothers envied and resented him.

Joseph came to his brothers where they were feeding their flock at Dothan. The brothers decided to kill him and threw him in a deep pit to die.

But Judah saved Joseph's life. The Bible says:

> Judah said to his brothers, "What will we gain if we kill our brother and cover up his blood? Come, let's sell him to the Ishmaelites and not lay our hands on him; after all, he is our brother, our own flesh and blood." His brothers agreed... They sold him for twenty shekels of silver to the Ishmaelites, who took him to Egypt...
>
> Then they got Joseph's robe, slaughtered a goat and dipped the robe in the blood. They took the ornate robe back to their father...
>
> He recognized it and said, "It is my son's robe! Some ferocious animal has devoured him. Joseph has surely been torn to pieces."... He refused to be comforted. "No," he said, "I will continue to mourn until I join my son in the grave. " ...
>
> At that time, Judah left his brothers and went down to stay with a man of Adullam...
>
> *(Genesis 37:26-35)*

Judah speaks to us as he prepares to leave Jacob's camp, as Jacob continues to mourn for Joseph.

These colors flash and melt before me. When my eyes are closed, they form shards of taunting brightness, too brilliant to allow me to sleep. When my eyes are open, the colors stain my view, distorting all that I see. These are the shades of betrayal, of guilt: the blue of distant sky and ocean water; the gold glare of the scalding sun reflected by the signet of a king; the green of the smears of grass on linen, on the robes of a father kneeling, crying in a field; and, smearing and mocking all the other hues, the visceral crimson of lambs' and humans' blood.

Even when I close my eyes, I can feel the presence of my father, Jacob, a fading cloud of a man where once there was a star. His feet drag as he walks among his tents, his voice hoarse and mumbling as he does what little business he can still maintain. When he heard that our brother, Joseph, died, it seemed that most of our father died with him. (I notice, recognizing resentment in my noticing, that it is as if he did not have another eleven sons and a daughter still alive.) An aura of permanent mourning hovers around him, a darkness that turns day into twilight for anyone who comes near.

I can not tell him, and none of the others will tell him, the truth, that our brother did not die at Dothan. None of my brothers seem to care. They seem happy in their lives, glad that the burden of our brother is gone, immune to the pain that what we did had caused.

All would agree that our brother was beautiful, with the look and the bearing of the child of a god, more striking than any of us. When we brothers would walk together into a room, those gathered there would see him enter alone.

And with that beauty came his arrogance and insolence, his way of working the desires of others to get the things that he wanted, ignoring and insulting those who did not fit his needs. He could not have failed to see that his telling us of his self-inflating dreams would sting like blinded bees exploding from their hives. He must have known that his shirking of his tasks, wandering up to us late, after the labor was done, to share in our meal without working as we had, would cause us to hate him, to want to be rid of him and his taunting pretenses of innocence.

So on that day at Dothan, when our brother came to our camp at evening after we had worked all day, we brothers conspired to deal with him no more. Most wanted to murder him in that moment, to cut his robes from him, to slash away his life. But our oldest brother kept us from spilling his blood directly, and threw him into a desert pit instead, with no water, where there would be no refuge from the next day's sun, so that we would be rid of him but our hands would be clean.

I, too, shared in their hatred and anger, and I did not speak up when they threw him in the pit. But when, emerging from the evening haze, a caravan of merchants passed us on the road, I saw a way that he might live but be gone from us. So I convinced my brothers to sell him to the merchants as a slave, to have him taken away where we would never hear of him again. They gave us twenty silver coins. Each of the ten of us took two apiece, though many of my brothers may have spent theirs quickly on harlots and on wine.

Then my brothers took his coat, the beautiful one, the one that our father had told the clothier to sew for him alone when all the rest of us would have benefited from better robes, and smeared it with the blood of a newly slain goat.

When we came home, we all entered as if in mourning, presented the coat to our father, and told him that our brother was dead. As I stayed with my father, I saw his soul crumble, and saw him become as one of the dead himself.

Yet I could not tell him what I knew, that our brother was alive, though gone. The guilt of what we did crushed me, locked my mouth shut and made it impossible to breathe those words. The guilt should have spread among all of us evenly, perhaps less for me than for the others, for I was the one who had kept our brother alive. But I was the one who made the final move, who sold our brother, banished him to a foreign land. As painful as it is to see my father grieving, I cannot confess, cannot tell him that he has not lost his favorite son to an unthinking wild beast but to the intents and actions of his other sons that he also loves and trusts.

Now my father is a living ghost, and I cannot bring him back. And I cannot get my brothers to care, to acknowledge that they had cast away their own brother, not a dog that they had kicked away and then dismissed.

But the guilt haunts my life, my every action. The colors of his coat swarm and smear before my eyes as I sleep and when I wake. I cannot banish the visions, the guilt, cannot join in my other brothers' laughter, in the unfeeling carrying-on of their lives.

So, in the night, as this full moon illuminates the grave of Rachel, our brother's mother, and amplifies my father's cries, I must leave. I have packed what few belongings I care to take with me and, leaving the rest of my life behind, will creep out of my father's camp, down to Adullam. I will come there as a man without a past, without a name, and try to work, to marry, to have sons of my own, to give myself the life of a quiet, guiltless man.

But I do not know if I will escape these fears, these colors.

The pack on my shoulder has three days' food, a robe, and a scroll that I have written as a will, as words to remember in my new life. In my hand, I clutch only two coins, the pieces of silver that are all that remains of the brother that I had betrayed. I cannot leave them behind, cannot forget. And I will ask that, when I die, these coins will be placed on my eyes when I am dropped into the earth. Perhaps, if I see my brother in the mists of the afterlife, I will be able to return these coins to him, and pray that he can forgive me, so that I can forgive myself.

For comments and discussion about the tale of Judah and to hear the audio version, please visit http://www.thebookofvoices.com/Judah

BENJAMIN

בנימין

Benjamin was Jacob's youngest son. Both he and Joseph were the sons of Jacob's favorite wife, Rachel, who died when Benjamin was born.

The Bible says:

> Rachel began to give birth and had great difficulty. And as she was having great difficulty in childbirth, the midwife said to her, "Don't despair, for you have another son." As she breathed her last—for she was dying—she named her son Ben-Oni [son of my pain]. But his father named him Benjamin [son of the right hand, or son of the south]
>
> *(Genesis 35:16-18)*

When a famine struck, all the other sons of Jacob went to Egypt to get help. Jacob insisted that Benjamin stay back with him. The brothers went to meet the official Zaphnath-Paneakh, unaware that he was really their brother. Joseph, benefitting from his ability to interpret dreams, had risen from slavery within Pharaoh's court.

Benjamin speaks to us as he awaits word from his brothers.

Picture my face. Age it by a few years (though fewer than before, since I am now almost as old as she was when she died), make it thinner, with sharper eyes and straighter, paler hair, and make it, of course, female. That was the face of Rachel, my mother, or so I am told.

Picture me again, a few years younger than I am now, the face now rounder, the eyes perpetually lost in waking dreams. That was my brother, Joseph, at the time that he died. Or so, again, I am told. I was so young when he died, barely able to speak sentences on my own, that my memories of him are as vague as the memories that I seem to have of my mother. And I know that my memories of her are false, since she died (as I am so often told) when I was born.

All the memories I have are second-hand. I have experienced nothing of my own. All my life, I have been cradled, been trapped by my family. My life is blankness, my face described only by reference to the memories of others. But there is no silence within me: I hear the noise between the cracks in the stories they tell. I listen for the truth, and sense how it may shatter the reality that they try so carefully to construct.

This is a family of instant legends. Everything that happens seems to be of catastrophic significance, as if the entire history of mankind hangs on whether one ate lentil soup at dinner. Every tale is told and retold, embellished and altered, until whatever truth there was is drowned in the resonance of the event.

So many of the stories speak of death, so few of birth (except, of course, my own, since my birth was woven into the tale of my mother's dying). So many of these stories tell of armies and slaughter. And the slaughters grow greater in each retelling: the death of a few soldiers becomes the destruction of a city. What may have been a house fire and an earthquake becomes the sulfurous earth devouring tens of thousands at our god's command.

And so many of the stories involve Joseph, my brother, my only full brother, the beautiful, the brilliant, the arrogant, the unsocial, the magical, the lazy, the dreamer, the reader of dreams, and, most importantly, the dead, torn to shreds, I am told, by animals in the fields near Dothan.

But as I listen to the stories, remember them, and compare them, I hear the spaces between the uttered truths. Some brothers will not speak of him at all: some become dismissive when he is mentioned; some grow pale and rush off, or quickly speak of something else. Most who tell the tale agree that he died at a pit, but each eyewitness recalls it differently: some say that he died at the lip of the pit, some that the beast had dragged him down, some that he had gone down into the pit on an urgent errand, and some that he had wandered down there in his dreamer's daze. Some say that he was killed by a wild bull, some by a lion, some by a creature the likes of which they had never seen; some that he struggled valiantly, some that the beast, too, was killed, some that he had had no chance to fight; some that he was killed by a single blow or swipe or bite, some that he was dismembered and devoured. That they only brought a swatch of his robe home with them has had many explanations: that he was buried on the spot, that there was too little left to bury, that the beast had carried his body off to its lair.

I always ask the unanswered questions, enjoying the ways that the stories distort, sticking pegs of doubt into the points where they don't agree and watching my brothers improvise evolving myths to make it seem as if the stories cohere.

And I gather the testimonies of others as they visit. My uncle Esau comes by every few years, full of gifts, as gracious to our family as my father, Jacob, is curt and wary of him. He tells me that he has seen no graves in the fields near Dothan, makeshift or otherwise, and that few beasts are ever seen there. When I tell him of the stories, he smiles and sighs and tells me to let my brothers have their tales. Each, he says, has grown the story that he wants to believe, and the more time passes, the less important the actual truth becomes. And he tells me stories of the world outside our family's lands, of the larger lands that he controls and the even greater lands of our great-uncle Ishmael, lands that I have never seen.

Now my brothers are gone again, all of them gone on a journey to the kingdom to the south of us, all the brothers gone except for me. Though I am grown, am able and eager to travel, my father insists that I stay home, thinking of urgent tasks in our own territory that only I, he says, can do. So I remain at home, keeping an eye on the servants, doing yet another inventory of what little grain and crops have survived these famine years.

But the lands to the south call to me, beckon me. I feel the pull to travel there, growing in the night, building through my haunted dreams.

I rarely dream, rarely have dreamed. But what dreams I have are always the same: flashes of color, of cloth, of blood, and a voice like my own, as if echoing from distant memory. The voice speaks, not in words but in sighs and resonances. It tells me not to forget, but not what I should not forget. It tells me to be awake, to listen for sounds, for words from afar, for the fragments of truth that escape when the walls of storytelling part.

This part of the dream always looks the same: the field of color is slashed by brilliant streaks like lightning, like the swipe of a lion's claw. But unlike lightning, the slashes do not disappear. Instead, they hover in the space and build into patterns, as if they are words carved into an alien sky in an alphabet that I remember but do not understand.

I awaken from these dreams with a thirst for knowledge, for the words that pass between the traders who come to us from foreign lands. I listen, I compile, and I analyze the news, suggesting things that my father should do, suggestions that he sometimes follows and sometimes ignores. It was I who heard the word of the traders from the lands to the south, word of the ruler there, Zaphnath-Paneakh, second only to the king, who had organized their storehouses, who had established the methods that saved them from the famine.

The traders envy and resent this ruler, who came not from the king's family but from some mysterious other land, first as a servant, then a prisoner, then the ruler of the kingdom's stores. Their stories, too, resemble rumor, resemble myth, and, like my brothers', do not make sense. But they are consistent in their incongruity, and I sense that this lack of logic somehow is indeed their truth.

But I am trapped here by my father's orders, trapped by duty within my father's home. I feel the call to travel where only I am forbidden to go. I feel the need to study, to investigate, to discover what exists in the larger world, outside this web of myth and innuendo that stifles me within this tiny land. But I am always, have always been the dutiful youngest son. In my father's eyes I will always be a child, endangered by a savage reality that has already devoured my mother, his most beloved, his dearest wife whom he desired from the beginning, and his previous youngest child, my only true brother, the only other child of that beloved wife, who inherited his dreams, embodied his dreams, and now exists only in family legend, only in my family's dreams.

Yes, picture my brother's face, or picture my mother's. Take what is most distinctive from them and subtract it, average it and remove it, leaving that which is least interesting, is easiest to forget. What remains will be my own face, will be nothing at all. For someday that blur of what remains in the absence of legend will vanish, will merge with the colors, with the slash of knowledge that inhabits the star-abandoned sky of my long internal night, and I will be gone, off to the south, off into history, to escape or to join the family legend. I will meet this destiny, will step once into and once out of this book of stories forgotten and retold.

Then, like my being dissolves in a fog of description, like my face in this mirror blurs in a mist of breath, I will be free of these legends. I will be free of this family. I will completely, finally, disappear.

For comments and discussion about the tale of Benjamin
and to hear the audio version, please visit
http://www.thebookofvoices.com/Benjamin

JOSEPH

יוסף

Joseph was the son of Jacob and Rachel.

His brothers, who envied him, threw him in a pit then sold him to traders who brought him to Egypt. (The story of his capture and his survival echoes earlier myths in nearby cultures in which their gods died and were resurrected.) His ability to interpret dreams helped him rise from prison to become a leader within the court of the Pharaoh, the king of Egypt.

When a famine struck Canaan, where his family lived, his brothers traveled to Egypt to seek the help of the Pharaoh's second-in-command, Zaphnath-Paneakh, not knowing that he was actually Joseph.

The Bible says:

> Now Joseph was the governor of the land, the person who sold grain to all its people. So when Joseph's brothers arrived, they bowed down to him with their faces to the ground. As soon as Joseph saw his brothers, he recognized them, but he pretended to be a stranger...
>
> *(Genesis 42:6-7)*

Joseph speaks as he awaits the meeting with his brothers.

At times, I cannot remember if I am real. Much of what I know about myself comes from stories told about me; I doubt my memory if it conflicts with them. I have always lived in a world built half from matter and half from dreams. Neither seems more lucid than the other. When I wonder if I am dreaming, I too often forget to check whether I can fly. And

81

I sometimes forget whether flying would show me to be dreaming or to be real.

My life has always seemed tenuous, disconnected, made up of states without transitions, disjunct moments threaded together by the logic of dreams. For a seeming instant, I was a child. Then I was grown, with a beautiful coat, but with vengeful brothers, once Rachel, my mother, was gone. Then I was in a pit, my coat torn from me. Then I was sold to the Ishmaelites, then sold to the Egyptians. Then I went from being a slave of an Egyptian to running his household, then from being a prisoner to running the prison, then from being dragged in front of the king to running the kingdom. Everyone has always seemed to like me, though I don't know why—everyone, that is, except for my brothers, whose distaste for me was as baffling as everyone else's trust, and except for the wife of my first captor, my first employer, who liked me perhaps far too much: the effects of that love could not be distinguished from the effects of equal hate.

I try to remember my life, but true history gets tangled with other editions, other incarnations, other fantasies of myself. I see myself saved from the pit at Dothan and sold, my bloodied coat shown to my father, evoking his anger, his grief. But I also see myself dead in the pit, then raised from the dead, and I see my coat shown to my grieving wife (though I don't recall being married at the time). And I see an earlier, parallel history in which I am not human but a god, an emblem of my tribe, of fertility, and I hear the story told of my death and rebirth at the same time every year.

In my dreams, in my memory, I hear my brothers arguing above the pit, shouting that I am dead, shouting that I should be dead, that I must die, that I must not die. The voices have changed over time: At first I remembered Reuben calling for my death, then I remembered Levi, but now the memory is mostly of Simeon, as angry and vengeful as Levi, but without Levi's gift of using his voice to lull, to convince, to coerce.

I see my memory of Jacob, my father, wailing and clutching the shreds of my coat, calling my name, refusing to be consoled. Yet clear as that memory is, I know that it is a fabrication, perhaps the memory of a dream, since had I been there to experience it, it would not have happened.

I hear a voice arising from Ramah, my mother wailing for me, though I know that she is long dead, crying for all of her children, for the children of my father, as if they, too, were gone, though they all now are well, are alive.

I feel the gentle touch of my only sister, Dinah, now departed from the family, living in the city of women, a survivor of their brother's violence, making peace with the survivors of our brothers' violence toward them. Her city, her people cycle in time, the city forever destroyed and repeatedly rebuilt, its well always standing, its water circling, streaming across the memories of my bones.

And I remember my little brother Benjamin, my mother's only other son, as he crawls to my father's side to pull on his robes, as he stays away, crying, at the far side of the room, frightened by the ferocity of my father's grief. In some memories, he is not there at all, too young to remember me, not knowing that I had been there, that I had gone. And I see him growing up, attached to our father, yet resenting our father for his refusal to let him be an adult, to let him out of his grasp, needing my father to see him not as an echo of my mother, of me, but as a singular person himself. And I know that these memories, too, must be false, since I was not there, could not have been there when all this had gone on.

Now my brothers are coming here, coming to see the mighty vizier Zaphnath-Paneakh, not realizing that I am he. (Have I always had that name? Have others had it before me?) Yes, I know that they are coming, as I have known what has happened with the family over the years. The reports have had gaps, have conflicted with and contradicted one another, though the contradictions may only have been with my memory of them, with my memories of dreams of them.

I have often imagined this moment, playing out fantasies and scenarios of our meeting: I am kind to them, I am cruel to them, I comfort them, confuse them, torture them, torment them, I seek revenge, I refrain from seeking revenge, all in imaginings rehearsed so often and so clearly that I remember them as perfectly as, more perfectly than things that have already happened. Perhaps, in their conversations (conversations that I have imagined, dreamed, remembered), they have considered the ways in which they might encounter me, whether they might find me as a servant, a slave, a beggar, as one who has blended in, passing as an Egyptian, as one who has taken revenge by enslaving those who had enslaved him, as one who has come to the fore to free our slaves. (Do I recall having done so in my alternate lives? Does one of my descendants do this, or a descendant of one of my brothers? I have future memories of a descendant of Levi, his history scrambled with mine as a son of our father in a Pharaoh's court—but he stammers, without his family's magic tongue, so this may not be a child of Levi but my imagination's parody of one.)

They have probably forgotten me, have not imagined that I might still be here. I will begin by greeting them as foreigners, as strangers, as if I have no idea who they are. Then I will glide through the moments along the branching paths of what might happen, reading my script from the forking stele chiseled deep within my heart.

For now, my mind is clear. I must stay focused on the real moment, the real reactions, the real conversation. I will remember my scenarios, my imaginings, my future memories of what will happen. But when things happen here, in the time and space of the inarguably real, I must be prepared to react, to respond. There will be time in the night to digest what has happened, to determine what must happen next, to dream.

I can hear my brothers approaching. My eyes are open, my back straight, my visage stern as I glare (the image of sanity, of order, of control) out through the door, above their heads, as if barely noticing that they are here.

This is the moment to which all other moments have led. We meet at the center of this labyrinth of time. Let them all speak. Let the performance begin.

For comments and discussion about the tale of Joseph and to hear the audio version, please visit http://www.thebookofvoices.com/Joseph

ELISHEVA (INTERLUDE 3)

אלריאבץ

I awaken with images of branches, of vines, with the echoes of flows of sound, multiplying, crossing, blending as if in music not yet made, not yet heard. The branches, the melodies carry words, endless, teeming words, spreading and crossing as they comment on each other, comment on themselves.

I awaken and remember to breathe, sorting out from this tangle of words those that must begin each day. (For your mercy and faithfulness in restoring this soul to me, thank you). I open my eyes to light without source or shadow, in this softly lit room without windows or fire.

There, before me, above me, I see another forest of words. They sail across the ceiling, crossing and challenging one another in junctures of meaning or commentary, flowing down and along the walls then streaming across the floor in seeming spirals that never converge or reach an end.

I move my lips and read these words in silence, tasting each invisible vowel, feeling the texture of each consonant with my teeth and tongue. I realize and recall that these are sacred words, the words of the texts that I have grown to protect, learn, obey, and employ, some in the language that I must have learned as a child, some in the more ancient tongue of study and prayer.

I read these words in silence, but hear their sound through the ears of memory. The voice is not mine, but that of Aspaklarya. She heard and remembered all. She was our textbook. Once a teacher had read a text to her, it was hers forever. If prompted with the name of a text and a few words with which a segment started or the numbers of its chapter and verse, she could recite the text from that point until, if needed, its end. If prompted for the commentaries, she could recite what each of the sages

85

had said about the text, as well as repeating the lectures and discussions that she had heard about the text within the school.

Yes, she could recall any text that she had heard, but she could read none of them herself. She was blind, had come to us blind. Her pale eyes, which showed so much understanding and feeling when she spoke in remembered voices, saw nothing of what was within the room with her. Our doctors told us that her eyes responded to light, but the path of the light from her eyes to her mind had failed.

At times, I would hear the teachers or others of us talking about her (as, at times, I would hear them talking about me). Newcomers would ask why, if her eyes still functioned, Aspaklarya could not see. Had she seen something so horrible that she could no longer bear to see what was around her? Perhaps, the teachers would tell them. But perhaps she had seen something of such terrible beauty that nothing else could replace its image within the eyes of her mind.

I only sensed once what she might have seen. Late one night, I awakened to hear Aspaklarya crying out in her sleep. I went to where she lay, across the room, and saw her writhing and shaking. I placed one hand on her forehead and one on her chest to see if she was burning with fever, but felt no unusual heat.

I leaned farther forward and rested my head on her chest, to comfort her, to comfort myself. Suddenly, her hands came up and grasped my shoulders. Her eyes opened wide and seemed to be seeing me, seemed to be glowing, seemed to be seeing everything. She whispered one word, then spoke it again and again, her voice getting louder, the single syllable growing longer: *"Eysh!"* she said, "Fire!"

I looked around in a panic for fire within the room, within the school, but I felt no heat, smelled no smoke, saw no flame. Her cries grew higher, more fierce, until I feared that she herself might burst into flame. Then she sat upright and pulled me forward, my face close enough to hers to taste her breath. She spoke one verse quietly, in a deep, majestic voice, the voice of a king, the voice of the Psalms: "The voice of the Lord," she said, "kindles flames of fire." And the look on her face was not of terror, but of deep joy.

Then she fell backward, back to lie upon her bed, back to an almost gentle sleep. I fell back with her, holding her, and spent the rest of the night in her bed, as if to shield her should other nightmares come to shatter her peace.

She awoke before me, and I awoke to find her returning the embrace. We rose and began our morning ritual of cleansing and prayer. She showed no sign of remembering what had happened in the night, and my memory, as it always did, swiftly faded away.

But I remember now. And I wonder what she must have seen to cause her to lose her sight, to lose her own voice, as I had lost my voice, my memories. Perhaps the face of an angel? No, I have seen the face of an angel and retained my sight. Perhaps the face of God? But no one can see the face of God and live.

I return to this present room, this present moment, letting the sights and subtle sounds around me softly replace my memory of Aspaklarya. My eyes catch the thread of the words of a psalm as it drifts along the ceiling and down the wall: "The voice of the Lord kindles flames of fire; the voice of the Lord makes the desert tremble... The Lord will give strength to his people; the Lord will bless his people with peace..." The verse branches off into references and commentaries as it reaches the ground and more words (though never the name of God) stream across the floor.

I must arise now, to care to my daily cleansings and prayers. I focus my heart, my soul, my mind on the breath of the moment. But a part of myself finds itself continuing to dwell upon magic, light, and fire: the magic of our memories and powers, the sourceless light that fills this vibrant room, and the fire behind Aspaklarya's eyes.

THE BOOK OF EMERGING
ספר היוצאת

MOSES

צֵאה

Moses was born some 400 years after the time of Joseph. In that time, the Israelites, the descendants of Jacob, had moved to Goshen, a fertile area in Egypt. When their fortunes turned, they became Pharaoh's slaves.

Moses was born to descendants of Joseph's half-brother., Levi When he was born, the Pharaoh declared that all male children born to the Israelites would be killed. His mother hid him in a raft on the river Nile. When Pharaoh's found him there, she named him Moses and raised him as her own. Moses's mother served as his nurse, never letting his adopted family know who she really was.

When Moses had grown, he killed a taskmaster who was beating an Israelite slave. He fled to Midian.

There, the Bible says:

> The angel of the Lord appeared to him in flames of fire from within a bush. Moses saw that though the bush was on fire it did not burn up... When the Lord saw that he had gone over to look, God called to him from within the bush, "Moses! Moses!"
> And Moses said, "Here I am."
> *(Exodus 4:2,4)*

Moses speaks as he approaches the burning bush.

I am standing in the desert.

I am standing in the desert,
and a bush is burning before me.

A bush is burning,
and it is not consumed.

It is not consumed,
as smoke is rising from it.

It is not consumed,
as a voice is rising from it.

A voice is rising from it,
and it is calling out my name.

It is calling "MOSES."

It is calling "Moses"
and I am afraid.

But then, more gently,
it is calling my other name.

It is calling my other name
that no one else knows.

It is calling my other name
that my mother gave me
before she gave me up,

That my mother gave me,
before the princess found me,

before the princess found me,
and named me "Moses,"

"Moses,"
a name from the oppressors,

"Moses,"
a name that everyone would know,

"Moses,"
a name that I knew was not my own.

But when I had asked my mother
what name she had given me,
what name she had meant me to bear,

she said, "You are Moses now,
and you must live with kings

You are Moses now,
and you will be a leader.

You are Moses now,
because you have to be

You have to be true
You have to be strong
You have to be strong for us."

And the bush is calling me,
And the bush is calling me "Moses,"
And the bush is calling me by my secret name,
the secret name that I never knew

But when I hear the bush say it,
When I hear the bush sing it,
when I hear the bush whisper it,
I know the name is mine.

And as I suddenly know my name,
I suddenly know my destiny,
I know my future,

of struggle,
of struggle, and plagues,
of struggle, and plagues, and faith,

of struggle, and plagues, of faith,
and of freedom.

And I will go down, now,
I will go down to Egypt's land
I will tell Pharaoh
to let my people go.

But first,
But first I will go home
I will go home to my mother,
back to my mother's arms,

And she will hold me,
As she held me before she let me go,
As she held me when I was a child,

And I will whisper to her,
I will whisper to her
that I now know who I am,
I will whisper to her my true, my secret name,

And she will tell me
"You now know who you are,
You now can be a man,
can stand up to kings,
You now can lead

And people will know of what you will do,
and people will sing of Moses

And maybe, at the end of days,
when all good things are known,
we all will gather back again,
will gather by the river
that leads us to heaven,

where we will sing of our lives,
of our past, of our history,

and we will sing of Moses,
and then in a loving whisper,
we will all sing our true names."

For comments and discussion about the tale of Moses
and to hear the audio version, please visit
http://www.thebookofvoices.com/Moses

PHARAOH (OF THE EXODUS)

פרעה

Pharaoh was the title of the king of Egypt. The people of Egypt believed that their Pharaohs were gods.

This particular Pharaoh was the son of the Pharaoh whose daughter rescued Moses. He was raised in the same household.

Moses returned from Midian and demanded, in the name of a God that had no name, that Pharaoh free the Israelite slaves and allow them to leave Egypt. When Pharaoh refused, God unleashed a series of plagues that attacked the sacred symbols of Egypt.

The Bible says:

> Now the Lord had said to Moses, "I will bring one more plague on Pharaoh and on Egypt... Every firstborn son in Egypt will die." ... But the Lord hardened Pharaoh's heart, and he would not let the Israelites go out of his country.
>
> *(Genesis 11:1,5,9)*

Pharaoh speaks to the people of Egypt just before that tenth plague.

I am Pharaoh, ruler of all Egypt and god to all the world. Let all the world hear me: I am Pharaoh. I am known to all by many names, some shouted, some more powerfully whispered. But the only one that need survive, the only one that matters, is this: I am Pharaoh, as my father was Pharaoh and his father before him. We are all one god in this succession of bodies. This body may be destroyed, may be lost, or may be laid to sleep beside its ancestors in the grand tomb that my people are building in gratitude, in praise. But the god-king Pharaoh can never die, as this land, this people, this Egypt can never die.

We are a strong people, loyal, good, and proud. Let all the nations of the world know this: We are a strong people. No other nation in the world is like us: when another nation might seem to wound us, we return to the fight stronger than before. When fate seems to tear us away from our belongings, from our families, from the very air and water and earth that we worship and maintain, we flourish, making our gardens, our armies, our culture more vibrant than before.

We all know our places in this world of stones, plants, and animals, demons, gods, and men. We know that our world depends on this order. We all work together to maintain our world for the glory of our gods, and the gods work with men to maintain the world as a place where we can live.

Now we have been attacked, without provocation and without cause, by magicians of the lowest of tribes, by people who have returned our generosity and acceptance with slander and assault. They aim to tear apart the very fabric of our society, shirking the work that the gods have given them, so that they might worship a new puny, cowardly god of their own.

We have not forgotten the history of these tribes. They ran from their own lands to enter ours when they were too weak, too disorganized to survive in the face of famine. When they came to our land, we welcomed them, giving them some of our richest fields in Goshen to maintain as their own. And when they failed at even that task, we gave them honest work. We employed them to build our glorious temples. tombs, and cities, with duties and pay comparable to those of our own people there, those who knew that their place in society was to be on the necessary lowest tier, without whom no society can survive.

Yet now, without reason, without sense, they have decided to quit their work, to tear themselves out of society as one might try to whisk away the lowest few cubits of a pyramid—while the structure might survive, it would have to fight to maintain its stability, and the removed layer, made useless, would collapse on its own. So, too, would our society be shaken, though it would survive, and this layer of people, this lowest of tribes, soon would surely die in the desert, without preparation, without water, without food, without the shelter with which we honor the sun god and protect ourselves from his rays.

They claim that they have been commanded to do this by a tiny, ridiculous god, one so unformed and so vague that they cannot even say what his name is, cannot draw any pictures of him or say where he might live or what aspect of nature he represents. He has no face, no being of his own, and tries to make himself known instead by sneak attacks, by subversion, by whittling away at a grand society from within and trying to turn its own symbols, its own gods against it.

Its chief magician, its supposedly greatest representative, I know far too well. I knew that this Moses was evil from the moment that I first saw him, when he was a baby and I was a child.

We should have killed him, by my father's command, when he first appeared. He was born to be a slave, the child of slaves, in a year when the god-king had declared that no boys dare be born to those tribes.

But his power to twist men's will was strong from the instant that he was born. The midwives could not bring themselves to kill him, and, when they tried to hide him by the river, my sister found him. She should have drowned him then and there, but her will to act justly was subverted. She brought him home, where he even struck at the soul of the god-king. My father let him live, let my sister raise him by my side, brought the boy's own birth-family in to cater to him, to pollute the palace with their presence.

He was always the darling of the court; I, though certain to be the next Pharaoh, was almost forgotten. His every action was seen as charming, as brilliant. When, as my father played with him, the boy tore the crown from his head and stomped it flat, people laughed. When he argued with the teachers, giving no respect to the teachings of the gods, people applauded his wit, even though he needed his brother to speak for him so that people could understand what he barked and mumbled. And when he proved himself to be a soulless killer, striking down an Egyptian for merely doing his job, no one in the palace bothered to say a word to him. He only fled when one of his fellow Hebrews had enough of a sense of justice (so unusual for one of them) to confront him with the evidence of his immorality.

Now he is back, returned from Midian, where he twisted the souls of the priests and got himself married into their highest family. He says that he brings the word of a new god, but his story is so confused that he cannot even recall this supposed god's name. He says that this god spoke to him not in thunder, not in the roaring of the waters or in the trembling of the earth, but in a tiny voice from a shrub on fire. And he demands that I end the service of his thousands of people, of this entire caste, without preparation, without a replacement plan, without even the slightest restitution for the damage that it would cause to our society, to our economy, to our world.

My first instinct, when we first granted him an audience, was to laugh. I laughed even more when he tried to make his point by having his brother perform an irrelevant stunt with rods and snakes. But then his demands turned to threats, and when we threw him out of the palace, his supposed god began its assaults.

This god has no signature powers, no symbols of its own, so it has to make do with perverting the symbols of our own powerful gods. He changes the water of the life-giving Nile into blood; he causes the frogs to swarm and occupy our houses; he kills the frogs and causes them to stink and bring lice, then for the lice to become flies, then to have them bring sickness to our beasts. And then he attacks and perverts the very sun and rain and sky, bringing us darkness and thunder and hail.

And Moses and his brother come to us each time and present their increasing demands. And each time he twists our will a little more, and not only do we not kill him on the spot, but we weaken and accede, for the moment, to his demands.

But our gods are strong, and their ways are just, and each time, once we are out of the power of his soulless eyes, reason returns. And the gods strengthen our hearts, and we return to the right paths, standing up for the truth of our gods' ways against the oppression of that puny supposed god, and we stand firm, as our towers, as our temples, as the truth of our lives must stand.

He claims that there will be one more plague, that his god will attack the very heart of our houses. He claims that he will attack the truth of our dynasties, that the first-born sons of our families will die.

He will have no effect. We are strong, and will not bow, will not bargain with those whose only power is the will to bring terror to our land. I am a first son, and I declare that I am prepared to die, if I must, to affirm the truth of our gods. And my own first-born has sworn that he, and his own infant first-born, would happily sacrifice themselves for the glory of our gods.

For we know that we go on to life beyond life, that this life is but a preparation for the glories of the everlasting life to come. I am a god, but I have incarnated myself as apparently human so that I might guide my people into building our cities of tombs, so that the wonders that we accumulate may accompany us when we return to the next world. Those of the people who are not or are not yet gods have this same belief, this same knowledge in their hearts that whatever they might suffer in this life will make their lives stronger and sweeter beyond the grave.

Let them strike us, then, from all directions, from within and from without. Let them cause our bodies to burst with boils and our souls to fester with the madness of the dark. We will prevail. Our gods will prevail. Our truth will prevail.

For I know that this is what history will remember, will say of me, of my people (for I and my people are one): that the more he was oppressed, the more he increased his power and extended his reach. For on the day when time ends, all Pharaohs, all the people of this land will arise and rejoice across all history. On that day, we will be the kings in every land. On that day, we will all be gods. We will be one. Our name will be one.

For comments and discussion about
the tale of the Pharaoh of the Exodus
and to hear the audio version, please visit
http://www.thebookofvoices.com/PharaohOfTheExodus

Aaron

אהרן

Aaron was Moses's older brother. Moses had trouble speaking (legends say that he burned his mouth as a child), so Aaron spoke for him.

After the Israelites fled Egypt, Moses led them to Mount Sinai, where God gave them the ten commandments and other teachings. God designated Aaron and his sons as his priests, and gave them many rules to follow in doing their tasks.

The Bible says that, soon after they received these rules:

> Aaron's sons Nadav and Avihu took their censers, put fire in them and added incense; and they offered unauthorized fire before the Lord, contrary to his command. So fire came out from the presence of the Lord and consumed them, and they died before the Lord. Moses then said to Aaron, "This is what the Lord spoke of when he said:
>
> "'Among those who approach me
>   I will be proved holy;
> in the sight of all the people
>   I will be honored. '"
>
> Aaron remained silent.
>
> *(Leviticus 10:1-3)*

Aaron speaks as he mourns his sons.

"Strange fire"... and so my sons have died. And so I sit in silence, and so I mourn. I have always been the quiet one.

I leave it to Miriam, my sister, to exclaim and to dance; I leave it to my brother Moses to lead; I only serve. When I speak, the voice is mine, but the

101

words are the words of my brother; when I give blessing, I echo the texts of the Lord.

"Strange fire"... I had always raised my sons to be righteous, to be good, to make each action more true than it easily might have been, to make each moment more sacred than the one before. I raised them to examine, to devour, to dissect and reinvent each particle of the law that my brother wrote, each breath of wisdom whispered by the breezes that swept past those eloquent tablets of stone.

My sons knew that God's love increases when people reflect it with love for him. They knew that we enhance and confirm God's sabbath by resting with him on the seventh day. So when they saw the fire descend from heaven, consuming the bull, the calf, and the lamb, they rushed to the altar with fire of their own to expand and combine with the fire of the Lord.

And it did expand, and it did combine, and then it engulfed my sons and burnt them as it burnt the offerings. Then the fire returned to heaven, and all that was left was ash, the ash of their bodies and the cries of their mother. And the wind returned from the north and drowned the cries in the howls of the ringing stones, and it mixed their ashes with the sand that covered our resting place, removing from them the promise of ever reaching the land of our dreams, making them forever a part of this now-cursed land.

And I held my peace. Yes, let history read that I held my peace. For that is my lot: I am the quiet one, the one in the middle, loving peace and pursuing peace.

But I am listening. I am listening and learning how to speak my own words. And though I will continue to pray, and will continue to love the Lord, I will hold my peace no longer. And on the most sacred of days, in the most sacred of places, as I stand beyond the veil in the presence of the Lord, a new strange fire will burn within my eyes. And he and he alone will discover what I feel.

For comments and discussion about the tale of Aaron and to hear the audio version, please visit http://www.thebookofvoices.com/Aaron

MIRIAM

פֹרִים

Miriam was the sister of Moses and Aaron. She brought the infant Moses to the river where Pharaoh's daughter found him. She and their mother helped raise him within the palace.

She became known as a prophet. When the Israelites fled Egypt, she led them in the triumphant "Song of the Sea."

But, as the Bible says:

> Miriam and Aaron began to talk against Moses because of his Cushite wife, for he had married a Cushite... Then the Lord came down in a pillar of cloud; he stood at the entrance to the tent and summoned Aaron and Miriam... When the cloud lifted from above the tent, Miriam's skin was leprous—it became as white as snow... Moses cried out to the Lord, "Please, God, heal her! "... The Lord replied to Moses, "Confine her outside the camp for seven days; after that she can be brought back."
>
> *(Numbers 12:1,5,10, 13-14)*

Miriam was reunited with the Israelites after seven days, but the Bible tells of her death soon afterward.

As the Israelites traveled through the desert, a magical well, associated with Miriam, traveled with them. It disappeared when she died.

Miriam speaks from the well, toward the end of her seven days' exile.

A n infinite moment of silence. In the deepening darkness, here within the well, I am falling, falling, past where I should have struck the water, past where I should have struck the earth at the bottom of the well. I have been falling for so long that I no longer feel myself fall, save that my hair (long, suddenly white) is trailing above me in my wake. Features within the walls shoot past me, helping me see the direction in which I am falling. But when I close my eyes, I feel as if I am floating, adrift on dry water on a sea of muted wind.

The life from which I have fallen – in huts, in palaces, in hiding, in the desert – seems as far from me now as the vault of heaven is from the lands where I have dwelled. But the distance, the time over which I have fallen cannot erase the senses and memories of life. Memory is seared into the milk whiteness of my flesh, my hair, in the exhaustion of my voice, raw from singing, from shouting, from celebration, from tears.

If anyone had the right to confront my brother Moses, to criticize him, it was I, the one who had saved his life so soon after his birth, who had taught him, who spoke for him before the people as our brother Aaron spoke for him before kings. When Moses needed to sing, I led the people in his songs. When he summoned water from the rock, I formed the rock into this well, which has followed us in our travels through the desert, from Horeb on to Hatzerot.

And when his wife Zipporah came to me in tears, in despair over how Moses was neglecting her, I went to Moses, bringing Aaron with me, to speak on her behalf before all the people, to remind him that above all, above his responsibilities to his people, even above his responsibility to his God, a man's first responsibility is to his family, to his children, to his wife.

Moses said nothing for himself. He stood silent, the image of meekness. When we were done, he simply opened his arms and looked upward. And suddenly he and Aaron and I heard the voice of God summoning us to the tent of meeting.

There we saw the pillar of cloud with which the Lord makes himself known. He summoned Aaron and me inside.

And there God rebuked me, his words slapping me in the face. Yes, he said, Aaron and I were prophets, but not prophets at the level of Moses. While God spoke to us from within dreams, within clouds, he spoke to Moses face to face. How, then, he asked, dare we speak against Moses?

And he left me as I am now, drained of all color. When I returned to the well and looked at my reflection, I saw myself as a sketch of absence: white skin framed by white hair against white clouds, then the near-white walls of the well, surrounded and completed by the desert's white sands.

They banished me from the camp, by God's command, condemned to stay here, in solitude, for seven days. While the people had planned to move on, they have refused to travel without me (though I wonder if they have done so in solidarity with me or out of fear of losing the well).

There I sat for six of the days, with no one to speak to, no sounds other than the wind. I took to sitting by the well, listening to how the wind, blowing across its smooth opening like breath across a flute, caused deep resonances to rise forth, groaning and rushing like the sighs and whispers of the desert itself.

Then, at twilight at the end of the sixth day, I heard the sounds coalesce into patterns. The deep hums brought forth higher tones, coming up and disappearing, forming phonemes, letters, a name: they were calling "Miriam."

I looked down into the well, and saw, as always, the reflection of my face. But the face was speaking, calling me, calling my name. "Have I gone insane so quickly," I thought, "that I see phantoms calling out to me?"

"No," the face said aloud, "I speak for the Lord."

"Have you come to apologize?"

"No," it said. "Not to apologize, but to explain, and to ask a favor of you."

I did not reply.

"You were right about Moses, about Zipporah," it said. "The Lord has told him to return to his wife. His relations with her would not compromise his holiness but will enhance it. But at this sensitive time, as he builds these tribes into a people and prepares to lead them home, they could not see his leadership questioned. So the Lord chastised you, banished you, punished you, bringing you to this place, to this moment."

"And now," I said, "I am to be returned to the people?"

"Not now. The banishment will last the full seven days in the eyes of the people."

"And in my eyes? In the Lord's eyes?"

"This is the favor that the Lord asks of you. You have an opportunity to step outside of time. You would be a teacher, a leader. You can create a school, a community of prophets, where people can come, can seek refuge and learn."

"Why would I receive this supposed honor?"

"Because you are a leader, a singer, a teacher. Because you care about doing what is right in the eyes of the Lord, but also care about the people. And, most importantly, you care enough to have challenged Moses, to have challenged the Lord."

"And what need I do to make this transition?"

"All you need," the face said, "is to step into the well."

"Do I have a choice in the matter?"

"Yes. You can either accept or decline the offer."

"Does the Lord know which choice I take?"

"The Lord sees time from outside of time. You would learn to do so also. He knows whether you come to accept the offer. But the choice is yours."

"Both cannot be true," I said.

"Look at the path that a serpent has left in the sand," the face said, "or the path that a river has taken in its voyage from the mountains to the sea. Each is made of a multitude of tiny chances and decisions, but viewed from outside the voyage, the resulting path is clear."

"And if I do not choose?"

"That in itself is a choice. In either case, at sunset tomorrow, as you measure time, you return to your people, healed."

"If I step outside of time, do I live forever?"

"Not forever, but for a very long time. The doorway out of time opened in your world when the Lord gave the tablets of the Law to Moses. When they return to heaven from this world, the doorway closes. But that happens after more years here than, according to your histories, have elapsed since the beginning of recorded time. You would live for a very long time, but you would not age further. When you would return to this world when that world ends, it would be as if no time at all had passed."

"Would the work there have an impact here? Would it be remembered by history?"

"No, not by history. But traces of your actions would be felt in legends and in songs. To be most effective, you would work in secret. But when people need you, they would find you. And when the Lord would need to remember his covenant with humanity, you would be there to guide him, remind him, and, when appropriate, challenge his decisions."

I sat in silence, contemplating. When next I looked into the water, the face within the well was silent. I opened my mouth to sing a long tone, to hear it resonate in the depths of the well. The reflection of my face opened its mouth as well, then shattered as the water responded to the vibrations of my voice. When I fell silent, the reflected face returned to being identical to my own.

These were the choices: I could jump or I could stay. I knew that I would not die in the descent, since the face had said that, either way, I would return to the people, healed, tomorrow. I knew that the voice was telling the truth, knew that the voices of prophecy, though they might confuse, would never lie.

I had asked the right questions. I had received appropriate answers. The choice was mine.

I sat by the well for a long time, long enough for the sun to finish setting and for the full moon to rise. As I saw the moon's reflection move to fill the surface of the water in the well, I heard its voice whisper to me, "Miriam, your sisters await you."

The well filled with a brilliant glow, as if the light of the moon had transformed into a milky lantern. I knew that I would have to choose, but did not know what the choice would be. All that I could do would be to move to the point of decision.

Certain that I was alone, I dropped my robe by the side of the well, and stepped up onto its wall. For a moment that felt, itself, as if it was outside of time, I hovered there, between constancy and commitment, between time and infinity.

Then I felt my body decide: evenly, with a certainty that my mind did not yet share, my left foot stepped out into the air above the well.

I stepped out, and I fell, and I am falling, down farther than the earthly well could have gone. I hear echoes of sounds pass me (a distant gong, the wheeze of reeds, a resonance of deep sliding trumpets) as I leave the sound of the desert wind. Images flash around me, glowing from the walls (other women falling alongside me, a hare in human clothing, a circle of lesser angels shouting from and to a falling girl, a blue house in a whirlwind surrounded by leaves), as the light from the moon above fades away, and a glow from below grows more brilliant.

I fall away from the land, away from time, and see a multitude of destinies surround me. They spread out over all of time, as if a map has been laid out showing histories past and future, extending in more directions than I can name. Endless rivers of emotion flow through me, starting, perhaps, in fear or uncertainty, but all running toward an ocean of joy.

I know (though I do not know how I know) that this decision is the right one. I do not know if I will ever land, or where, or how, or precisely what awaits me. For now, I let myself sink into the luxury of this moment, away from the pull of time, of earth. I throw my head back, spread my arms, and let the ecstasy of falling overwhelm my soul.

For comments and discussion about the tale of Miriam and to hear the audio version, please visit http://www.thebookofvoices.com/Miriam

SICHON

סיחון

Sichon was the king of the city of Kheshbon.

As the Israelites wandered in the desert, they asked for permission to pass through Sichon's land.

The Bible says:

> Israel sent messengers to say to Sichon king of the Amorites: "Let us pass through your country. We will not turn aside into any field or vineyard, or drink water from any well. We will travel along the King's Highway until we have passed through your territory. "
>
> *(Numbers 21:21-22)*

But, as Moses says as he recounts the story to the Israelites later on:

> "Sichon king of Kheshbon refused to let us pass through. For the Lord your God had made his spirit stubborn and his heart obstinate in order to give him into your hands, as he has now done."
>
> *(Deuteronomy 2:30)*

Sichon attacked the Israelites and was defeated.

Sichon speaks as he decides how to respond to the Israelites' request.

Ours is the city of intelligence. Those whom we protect call us giants, claim we hold the ancient knowledge from before the flood.

Here we sit: arms crossed, feet planted, eyes forward, absorbing the world that we detect. The figures show the threats, the possibilities; our perfect information tells us what we must do to protect our homeland, to secure our borders from invaders and from within.

Yet I cannot reconcile my knowledge and my heart.

I see that these travelers intend no threat. They ask to walk through our country, keeping to the king's highway, buying all the food and water that they will consume.

But my heart refuses to let them pass. It defies my reason, the data, all rational views of what the travelers might do. My heart commands me, but with a new voice that I have never heard before.

What fracture in my soul moves me to unfounded judgment? What strange new god works its magic here to override my mind?

I think of where these travelers had been, a generation ago when they entered their desert from the other side. There, too, did they ask the king to let them pass. Then, too, did the Pharaoh clearly see that he should let these people go. And he, too, learned that his heart was growing hard, and he could not do what his reason knew was right. And he signed his decree, and he led his army, and he died there with them at the sea of reeds, as the travelers went free.

Then the rumors and the whispers began, that his heart had been possessed by the god of these strange travelers, that the one who asked the Pharaoh to let them free had not wanted that at all, that this god wanted to leave a path of destruction in the wake of his people as a sign and as a warning.

The whispers and the rumors began, too, that the king had merely gone insane, and led the best of his people to be pointlessly destroyed.

I feel that I, too, am going insane, whether by act of a god or through some more natural and frightening dissolution of my soul. For as my right hand writes these words, I feel my left hand moving forward with a reed pen of its own, reaching the parchment that bears the command to block these travelers from entering our territory, signing the decree with a harsh yet valid parody of my own royal glyph.

I see my left hand reaching for my sword. I feel this alien hardness that has possessed my heart and my hand flowing through to take command of the rest of my being. And I know that my soul is lost.

I will call for the people to defend our land.

There, by the banks of the three rivers that surround our city of intelligence, believing that my mind is whole and that my will is sane, they will stand with me by my command.

There we will fight.
There we will die.

For comments and discussion about the tale of Sichon
and to hear the audio version, please visit
http://www.thebookofvoices.com/Sichon

SERACH

ΗϤϷ

Serach was the daughter of Asher, a son of Jacob. The Bible mentions her in two lists of Israelites, several centuries apart:

> These are the names of the sons of Israel (Jacob and his descendants) who went to Egypt:... The sons of Asher: Imnah, Ishvah, Ishvi and Beriah. Their sister was Serach.
> *(Genesis 46:8,17)*

and then:

> These were the Israelites who came out of Egypt:... The descendants of Asher:... (Asher had a daughter named Serach.)
> *(Numbers 26:44,46)*

In the first instance, Serach is the only woman listed. In the other, the only other women mentioned are the daughters of Zelophehad, who figured prominently in another story.

According to legend, she was the person who let Jacob know that Joseph was alive and living in Egypt. She gave him the news gently, mixed into a song while she played her harp. In thanks, Jacob blessed her and said that she would never die.

Serach speaks from the desert, near the end of the time of the Israelites' wanderings.

They all died at sixty, all of them.

Not the few of us who were more than sixty years old when we left Egypt and crossed the Sea of Reeds: we did not die immediately when we reached the desert. We lived as long as we would have lived otherwise, dying suddenly or gradually, in pain or in senescence, by injury, by disease, or by the silent decisions of our bodies that their lives had been long enough. But when the rest of the people,who were not yet sixty years old reached that age, each of them died.

Now only the two of us old ones are left, Moses and I, here atop this mountain. He is one hundred twenty years old. I have lost count of my years, but they seem to exceed four hundred.

Moses lies here on a flat rock, sheltered from the sun and wind that assault this desert, this mountain top. I sit beside him, playing softly on my harp. This has been my role over these generations, these centuries: to play the harp, bringing comfort when people receive hard news, both news of sadness, and, as with my grandfather Jacob, news of joy that they might find as difficult as tears.

Those who lived most of their years in the desert came to accept death gracefully. When, in the first year, on the ninth day after the first full moon of midsummer, all those who had recently turned sixty died, the people were enraged, furious at God, imagining that a plague had struck. But Moses spoke to them gently, reminding them that all those who had died had died in their sleep, in peace. The people returned to their homes to mourn, but with less of the anger that they had originally felt.

Then on the same day of the following year, all those who had turned sixty in the preceding year also died, all in peace, all in their sleep. And again the people were angry, but less so, and more accepting of the sudden deaths.

In the third year, as the day approached, the anger began to build beforehand. But some of those who had just turned sixty gathered together and decided on a different course. On the eighth day of the month they had a party, with music, with dancing, with joyful recollections of their lives so far. As night fell and it became the ninth day, they sent their families away and slept in a group, there in a tent on a silent plain. They talked for a while, prayed for a while, then, one by one, fell asleep. The sound of human voices was gradually replaced by the voices of the creatures of the desert, by the voices of the wind.

In the morning, none awoke.

And, over that year, all accepted that this was our fate, that all of us would die peacefully on the same day of the same month of the year that each turned sixty. Traditions grew over the forty years that we rested here in the desert, here outside the outpost of Kadesh.

At first, all those about to die gathered for a party of remembrance on that day and died that night, and the survivors gathered to dig graves for them the next day. Then one of them suggested, mostly as a joke, that it might be more useful to dig the graves during the party, as people might built a settlement together, so that the mourners needed only to fill them in at the burials the next day.

And so, each year, we have gathered and celebrated the lives of those who were about to leave us. Those in good health helped to dig their own graves. The rest sat and watched and directed as their friends and families dug them. If any were seen to be working alone, others from the community came to them and helped dig the graves for them.

When all the graves were dug and twilight approached, those about to die arose and dressed themselves in funeral shrouds of white linen. They placed in the graves mementos of their lives, things that they would want to bring with them if they were to be brought into some sort of future life. Those who were saying goodbye to them also gave them gifts to be placed in the graves, gifts by which the people who were about to die would remember them. Then the families and friends would leave, and those that remained would lie down together, each in his own grave, and one by one would silently pass into death.

So it had been for forty years. But this year, everything changed. As always, we held the party; as always, we dug and decorated the graves. I was in my place, as had become the custom, at the center of the new section of the cemetery outside Kadesh, playing the harp for the community. Occasionally, some would come and sing the tones that I was playing. The rhythm of the digging mixed with the waves of voices as, at one point or another, almost all of the people would sing the tones.

Then the time of the last watch arrived. Those who were to lie down in the graves lay down. The others dispersed.

Then, when the sun arose and the roosters crowed, the sleepers awoke. All were confused, concerned. Expecting death, they were baffled by their continuing life. Some arose and walked around, not knowing where to go. Others continued to lie in their graves. Some of their families returned to the cemetery to fill in the graves. Seeing people walking around, none came close, fearing contact with what they believed must be the walking dead.

For years, my tent had been at the edge of Kadesh. I rarely went into the center of the camp. People would come to me, to hear my music, to speak with me. Since I had lived for all these centuries, I suppose, people had come to believe that I had accumulated wisdom. Perhaps it was simply that, having a more relaxed relationship with time, I had developed a willingness to listen to them without needing to speak more than needed to be said. When they would come, they would bring me manna that they had gathered for me, would bring me clothing that I needed or that they believed would suit me well.

On the night that followed that morning, as I sat outside, listening to the wind, to the sand, and speaking with the stars, I heard sounds from the cemetery nearby, voices of confusion, voices of surprise and pain. I arose, answering what I felt to be a call. I had little fear, having played the souls of the dead into their next stages many times before.

This time, however, I found not the dead but the living. They asked me how this could have happened, how they could be alive, what they should do. I had no grand answers, but was willing to serve for them as a focus of listening.

In time, one of those in the field, one who had studied astronomy as a child with magicians who had come to visit Egypt from the city of Ur, spoke: "Perhaps our calendars are wrong," he said. "Our study of the stars is inexact. We have seen, over the years, the times that the sun has lost pace with the moon, when we have needed to intervene and redefine the days so that they would meet again. Perhaps we have lost track of the days, and last night was not truly the ninth of the month."

I sat silently, then asked everyone, "Truth?" One by one, the people nodded and echoed, "Truth."

Then another person spoke: "I will lie down again. Perhaps tonight is truly the last night." And he went to his grave and lay down.

I watched as others did the same. Then I picked up my harp, played a chord slowly, repeatedly, and sang a tone from it. Others joined, breathing the same tone, a tone of release, a tone of acceptance and peace. Then, one by one, all lay down. I played them to sleep.

But again, in the morning, they awoke. Most were surprised, again, and even more surprised to find themselves hungry and thirsty. When friends came to my tent, bearing manna and water for me, I asked them to gather more and to bring them to the new cemetery.

"You wish us to bring food and water to the dead?" they asked.

"They may not be dead," I said, "or do not believe themselves to be dead.

Something new may be happening, something wonderful. We do not yet understand. But maybe we do not need to understand."

And thus it happened for a third day, a fourth, a fifth, a sixth.

Then, on the seventh night after they first lay down, the full moon rose, unmistakably, inarguably. It was the fifteenth day of the seventh month. The pattern had been broken.

They came to me for answers. I had none. But we knew that they were alive.

Together, we all walked to the center of the camp, to the tabernacle. I had put on the colored tunic that I wore when approaching the officially sacred. The rest walked alongside me, all dressed in their linen shrouds, all smiling, singing. The people of the camp came out to see our procession. They stood by the side of the road, letting us pass, uncertain of what was happening, but knowing that it was a moment of joy.

When we got to the tabernacle, the priests could tell us nothing. Even the high priest had no idea that we would be coming, had no idea what had become of the pattern that we knew.

So we went to Moses. When we got to the tent, he had already come out to meet us. "I have awaited this day. The time for which we had hoped has come. It is time for us to return to the land of our fathers, to Canaan."

At the end of a year of preparation, a year of celebration, Moses stood before the people. He reminded them of all that we had experienced, all that we had learned. He let us know what we might find, what we must do, and what we must not do. And he told us that his work was done, that he would not be leading us into the land that had been promised to us.

And on that night, this night, as I lay in my tent on the edge of sleep, I heard Moses's voice calling to me from outside. "I am leaving tonight. Will you journey to the mountain with me?"

I rose, stepped outside, and looked at him. He stood there dressed in his simplest robe, carrying no satchels. "A journey? And you are not bringing anything?"

He opened his arms wide. "I have everything that I need."

I took my harp and walked with him, along the road, out of the camp, up the gentle path on the less-steep side of the mountain.

We came around to the cliff side overlooking Canaan. "Here we are," he said.

"And now we sit?" I asked.

"And now we sit."

We sat alongside each other silently for much of the night. Then, as the morning star rose, he asked me to play.

Now we sit. Moses rests his head on my shoulder as he listens. With each note that I play, I feel him tremble gently, a different quiet shivering with each tone.

As the morning light grows, I feel his own light fade. He is speaking softly, saying things that I cannot remember, that I cannot understand. Some are words in the language of our people, some in the language of those who oppressed us, of those with whom he was raised. He speaks words of his brother and sister, of his mother, of dreams of rebirth, of dreams of reunion.

The sun is rising now above the horizon. As the direct rays shine on Moses, rays of light emerge from his face to meet them. He has stopped speaking. He is gasping, repeatedly, slowly, shallowly.

"Moses?" I ask.

"Here I am," he says, in a high voice, a child's voice. "But my name is not Moses."

"What is your name?" I ask.

The light from his face grows richer, brighter. "My name is—" he says. Then he sings a pure, high note, a note with the sound, the color of the rays of the sun.

I join and sing the note with him, clearly, joyously. Although it is impossible, every one of the strings of my harp resonates with this pitch and vibrates with it, a chord of every note that we know, shifting and shimmering with the slightest difference in the music, in our breaths, in the wind.

Then, from all around the mountain, we hear voices, thousands of voices, singing with us. We look down and see all the people who had died in the desert over all these years, their souls taking the form of the bodies in which they once were clothed.

One by one, the souls rise from the ground until they are at our level, surrounding us, floating in the air. Moses looks at them and stands, as strong as he had been as a youth, glowing with rays so bright as to be almost unbearable. "No, we will not be entering the promised land. But all here may join me in traveling to the world to come!"

He walks forward, off the edge of the cliff, but he does not fall. Walking through the air, he embraces the soul directly in front of us, wrapping his arms around her and whispering in her ear. The soul moves even closer to him, merges with him, until it comes to share the body with Moses's own soul.

The next soul moves toward Moses. Moses embraces that soul, too, whispers to it, and merges with it. Then the next comes forward, and the next, and the next, all the thousands of souls embracing Moses, becoming one with him. He shines ever brighter with each merging soul, the note that they were singing becoming purer, clearer, more powerful.

Then, again, we are alone. He turns, steps back onto the cliff, and again opens his arms. "Will you join me?" he asks.

"Must I?"

"You may do so if you would like," he says. "But it is not required."

"I will stay, then," I say. "I believe that I will know when it is time for me to leave. It is not yet that time."

Moses nods. "Goodbye, Serach. Our souls will meet again, in time."

Then he throws his head back and sings the one pure note, not just with his voice but with the voices of all whom he has embraced, all whom he has touched, has taught, has led. The brightness of his glowing, the power of his voice grow ever stronger, until I must shade my eyes and block my ears.

Now, suddenly, his light and his song have vanished, though I can hear fading echoes of his voice reverberating from other mountains nearby.

Moses is gone. The ground on which he stood, the mountain wall in front of which he stood, have all melted, run, frozen, turned to the sheerest sheets of mirror glass.

I look into the glass and see myself reflected. But I do not only see myself as I now am. Visions of myself as I was, as I will be, join my current image in a dance that spreads out in more directions than those for which we have names. There I am, an infant, crawling across the carpet in the tent of my grandfather, Jacob. There I am, receiving the harp from my great-uncle Esau, who says that he carved it from the wood of a fallen Asherah tree. I am playing the harp to still my grandfather's confusion as he learns that my uncle Joseph is alive, to accompany the family as they move from Canaan to Goshen, to bless houses, to comfort the younger ones as their money fails and they are forced to live as slaves. And I play for so many births, and for so many, so very many deaths.

And then I have crossed the Sea of Reeds and am dancing with Miriam, then I am spending the years at my tent at Kadesh, then I am playing for those about to die, for those who do not die, and then I am here with Moses, here without Moses.

But the images do not end here. I see myself as I will be in the years to come: returning to the land of Canaan, playing the harp for Deborah, for Hannah, teaching my music to the school of women in the lavish caves in a valley among mountains, giving my harp away to a young shepherd in the fields of Benjamin. He touches it and immediately draws forth from it music finer than my own.

And that is all that I see. I do not know if that means that that moment is when I will die, or if I will carry on even longer. I will accept whatever happens. As long as I live, I will live. When I die, I will die. I am not eager to leave this life, but I have lived far more than most. When death comes, I will be ready.

The sun is now fully risen. As I travel around the edge of the mountain, I see that the cemetery is gone. The plain where it had been is now an oasis, rich and green, contrasting with the rest of the desert. I will walk through there on my way home. I may stop to pluck some olives and almonds from the trees.

And then I will come home, sit at the entrance of my tent, and hold my harp gently. I will listen for whatever might come next.

For comments and discussion about the tale of Serach and to hear the audio version, please visit http://www.thebookofvoices.com/Serach

ELISHEVA (INTERLUDE 4)

אלישׁרצע

The sense of a harp's music fills my mind, fills this room. Not the sound of the harp itself, but the emptied resonance where sound has been, much as the emptied shape of a memory of angels remains in sand where a child once lay and waved her arms.

The people from the East told us a name for it when they sat with me, with Aspaklarya, with... whom? I reach into myself, into the soundless sound that resonates within the emptiness of my memory. I reach back, look back, and feel a bit more of my memory appear, feel a dissipation, a new absence of that (protecting?) absence.

I am there, yes, and she is there. And there are more. Many more? I sit facing forward and see perhaps twelve more before me. Behind me, to my sides, there may be many more, or a few, or none. All that I see wear robes, similar but not the same. Each of us has added her own touch. (Her? All whom I see appear to be women, though I am not certain that there are no men.)

A scream suddenly slashes through the silence. All the others look at me. From the burning of my throat, I can tell that the scream was my own. I stumble to my feet and try to run from the room, but feel that a voice is about to be pressed out from my breath, my throat, my lips.

I do not hear what my voice says, do not remember. There is a break in time, as if I had stepped from one room into another. Then I am on the floor, not sitting as I had been but curled in a ball, closed in on my self, shaking, inert. Aspaklarya embraces me, comforts me, hums wordlessly to me, a music of solace as I am surrounded by chaos, by people staring at me or shying away from me in horror.

Then she stops humming, releases me, stands straight and tall there in the center of the room. "Sisters of Sarah!" a voice calls from her lips, "Sacred Sisters of Sarah, listen to me!"

All stop, fall silent, turn to face Aspaklarya. The voice is not her own (it is never her own), but is unmistakably that of the eldest of us, who is not now among us.

"Sisters," she says more quietly, though with no less power, "if these words are emerging from Aspaklarya's lips, a signal has arrived that my mission has failed. I will not be returning from Jerusalem. The city, the temple have indeed been destroyed once again.

"I assure you that the tablets of the covenant have not fallen into the hands of Rome. The cherubim have returned to their realm, securing the tablets with them, removing them from this land. The true heart of the temple is safe. The only things that burn here are wood, fabric, flesh, and stone.

"But it is time for us to leave our school, to move out into the world. We knew that this day would come soon, as our view of the planes of time ends not long after this moment. The power, the magic that holds the space for our school open, that connects it with its points of entry in the world of objects, will fade away. It came to our world when God gave us the tablets, and it disappears when it goes away.

"Now you must gather your belongings and depart from here. I know that many of you already had thoughts of where you might go, your destinations in other places in this world, perhaps in other times. Some in this group have the skills that you will need to help organize your departures. They will make themselves known.

"Do not mourn me now for longer than you must. If you need to do so, there will be time after you are gone. I do not know how I have perished, but my life has been good and has been long. And our souls will meet and merge again in time, as all souls again become one.

"Farewell, my friends. May God extend his blessings, and may the presence of God extend her love, through out all the places and all the times of all the world of creation."

Silence falls, a silence with the shape of the absence of the one whose voice has spoken. The shape is gradually filled with the sound of tears. Aspaklarya once again settles to the floor beside me. I reach out and we hold each other.

At the front of the room, the visitors, who had sat motionless through all that had happened, rise as one. "May that which is one in all of us, in all the many forms around us, bring you courage and peace."

The sound of the tears is punctuated by murmurs of "Amen." Then it falls away again to silence, a silence as deep as it is here, now, in this room with this angel. And the sense of memory falls away, gently, mercifully. All I recall is a sense of destiny, of loss, of the sound of harps, of voices now gone, of the presence of Aspaklarya's breath, the embrace of Aspaklarya's arms.

THE BOOK OF DWELLING
ספר אשבילנה

GIDEON

‏גדעון‎

Gideon was a leader of the Israelite tribes.

The tribes returned to the lands of their fathers not long after Moses died. They had no official government or leadership. Leaders arose as needed from among the people.

When the Midianites threatened the tribes near them, God called on Gideon to lead the fight against them.

Unlike most prophets and leaders in the Bible, Gideon was cautious about his calling, and asked God to prove that the orders were coming from him.

The Bible says:

> Gideon said to God, "If you will save Israel by my hand as you have promised—look, I will place a wool fleece on the threshing floor. If there is dew only on the fleece and all the ground is dry, then I will know that you will save Israel by my hand, as you said." And that is what happened. Gideon rose early the next day; he squeezed the fleece and wrung out the dew—a bowlful of water.
>
> Then Gideon said to God, "Do not be angry with me. Let me make just one more request. Allow me one more test with the fleece, but this time make the fleece dry and let the ground be covered with dew." That night God did so. Only the fleece was dry; all the ground was covered with dew.
>
> *(Judges 6:36-40)*

Gideon speaks on the day between these miracles.

I have never asked much of you. Well, rarely—I have rarely asked much of you. But that scarcely compares to what you have asked of me. And, yes, I realize that I asked you for another small miracle last night, and that you performed it, and for that great favor I am infinitely grateful.

But please, now, if it be your will, I ask you to show yourself again, so that my wife will let me go out and fight your wars. Please, if you will, perform for me just one more tiny miracle.

I have received your commands, or what I believe to be your commands. Perhaps it might help if your angels would wear the same body two visits in a row. As it is now, with them incarnating into a different apparent body each time, we cannot be certain when one appears that it is the same angel to whom we spoke last time. It is hard to tell whether a person really is an angel, and really was sent by you. And now that Chaim down the road suffered that prank where a visiting man, pretending to be sent by you, got him to stand naked and shout your names repeatedly in a field where the women of the next town were having a gathering, nobody particularly trusts that any angel or any orders from you are real.

So now this person (whom I do truly believe is your angel) has told me to leave my home, leave my fields, leave the wine press where I have to thresh the wheat (and I do look forward to the end of this war, so I can get back to threshing the wheat in the field). If you want me to take a small number of men with an even smaller number of weapons, surround both the Midianites and the Amalekites, and somehow vanquish them, I suppose that I can do that.

But my wife, my beloved Zehava, who is beautiful and strong and honest and, as I am frequently reminded, much smarter than I am, has her doubts. She needs proof that things are true. So she demands miracles. She knows that, of all the gods, you are the only one who can perform miracles, so she asks for them, as if for you to sign your commands.

The sacrifice that we set up for you where we tore down the Asherah and the altar of Baal? That was her idea. And she was the one who came up with the argument that saved me when the men of the city came after me: "If your god is so great, step back and let him trigger his own miracle and deal with me."

It worked. You know that I was terrified, but it worked. Now they cheer me, call me Jeruba'al, say that only Baal himself should contend against me. In truth, my Zehava should be getting the praise, getting the fame.

And now your messenger (or, at least, the person whom I believe to be your messenger) has appeared and given me new orders. The plan seems, if audacious, consistent with your previous commands.

But Zehava is rational, is prudent, is cautious. She reminds me that we have no proof other than faith that the messenger comes from you. She says that we cannot depend on faith alone if I am to risk my life.

So yesterday she presented me with a test, and I (shyly, tremulously, speaking from my small place to your great power) requested it of you: that we put a fleece out on the ground, and that in the morning there would be dew only on the fleece, but the ground would remain dry. Impudent, I know, for a human to demand not only a miracle but a specific miracle from you. But when Zehava presents her case, I respond, for with all her beauty and honesty, her wrath is second only to yours.

You responded as we asked: in the morning the ground was dry but the fleece was drenched with dew. We wrung a bowlful of water from it. (And Zehava made soup from it, perhaps her best ever: I am not sure whether is was her handiwork or yours, but, even though the chicken that we placed in the soup was not the plumpest and healthiest that we have had, that nagging cough that I had for the past week is now gone, for which I thank you and her.)

So once we had awakened, fed the herd, done the day's threshing, and had our meal, I prepared to pack for the trip and battle. But when I started to collect my clothes, Zehava stood between me and my pack and glared. "What do you think you are doing?" she demanded.

"I am preparing for battle, as the Lord's messenger commanded me."

"You are that convinced that he was from the Lord," she said, not as a question but as a statement.

I must admit that as her lovely brown eyes stared through me like daggers, my certainty in your word began to waver. "Well, he did tell us consistent things," I said carefully, "and the Lord did perform the miracle that you devised."

"You are convinced that it was the Lord," she demanded. "You are convinced that it was a miracle."

"Did it fail your test? Was there dew on the floor? Did the fleece remain dry?"

"The dew was on the fleece and the floor was dry. But that alone proves nothing."

I stood silent, attempting to follow what she might mean. I failed. "Was that not the test?"

"That was half a test," she said. "Tell me: have you ever in the past left a fleece on the threshing ground overnight?"

"No, I have not," I replied. "But the water—"

"So how can you pretend to know that what happened was a miracle? Is it not possible that when a fleece is left on the ground, it naturally absorbs the dew from the ground, drawing the dew up to collect on it?"

"I... suppose... that it is possible." I let the clothes that I was carrying fall to the ground. Zehava looked down, glared at the clothes, then at me, then at the clothes again, then back up at me, and crossed her arms. I bent down and picked the clothes up again, brushing them carefully to remove any dust that might have collected on them.

"So that proves nothing on its own," she said.

"What sort of proof do you need?"

"You will not leave today," she said, "but will remain home overnight. For the rest of today, the fleece will hang in the sun outdoors so that it will be completely dry. Tonight, you will place it on the threshing ground again. You will have the Lord, if that's who that is, do the reverse of what he did last night: this time, the ground will become wet but the fleece will remain dry."

"I cannot just have the Lord do something," I said. "I can ask him, pray to him, request actions of him. But no one tells the Lord what to do." I refrained from adding, "any more than anyone can ever tell you what to do."

"This must happen," she said. "For you to leave on this journey, he must show us a simple miracle. For a Lord that makes the mountains tremble, changing the behavior of dew is not too much to ask, is it?"

"I... suppose... not," I replied. "But what if both behaviors are natural? After all, last night was the full moon. It is waning tonight. What if the full moon draws dew to fleece, but it is too weak on other nights?"

"You are saying that only to be difficult. If the full moon draws dew to fleece, then the dew would be distributed differently on other nights. The only night on which the fleece would naturally remain dry would be the night of the new moon. Of course, he can decide to make the moon jump from full to new in a single night if he wants—but he would then have to deal with a world of angry women and disrupted tides. And even the Lord might not want to face that." (Let me hasten to say that I am not telling you this to incur your own wrath at my beloved Zehava or at myself, but rather to lay out the logic of her argument.)

I sighed. "Yes, I will ask him. Your way of thinking is, as always, reasonable and true. So if the floor is wet and the fleece is dry, you will let me leave for battle?"

"Yes, I suppose so," she said. "But only once I am convinced. You know that I only raise these questions because I care about you. You know that without some help from someone who can think clearly, you might wander off into some dangerous situation based on your imaginings, and might be hurt. I question you and challenge you because I love you."

"I know that, my beloved," I said. "But may I pack now so that I may leave in the morning?"

"Have you already forgotten that you were going to hang the fleece outside to dry? How can you lead men into battle if you cannot remember these simple things?"

I avoided rolling my eyes. "Yes, my beloved. Let me put these clothes on the table, and I will fetch and hang the fleece immediately."

"And at nightfall," she said. "We will place the fleece on the threshing floor together, then close the door so that no person can enter the room and disrupt the experiment."

She stepped aside. I put my clothes on the table, turned and kissed her on the cheek (leaning forward, since she did not uncross her arms), picked up the fleece, and came out here to hang it up.

So here we are now, just you, me, the sun, and the chickens. And I am asking you, humbly, nervously, to perform this one tiny miracle. It will make everything else much simpler. Oh, and please do not make rain tonight, or everything will be confused, and I will be stuck at home yet again.

Also: could you give me some inspiration as to how I might quickly find the three hundred ram's horns, torches, and earthen jars that I am told that we need for this battle? I will not ask why we need them; I am just collecting things as I am told. For I know that you are all powerful and all knowing, and have some sort of scheme in mind.

Maybe when I get home after the battle (and I am hoping that you are not just in one of your wrathful moods and that you do intend for us to avoid being slaughtered in this war), my vigilant Zehava will explain to me how this all made sense. For now, though, I will proceed on faith.

And could you please let Zehava and me know of, perhaps, some secret code word or handshake that your angels might use to identify themselves when they come around again, or some trivial instant miracle that they can do to show us that they are who they are? It will keep my home peaceful, and might even make Zehava happy.

That is all, I guess. I look forward to this miracle, if it be your will, and to what ever future wonders you choose to provide. Yours, of course, is the power and the glory and the knowledge of all things. I remain your trembling servant. If you have any further messages, you know where to find me: threshing wheat over in the wine press. Hallelujah. Bye. Amen.

For comments and discussion about the tale of Gideon and to hear the audio version, please visit http://www.thebookofvoices.com/Gideon

JEPHTHAH'S DAUGHTER

בַּת יִפְתָּח

Jephthah was another leader of the Israelite tribes, some time after Gideon. He led the tribes when the Ammonites attacked them.

The Bible says:

> Jephthah made a vow to the Lord: "If you give the Ammonites into my hands, whatever comes out of the door of my house to meet me when I return in triumph from the Ammonites will be the Lord's, and I will sacrifice it as a burnt offering. "...
> Israel subdued Ammon.
> When Jephthah returned to his home in Mizpah, who should come out to meet him but his daughter, dancing to the sound of timbrels! She was an only child. Except for her he had neither son nor daughter. When he saw her, he tore his clothes and cried, "Oh no, my daughter! You have brought me down and I am devastated. I have made a vow to the Lord that I cannot break. "...
> He let her go for two months. She and her friends went into the hills and wept because she would never marry. After the two months, she returned to her father, and he did to her as he had vowed....
> From this comes the Israelite tradition that each year the young women of Israel go out for four days to commemorate the daughter of Jephthah the Gileadite.
> *(Judges 11:30-40)*

Jephthah's daughter (whose name, like that of many women in the Bible, is never given) speaks as she wanders in the hills, resigned to her death.

131

I am dead, dead to the world, dead to my father, dead to myself. Here, lying on this cold stone slab atop Mount Moriah, on this peak where Isaac offered up his life to his father Abraham's god, I too have sworn to leave this world, to give over my spirit to my own father's god, to abandon this weary body and let my soul sink down into whatever fate this unyielding god has planned.

I have always been known only as my father's daughter. No one calls me by my own name. I have only seen what he let me see, learned what he let me learn. And now I am to die, by simple trivial fate: He went to war. He swore to his god that if he won, he would sacrifice the first living thing that came through his gate toward him when he returned. I saw him coming home. I ran out to greet him. So now I am to die.

It is dark here, under this shard of the new moon, and nearly silent. The only light comes from the stars. The only sounds are those of wind, of distant frogs, and of a single repeating bleating from nearby.

I want to fade, to silence my mind, but the repeating sound keeps calling me back, holding me here. I try to silence it in my soul by breathing in its rhythm, but that makes it stronger rather than causing it to blend and disappear. So be it. I open my eyes, sit up and try to find the sound.

I look to my left and, despite my grim heart, hear myself laugh. Yes, it is a bleating. There, in a thicket, a ram is caught, the brambles tangled with its fleece, its horns. Yes, a ram, here on Moriah where another ram, long ago, had appeared for Isaac. I laugh again, stand, and walk over to it.

It looks at me as I approach, silent now, great dark eyes comforting and pleading at the same time.

"You would like to be free now, wouldn't you?" I say, and, improbably, it seems to nod. "So would I. But it seems that you must be free first."

I reach down carefully into the thicket, grasp a bramble at a bare spot without thorns, and pull it free of the ram's wool. Some strands tear away from the ram as I pull. They hang in the breeze as if an absent-minded spider had abandoned its web there. I pull another branch, then another, becoming bolder with each tug, as with each loosed bramble the ram becomes free of the branch, the branch becomes free of the ram.

Finally only the horns are tangled. I grasp the bunch of branches that are holding the left horn (some thorns scraping my palms, but I do not care). I slide them carefully toward the end of the horn. "You have to move your head down," I say to the ram. It does, and this somehow does not strike me as odd. "Now left... now up..."

Together, we free its left horn, then its right. It rises to its feet, steps out of the thicket, and stands to my side. It bows its head and butts me very gently, in seeming thanks.

I pat it on its head. "You are free now. You can go." It nods its head again, but, rather than leaving, settles down onto the ground. I look at it for a long moment, then return to the slab and lie back down. I try to give myself permission to drift toward death.

Time passes. I remain alive, remain almost awake, though with the images and phantoms of the realm between waking and sleep drifting through my mind.

Then I feel a bumping against my side and open my eyes. It is night (again? still?). The ram has walked over to me and is butting me again, gently, though less so than before. "What do you want? You are free," I say. "We are finished."

It raises its head and looks deeply into my eyes. Then it looks down again, and, pressing its head against my side, gives a sharp shove.

I tumble off the slab and fall to the ground. "Why did you do that? What do you want?" I ask, standing.

The ram walks a few steps to the north, looks down the mountain, and bleats, twice, three times. It then walks back to me, walks behind me, and once, twice, butts me forward.

"Do you want me to go somewhere?" I ask. It bleats, again steps north, and looks back at me.

"Well, it seems that you will not leave me at peace here." I sigh and follow.

We walk for a long time, the ram usually by my side, though occasionally scouting ahead. Sometimes it pushes me onto or away from a mountain path.

We end up deep in a valley, by the steep rock wall of another hill, sheltered by the darkness beneath the branches of an asherah grove. "What now?" I ask the ram. "This is the end of the path."

The ram nods toward the rock wall, as if gesturing for me to continue walking, then settles again onto the ground. I sit alongside him, my back against an ancient silent well, and stare at the wall.

As the dawn brings more light into the grove, onto the wall, I look more closely. There is no way past it, around it, over it. "Why have you wasted my time?" I say to the ram. "I have no reason to be here. You should have let me die on the mountain." I stand, turn, and prepare to head back the way we came.

The ram leaps to its feet and runs in front of me, blocking my path. "Let me go. Now." I say.

The ram lowers its head, paws the ground, its muscles tensing.

"So this is how it happens? You use your horns to ram me now, to kill me?" I don't understand how this god could want this, but then, I have never understood this god at all.

I stand tall before him and open my arms wide. "Then do it now," I say. I close my eyes then open them, glaring into the ram's eyes. "I am not afraid."

The ram backs up the hill, pauses, then, with one long, loud bleat, rushes toward me. I see him coming, catch my breath, tense my muscles then release them waiting for the impact. But at the last moment, the ram dodges to the right, darts around me, and heads straight into the rock wall. I spin around, looking, listening for the collision, the viscous crash of flesh, horn, and bone against the rock.

And right at the point of impact, at the moment that the rock should have stopped the ram, I hear a rushing, see a shimmering. The rock shudders, becomes smooth, becomes a mirror, becomes glass, becomes water, becomes air. The ram passes through into the dim darkness behind it.

Then the shimmering fades, and the wall is once again silent stone. I walk up to the wall, look closely at it, slap my palm against it. Nothing changes. In confusion, in despair, I rest my hands softly against the wall, rest my forehead against the cool stone.

And I, too, feel myself falling forward. Instinctively, I step forward with my left foot and feel it pass through what had been rock, feel it rest against a flat smoothness, not grass, not dirt, not sand. With its unbraked momentum, the rest of my body follows, and I am inside.

It is dark, though not as dark as it should be, in this silent room surrounded by rock and earth. The distant walls appear to have high windows, though I see nothing through them other than streams of a moon-like light. My feet feel the floor as cool, dry wood. The air has the slight chill of morning, warm enough for comfort as I wear my simple funereal robe.

In the center, I see a simple stone table, similar in shape and size to the stone slab on which I had recently lain. And a body rests on it, as still as I was, in a robe like mine.

I step toward it gingerly, afraid of where I might be, afraid of what I might find. As I get closer, I see it is a woman, ancient, still, her breast rising and falling in the rhythm of sleep.

And then she speaks: "Yes, I am alive. And yes, you, too, are still alive." Her eyes open, and she slowly shifts until she is sitting up. Her white hair glistens in the apparent moonlight, her green eyes seeming to look deeply into my soul.

"What time is this?" she asks.

I frown. "It is—Outside it was just past dawn."

She shakes her head. "What year is this? What era? Who is king in Israel?"

"What year? I am seventeen years old. I don't know any other way of counting years. And we have no king, nor do I think that we ever have."

She nods. "So these are the years before Samuel, before Saul. What is your name? What is your father's name?"

"My name has fallen from me," I say. "My father's name..." I pause, find it hard to think of him, hard to say his name. "My father's name is Jephthah."

"And your father has not yet—" She stops suddenly.

"Killed me? No, though he is to do so soon. It is my fate."

"And you would let him do this? Would it not break his heart to have to kill his daughter?"

"I am resigned to death. No reason remains for me to live. And he would have less pain in killing his own daughter than in breaking a vow to his god."

She sits silently for a while. "Good," she says, "this is good. You are still alive, and are here. The story cannot be changed, but all is not lost. Give me your robe."

"My robe?" I say. "But—"

"Oh, yes," she says. "Not yet." She stands, turns, and rests her hands on the stone table. It shimmers in the dim light and becomes a wooden cabinet.

She places her hands under the lip of the cabinet lid and slides it back. Reaching inside, she pulls out a neatly folded robe of simple white linen.

I take it from her, look around to confirm that no one else is there, then quickly remove my old robe and put on the new one.

"Give me your hands," the woman says.

I reach out to her, palms up. She takes each of my hands in hers and touches my palms where the wounds from the brambles remain. Each of the wounds, painlessly, begins again to bleed. She rubs my hands together until each of my palms is covered in blood, then, picking up my fallen robe, presses them to its cloth.

She releases my hands and the robe drops again to the ground, two fresh palm prints of blood bright against the dark fabric. I look at the robe, then at my hands. The wounds have healed.

The woman slides the lid on the cabinet closed then knocks on it. The sound echoes quickly in the emptiness of the room. The ram emerges from a dark corner.

She folds my old, bloodied robe into a small bundle. With its cloth belt, she ties it to the ram's neck. She leans down in front of the ram, whispers to it, then playfully bumps her own forehead against the ram's.

The ram nods to her, then to me, then walks over to the wall through which we came. It calmly walks through the wall and disappears.

"The ram will take your robe to your father," the woman says. "When he touches it, he will believe that you are gone, will have the memory of having met you at Mount Moriah and sacrificed you as he had promised. This is the story that he will tell, the story that people will believe."

"And what of me? Do I continue to live as if dead, alone?"

"You are not dead. And you are not alone. You remain here, with me. I teach you what I know of time, of magic, of prophecy. And more will join us: this day, on which you are said to have died, becomes the women's holiday. For four days each year, your friends, then their friends, then women from across all these hills and deserts leave their towns to be alone, to be together, to remember who you were and who they are."

"Do I join them?"

"No. You do not get to leave this place. But each year, some women depart from the crowd. The lost, the lonely, those who feel that they cannot bear to continue with their lives as they have been, walk away to sit, to live, to die in silence. And the ram listens for them, finds them, and guides them here."

"Will this continue forever?" I ask.

"Not forever," she says. "Traditions do fade, and are forgotten over time. But by that time, we will have become a community, a school, the place where women come to learn to be teachers, to be prophets, to work wonders and to help to heal this broken world."

I nod. We stand still, looking around, until the silence is broken by my stomach's growl. Startled, embarrassed, I look away.

The woman laughs. "Yes, you would be hungry. We must have food."

I hear myself laugh, too. "There is food here?"

"Not yet," the woman says. "We must bring it into being. We have incantations to do that: the same words that function as prayer in the outside world, function as incantations here."

She reaches into a pocket of her robe and pulls out a scroll with brief writings on it. "Can you read this?" she asks. "Have you been taught to read?"

I shake my head. "I have never been taught much at all."

"Then you will soon learn. There is much to read." She gestures around us. I suddenly realize that the smooth wooden floor is full of inscriptions, in complex patterns that I cannot yet understand.

She rolls up the scroll and puts it away. "All wonders, all wisdom," the woman says, "begin by blessing the Lord."

"I am to bless the Lord?" I say sharply. "The same god who fated me to die? How would I bless a god, and why?"

"The Lord did not condemn you to die," she says, speaking as sharply as I had just spoken to her. "That was your father. The Lord does not demand the lives of those who believe in him. And," she says more softly, " as you may have noticed, you are still alive."

I look down at myself and nod. "Yes, alive," I say.

"Good." The woman smiles. "And now we will bless the Lord, because the Lord needs to be whole, needs to be loved, as we need to believe that he loves us. These are the words that we speak."

And I listen carefully and repeat after her, feeling the first glimmers of a slim, healing thread of love begin to form, flowing from me, flowing from this god, from the Lord, who could have taken my life, but has kept me alive, has brought me to a new life. "You are blessed, Lord," we say, "our god, ruler of the world, who brings forth bread from the earth."

I close my eyes and breathe deeply, and smell the scent of fresh bread. I look down at the top of the cabinet, and see a pitcher of water and two simple loaves. The woman and I each take one loaf, tear off a chunk of bread, and place it in our mouths.

And I feel my soul return. Apart from fate, distanced from what that person had promised to this god, hoping to feel what the Lord has promised to all people, I fall into, absorb, am absorbed by the simple warmth and sweetness of the bread upon my tongue, of the fresh robe upon my body, of the smooth wood against my feet.

"Yes, I am alive," I say aloud, again, to the woman, to this god, to myself. "Yes, alive."

For comments and discussion about
the tale of Jephthah's Daughter,
and to hear the audio version, please visit
http://www.thebookofvoices.com/Jephthah'sDaughter

ACHINOAM

אֲחִינֹעַם

Achinoam was the wife of Saul, the first king of Israel. She is mentioned only twice in the Bible. The first is in a listing of Saul's family, where it says:

> Saul's sons were Jonathan, Ishvi and Malki-Shua. The name of his older daughter was Merab, and that of the younger was Michal. His wife's name was Achinoam daughter of Achimaaz...
> *(1 Samuel 14:49-50)*

The second is when Saul is yelling at his son:

> Saul's anger flared up at Jonathan and he said to him, "You son of a perverse and rebellious woman! ..."
> *(1 Samuel 20:30)*

King David also had a wife named Achinoam. Opinions differ on whether this is the same person. But David married Michal, Saul and Achinoam's daughter, too, though, and his marriage to both a mother and her daughter would have made the family tree all too complicated, even by Biblical standards.

Achinoam speaks to us on the night before Saul's coronation.

The people of Israel want a king. I'm not sure why — maybe because everybody else has one. And they want my husband, Saul, to be that king. I'm not sure why — maybe because every other woman around here has had him.

(Yes, I know about that son of his that that woman in Gilead bore. I take some scornful pleasure in one of the few things that my friends who can see the future have told me: that long years from now, the memory of the boy's name will be garbled, and people will remember him, if at all, as Ish-Bosheth — Embarrassment Man.)

Tomorrow we will be moved into a fancier house, and, I am told, be granted servants and other benefits of royalty. Tonight, in our last night in the freedom of our own house, we have chosen to sleep away from the clutter of the move, Here, outdoors, in our courtyard, we are lying atop a comfortable layer of skins, beneath the stars. Saul is snoring beside me as I stare into the sky, wishing that the moon would rise.

I know that Saul isn't perfect. Far from it. He does have his rages, though he always apologizes later, saying that "an evil spirit from God" had come over him. (I think the evil spirits are in what he drinks.) We have had to cover over too many holes in the walls of our house from when he threw his spears at things that we couldn't see. The children and I have grown attuned to when his rages are coming, though. Before leaving or cowering in another room, we try to hide his spears where he won't find them.

He is far too zealous, also, in defending his God, whom he insists is the only one. I still believe in and love Asherah, the goddess, alongside his God, but I have learned not to mention her in his presence or to have any items in the house that he would know to be sacred to her. That is all right, though. I know that I am with her whenever I am outdoors among all the trees of this world that she has blessed.

When I am indoors, wishing to be far away, I close my eyes and imagine myself to be in my favorite place, the grove of Asherah trees near Miriam's Well, the Well of Generations.

It was there that I had wandered so many years ago, during the four days of the festival of the forgotten girl. We all would go out then, all the girls would otherwise be stuck at home with our families.

Each year they had to let us wander. They would give us our packs with food and provisions for four days. We knew that we would be safe. No man dared touch us if he encountered us then. Even the beasts of the forest kept their distance. (Whether this was by the doing of Asherah or of our fathers' God was a matter of much chattering debate among us, though we would always come to the conclusion that it didn't really matter whether it was due to either, both, or sheer luck.)

I was always glad when these days came, and never more so than in that year. I had grown to be just a bit more than a child, and the way that the men in my town looked at me seemed even more menacing than before.

My father had taken to picking fights with men whom he suspected of looking at me askance. He won some of the fights. He lost many. Often the other men would just step aside or trip him when he attacked, leaving him sprawled in the dust or mud, leading them to speak to and of us even more jeeringly and harshly. Then my father would blame me for his shame, saying that the way that I was dressing or walking or speaking was enticing the men to approach me and leer at me.

I had wandered far that year. I found myself in a dense grove, facing a sheer rock wall. At the foot of the wall was a deep well. Within it, the water reflected the light of the full moon.

I stared into the well for a long time. After a while, I said "Hello" to the image of the moon.

"Hello" came back up from the well, in a voice not quite my own. The water shimmered with the vibrations of the voice, making the moonlight seem to spell a momentary message.

"Can you help me?" I asked. "I am tired of my family, of this life in which I am trapped. I don't want to return."

"Perhaps we can help," the voice said. This time, it came not from the well, but from behind me.

I stood and turned. A tall woman stood there, dressed in a simple robe. She smiled gently, the warmth of her voice enhanced by the fine wrinkles surrounding her oddly green eyes.

"I am Yael," she said. "We are here to protect you. Please, come inside."

"Inside?" I said.

Yael gestured to her right. There, where I had seen nothing but sheer rock before, a door had opened. The voices of more girls and women came from within.

Yael stepped through the door. I followed. There, in that room, many girls had gathered. Most carried the packs from their wanderings, though some had set them down. Scents of warm bread and healing teas filled the room. A few older women, dressed like Yael, spoke to individual girls or watched from a distance, gathered along walls that were engraved with endless texts.

"Where are we?" I asked.

"In one sense," Yael said, "you are a few steps from where you just were. In another, though, you are far away, safe from that world. Where we are is outside of the world of your birth, outside of its time. We can step out of here into many realms, though most of us stay inside. You are welcome to stay as long as you like. If you care to leave after a while, you can return to your world at the moment at which you left it, or step into the future or the past."

"The future or the past? At any time that I would wish?"

"There are a few limitations. You can't return to a time earlier in your own life, since there can't be two of a person in the world at once. And things grow far too unclear more than a couple of thousand years or so before or after your time. But other than that, yes, such things are possible."

"Have you been to the future? What becomes of my world, of me?"

"I'm afraid I can't tell you that yet," she said.

"Why not?"

"Because you may choose to return to your world. And without proper training, your knowledge of the future might compromise and complicate history too much. But if you stay long enough, you will learn of these things."

I sighed. "All right," I said.

"Come join the others and eat and drink with us. These girls, too, have needed to find refuge from your world. You all are safe here."

I set my pack down. With the other girls, I ate their bread and drank their tea. When we tired, they offered us each a simple room, and we slept.

I stayed there for what seemed like a long time. Months passed, perhaps, as I counted the days, though after a while I stopped counting. I lived and studied with the women there, learning the skills that too few of us learn in the outside world: how to read, how to write, how to work with numbers, how to do the simplest of magic, and how to speak to God and the other spirits of the world so that they might hear and might respond. Most importantly, our teachers taught us how not to be afraid, how to counter with our demeanor, our thoughts, our words and, yes, if needed, our fists and weapons the many assaults against our souls and selves that come upon us in this world.

Then one day, Yael came to visit me in my room. "Achinoam," she said, "it is time for us to talk. You have come to the end of the first stage of your learning. If you wish, you may stay and continue and become fully recognized as a Sister of Sarah. But you may also choose to return to the world as it was when we first met. The choice is yours. You may take time to decide, but you must make a conscious choice before you continue with your training."

I closed my eyes and thought, though not for as long as I would have expected the thought to take. "Yael, I love this place and the people here, But

I find that I miss my world and my family. I have a sister just a bit younger than me, and she needs my help and, if I can offer it, my protection. And I miss my mother and even my crude drunken idiot of a father. Will I forget and lose what I have here if I go?"

"No," Yael said. "You will not forget us and will not lose us. We will stay in touch with you over the years. Should you again need refuge, come back to the Well, and we will be here."

So I said goodbye to the school, to my teachers, and to the other girls who had chosen to remain. Yael brought me my pack, preserved exactly as it had been when I came there. Together, we stepped out into the grove.

I looked down into the well, down at the reflection of the moon, still full. "Goodbye," I said.

Yael's voice, behind me, said "Goodbye," then echoed from the well, "Goodbye." When I stood and looked behind me, she was gone.

I left the grove and rejoined the girls with whom I had been wandering. Most were as they had been. A few, though, whom I had seen in the school when I was there, seemed, like me, a little older, a little more serious, a little more prepared for the world to which we had returned. We gave a nod of recognition when we saw each other, but nothing needed to be said.

I returned to my village the next day, trudging up the road to my house. As I approached, I heard my father's drunken shouting. "Clean that up, girl!" he said. "It's enough that I have to feed the both of you. Make yourself useful! You are just going to end up like your big sister, lazing around the house, dressing to taunt the men into approaching her —"

"Stop." As I stepped into the house, I was surprised that the powerful voice came from me. "You will not speak to either of us like that again."

"Who do you think you are?" my father said.

"I know who I am," I said. "Who do you think you are?"

"I am your father!"

"Yes," I said. "But that does not give you permission to speak like that."

He stood there silently, mouth agape, then slammed his glass down on the table, turned, and walked out. I embraced my sister and we stood there, equally silent, until her tears and shaking stopped.

My father died not long after, worn out by his drinking and his fights. My sister grew into a fine woman. I tried to teach her all that I had learned.

But I may not have learned enough, since when I married, I married Saul. When we met, he seemed strong and charismatic, with a certainty about him that seemed to override all his faults. Now that we are wed, however, he has proven to be all too much like my father, too prone to drink and anger, unable to stay faithful to me. He has become a warrior and leader, but while he has helped to protect Israel from its enemies, all too often I find myself protecting my family from him. I'm not sure that I love him anymore. But he is my husband, and this is my life.

Yael comes to visit often, though never when he is at home. She has said that she has been told that they can never meet. She has helped me raise our children to be good people and strong. Someday one of them will become king or queen — probably Jonathan, our oldest, though he shows little interest in being king. Our youngest daughter, Michal, shows the strength to lead, though she has developed a streak of grimness, perhaps from seeing all too clearly her father's ways.

And tomorrow, her father, my husband, my Saul, will become Israel's king. I suppose that that means that I will become its queen. As I lie here beneath the summer sky, I look quietly to God, to my Asherah, and to my friends in the place beyond time to grant me wisdom, to grant me strength.

"You are awake." Saul's voice murmurs in my ear. So, apparently, is he. "What are you thinking, my queen?"

"I am thinking about tomorrow morning. I wonder if we have to go through with this. Saul, are you sure that you want to be king? Can't we just run off and not be home when they get here? We can duck away, just the two of us. Maybe we can go to the shores of that lake I showed you. I can bring those scented oils that you like..."

Saul puts a strong arm around me, pulls me closer, and quietly laughs. "You, my queen, are a perverse and rebellious woman," he says.

"But you love me," I say, moving closer to him.

"Yes," he says. "Yes, I do."

For comments and discussion about the tale of Achinoam
and to hear the audio version, please visit
http://www.thebookofvoices.com/Achinoam

JONATHAN

יהונתן

Jonathan was the oldest son of King Saul and Achinoam.

Saul disobeyed God's orders, and God caused an evil spirit to come upon him and torment him. David, a young man from Bethlehem, came to Saul's court, and played his harp to calm the king.

When David went into battle and killed the giant Goliath, he was accepted into the king's home, where he met the king's son, Jonathan.

The Bible says:

> Jonathan became one in spirit with David, and he loved him as himself. . . And Jonathan made a covenant with David because he loved him as himself. Jonathan took off the robe he was wearing and gave it to David, along with his tunic, and even his sword, his bow and his belt.
>
> *(1 Samuel 18:1, 3-4)*

But Saul grew jealous of David and tried to kill him. Repeatedly, the "evil spirit from God came forcefully on Saul," and he threw his spear at David, threatening to pin him to the wall.

David went into hiding, a day before he was supposed to appear at King Saul's feast for the new moon.

The Bible says:

> Jonathan said to David, "Tomorrow is the New Moon feast. You will be missed, because your seat will be empty. The day after tomorrow, toward evening, go to the place where you hid when this trouble began, and wait by the stone Ezel. I will shoot three arrows to the side of it, as though I were shooting at a target.

> Then I will send a boy and say, 'Go, find the arrows.' If I say to him, 'Look, the arrows are on this side of you; bring them here,' then come, because, as surely as the Lord lives, you are safe; there is no danger. But if I say to the boy, 'Look, the arrows are beyond you,' then you must go, because the Lord has sent you away."
>
> *(1 Samuel 20:18-22)*

Jonathan speaks as he heads out to the field with the boy.

This bow, these arrows weigh heavily on my back. My quiver can hold many more arrows than the three that it carries now. But each arrow is laden with the message that I had prayed that I would not have to send, the message of goodbye, goodbye, goodbye.

An attendant walks beside me. But this boy is too small to carry my weapons, too small to know anything, to do anything other than follow the clear directions that he will be given.

We walk slowly eastward through the forest, toward the barely risen sun. away from the dim pale sliver of the setting moon, to the edge of the dew-dampened meadow. Arriving, we set down our packs and wait until enough light appears for us to see the target.

There, off at the far edge of the meadow, the marker stone gradually shows itself: white, taller than most men, slightly wider than it is tall. On the far side of the stone, I know that a man awaits: my beloved, David, huddled against the morning chill as he listens for my sounds, for my words.

We had set up this meeting four days ago, a lifetime ago, it seems. Then I went back to the palace, to my home, to sense the state of the madness of my father, the king, to learn whether it would be safe for David to come home with me, or whether he would need to flee to other lands, to save his life, to be able to continue with his sacred destiny. Now I am here, and I know that he is here, though I cannot see him in the distance, silent as he is amidst the sound of the morning breezes against trees and grass, amidst the chatter of the morning birds.

I kneel and pick up the bow from the ground. I pluck the string to test its tautness. It sounds a clear note, resonating with my memories of the sound of David's harp. "Boy," I say to my attendant, "pick up the quiver there, and be ready to hand me each of the three arrows, one at a time, as I ask you for them."

I rise to standing. He picks up the quiver and stands near me, but not too near, off where he is away from any danger from sudden motions of the bow.

"Boy, hand me the first arrow," I say. The boy reaches into the quiver, lifts the arrow out, and hands it up to me, careful to keep it pointed down and away from us.

I take the arrow, position it on the bow, and pull back on the string. Focusing on the target, focusing as if I, too, were to launch with it and fly, I let a full breath out and take a full breath in. With an instant of clarity, of prayer, I let go of the arrow, and let it fly. My eye is sharp and my aim is true. The arrow arcs and lands precisely where I sent it, directly in front of the marker stone.

I reach back down to the boy. "The second arrow," I say, and the boy hands it up to me. Again I set the arrow on the bowstring. Again I pull it back, breathe out, breathe in, and let it fly. It sails, arcs, and lands, several strides nearer to me than the first arrow and slightly to the left.

I reach down, and, without needing me to say anything, the boy hands the final arrow to me. I launch it, watch it fly, and see it land, several paces to the left of the other two, forming a perfect triangle, exactly as far from each of them as they are from each other. But rather than feeling any pride in the accuracy of my archery or joy in the mathematical beauty of their pattern, I feel only pain, pain as if each of the arrows had pierced my own heart.

I look down to the quiver and see what I already know, that there are no more arrows left to shoot. For a moment, I am tempted to turn and run away, away from David, away from our destiny. But to run from him now would be to leave him with no news, which would be harsher than the foul news that I have to convey.

I put the bow on the ground and crouching, speak more quietly to the boy. "Run ahead now, to the arrow nearest us. Pull it from the ground and wait for me to tell you the next thing to do."

The boy runs on ahead. His short legs carry him toward the arrow as swiftly as they can, but the furrow that they trace through the long wet grass takes a eternity to grow toward the arrow, toward David. It takes an eternity, but not nearly long enough.

The boy reaches the arrow and, trying first with one hand then with two, pull it from the ground. He stumbles backward slightly as it comes out, but does not fall. Turning, he waves the arrow in the air for me to see.

This is the moment for which I had waiting, the moment that I had been avoiding. David and I had established two signals. If David hears me tell the boy that the arrows are off to his side, he will know that he is free to come home. If I tell the boy that the arrow is beyond him, David will know that he must run. And if… is there a third option? Might I say something else or say nothing? Might we avoid or change our fate?

My heart and mind thrash through the spectrum of possible futures, searching for a possibility of possibilities. But none appears. My father's heart has hardened, and if he ever finds David, David will die. The future has constricted to one small truth. The words that I must speak are cast in stone.

I call out to the boy, "Aren't the arrows –" My voice breaks. I pause and try again. "Aren't the arrows beyond you?"

The boy turns and walks toward one of the arrows. I call out to him, but even more so to David, "Quick! Hurry! Do not stand still!"

The boy runs as quickly as he can and retrieves the remaining arrows, yanking first one and then the other from the ground. He turns again and, looking toward me, sees me wave, signaling him to return to me, to return the arrows to me.

He runs back to me, back along the furrow of trampled grass that he had made while running out across the meadow.

He reaches me and hands me the arrows. I pull a soft cloth from the quiver and wipe the arrows clean of the dirt from the ground that they had pierced.

I crouch down to his level and hand him the arrows. "Bring the arrows back to where we store them. I will bring the bow back myself."

The boy takes the quiver, takes three steps away from me, turns away, then turns back. He stands silently for a moment and looks deep into my eyes. "Have you lost something?" he says. "You look like you have lost something. Is there something that I can help you find?"

I place my hand on his shoulder. "No, I have not…" I say, then, "Yes. Yes, I have lost something. It isn't anything that you could help me find. But I hope that someday you might find it for yourself."

We look into each other's eyes for a moment longer. Then I stand, and the boy takes three steps backward, then turns and runs off.

I shade my eyes and look to the east, toward the now fully risen sun, toward the marker stone behind which my David hides. I take a deep breath, start to call out his name, then refrain. If he feels that it is safe to come to me, he will come. If he feels that he must run, he will run.

My mind prays that he will run far away from me. My heart prays that he will run swiftly toward me. And my soul prays that God will grant us magic and grace, that he will change the world, change time, change my father's vicious will, that David and I will dance once again, under a new moon, there in a new tomorrow.

For comments and discussion about the tale of Jonathan and to hear the audio version, please visit http://www.thebookofvoices.com/Jonathan

SAMUEL

אשמ1אל

Samuel was a leader and a prophet in Israel. When the people of Israel insisted on being led by a king, Samuel anointed Saul. When Saul disobeyed God, however, God told Samuel to anoint another king. Samuel anointed David.

David had lived in Saul's court, had loved Saul's son, Jonathan, and had married Saul's daughter, Michal. When Saul was driven into insanity as a result of having disobeyed God, David was able to calm him at first by playing the harp for him. But when Saul tried to kill David, David fled from Saul's court. David allied with Saul's enemies to fight against him, but refrained from killing Saul when he had the chance.

Samuel lived and died at Ramah, where Joseph's mother Rachel was buried.

After Samuel's death, the Philistine army attacked the army of the Israelites, which was led by King Saul.

The Bible says:

> When Saul saw the Philistine army, he was afraid; terror filled his heart... Saul then said to his attendants, "Find me a woman who is a medium, so I may go and inquire of her."
> "There is one in En-dor, " they said.
> So Saul disguised himself, putting on other clothes, and at night he and two men went to the woman. "Consult a spirit for me," he said, "and bring up for me the one I name."...
> The woman asked, "Whom shall I bring up for you?"
> "Bring up Samuel," he said.
>
> *(1 Samuel 28:5,7,11)*

Samuel speaks to us as the magic worker at En-dor (The Well of Generations) summons his soul back from the dead.

This cannot be happening. This does not happen. I was dead, am dead, my body buried, returning to dust at Ramah, my spirit at rest, dissolving into the universal soul, the loam of Sheol.

Now a vibration is disturbing the surface of this substance of souls. I—the specks of this substance, once part of a separate soul, now coming together, now restored to an earlier order that remembers that it once formed a single being, that it once had an identity—can feel this vibration focusing into sound, this sound into a voice, the voice of a person, the voice of a woman, of a woman whose soul once knew mine, who once had run and shouted and sung with me in the circuit of prophets.

She is chanting a cycle of long sounds: a voiceless hush, then a hum, then a sustained voiced vowel, moving in stages from the back of the mouth to the tip of the tongue before it fades and the cycle starts again with the hush. The cycle moves faster, the sounds resolving into letters, gaining meaning, becoming a word—sh'muel—becoming a name, a name that resonates within me, that awakens me. It was, is, my name. I was, am, Sh'muel: Samuel.

I am drawn up, drawn out, drawn forward, from this existence without place or direction, back through the barrier that I had thought could only be crossed from there to here, drawn back into the world of objects, the world of temporary life. I cannot touch things, cannot smell, taste, hear, but the light (created before objects, before life) comes through to me, reveals to me the images of this world, reveals this room, with two people, three candles, a talisman, and an air of wonder and fear.

I still hear the voice, what seems like a voice. The thoughts of the woman echo as she who stands before me. She is turning slowly, her right arm outstretched, brandishing the talisman. Shadows hide her face from the candles' light, but I recognize the tone, the signature of her thoughts.

I call out her name. I cannot speak, but the motion of my mind that, when alive, would cause my mouth to speak sends the name across to sound within her soul. "Yael," I call. "You were, are, Yael."

She stops her turning, and faces the three candles. "And you were and are again Samuel."

"How am I here? How have you torn me back into this world of the living? The prophet that I knew you to be could not, would not have done this."

"Time has passed, Samuel. The prophets have been driven into hiding, all but those who swore everlasting service to the king. I have been living here, with my sisters, at the Well of Generations. And yes, we have learned the unspoken arts and hidden magic, to call out along the paths between the spheres and to reach across the membranes between the worlds. And the pain within the heart of this man who sits before me called out to plead for my help, despite the danger that revealing myself might bring, despite the threat of death declared by King Saul himself."

"By King Saul? Do you know that that is Saul who sits before you?"

I feel shock and fear come from Yael. I see her cry out, though I do not hear the sound. She speaks to Saul and he responds, though I can only hear a faint murmur of his thoughts. Yael gestures toward the candles, shows that she sees me between them, an image that only she can see in the refraction of their light. He falls to his knees, then to the ground, head bowed, facing them, facing me.

In terror and unaccustomed humility, his soul is open to me. Yael channels a connection between us. The tale of his life is spread out as a single image outside of time. His birth; his boyhood; my anointing him king; his rise to power and corruption by it; the illness that causes him to believe that he, rather than God, can be the ultimate power, causes him to believe that those who love him are plotting against him; his wars, both righteous and insane; the act that doomed him, early on, not caused by trying to evade God's will but by trying to improve on God's command; his inevitable, imminent death—all these appear in a single brush stroke, in all possible colors, all painted at once.

Yael turns again to face the candles, to face me. "He swears that no harm shall come to me, though I know that his will is mutable, that those that he embraces in one moment might face his spear in the next."

"Why has he called for me? The living fear all contact with the dead. He had ignored me, had not spoken to me nor summoned me to his court in decades before my death. Is there no one else he can trust, no one else that he can ask what lies before him?"

Yael turns and repeats my question so that the living man could hear. The king raises his head to look at her, to respond, and I can see that his eyes are weighted with the beginnings of tears. He speaks, stops, closes his eyes, opens them, speaks again.

Yael nods to the king, then says to me, "In the noise of war, all has fallen to silence. He asks his generals how he might evade defeat, and they cannot answer. He has lost all contact with the voice of God. His advisors and prophets can tell him nothing at all. The priests consult the gems of revelation, plead with them to hint at the future in their patterns and their lights, but they remain dark, remain static. He looks to his dreams for omens, but all he sees is abstract, unfocused, the red of blood across skin atop grass and dust, the blue and black of empty skies from which no clouds or stars will spell out what might be. And even when he listens within himself, he finds dark silence. No roar of certainty nor whisper of hope, no inner voice, however still, however small, sounds within him. In a mind that once swarmed with voices, he is terrified, alone. So he turns to you, the one who found him in the crowd and declared him king, the one who led the people, the one whose advice he knew to be true even when he disobeyed. He needs one last word of truth from you before he is out of reach."

"Yael," I say, "when I look at this king, all I see is the blankness of sealed fate. I need to speak truth to him, but I fear that the words will be harsher than silence. His sole good fortune is that he has come to you, who have always been known as the prophet of compassion, the one who speaks truth gently. Tell me what I might say to this man."

Yael stands silent, looks at the king, at the talisman, at the candles, at me. "Perhaps I can speak for you, can speak as you, can be the filter that translates what you must say into what he can hear. Open to me the wisdom that had lived in your heart, and I will endeavor to blend it with what wisdom lies in mine."

She raises the talisman above her head, then brings it down, touching it to the crown of her head, to her forehead, to each of her eyes, to her lips, to her throat, and holds it to her heart. I see her aura glow and widen, and feel drawn into her.

Some of what had come together to form this temporary soul pulls away from me, leaves me forever, speeding into her physical world. Focused between the candles, it collects at the center of their space then is pulled to the talisman, to her, forming a cloud of all the colors and degrees of light. It surrounds Yael, encloses her, then gradually merges with her aura, till she and what had been part of me are one.

Yael looks down and speaks to the king, echoing her words back to me as she says them aloud: "Thus says our teacher Samuel, whom you have drawn from beyond the grave:

"I know no more than you know; what we both know, you refuse to believe. Yes, your kingdom is ended. You have known from the moment when, newly crowned, you immediately disobeyed the Lord, that your line would not continue as kings. The one that you loved, then resented, then sought to kill, the one that always loved you, that your son and daughter love, will fight this enemy and defeat them. He will continue the kingdom and will make certain that your name is honored and not forgotten.

"You know that you will not see the sun set again. By this time tomorrow you and your sons will be as I am, though your daughters and many grandchildren will survive. You can do no more to change this outcome. You may choose to tell your sons; you may decide for yourself whether it is a greater act of mercy to tell them when their lives will end or to let them fight without knowing.

"Take this night for yourself: eat, sleep, pray, cry if you must, set your affairs in order if you can. Trust Yael to guide you and comfort you through this final night. If this woman embraces you, accept her embrace, as I too am embracing you, both now as you reach across the chasm between our worlds and tomorrow as you step from the world of objects into this unseen world of the substance of souls."

The king lies on the ground, his face hidden from me. He curls up slowly, his arms and legs drawn into himself as he shudders and rocks.

"Yael?" I ask. "What is he saying?"

"There is nothing left for him to say. All that he has, for the moment, are tears and certainty. His soul has faced what it can. What he needs now is to be comforted, to eat, to sleep, so that he may face his final day."

Yael kneels beside the king, places her hands on his head, on his back, and softly sings a wordless melody, the song that the king's successor first played on his harp to calm him when his madness had first set in. Gradually the king stops rocking on the ground and lies quietly, taking in the blessing of her presence, of her song.

As I watch, I see them fade, become unclear, as if their world is painted on a sand dune being eroded by the wind. I feel myself start to come apart, breaking into the tiniest granules of the substance of souls. I am overwhelmed by fear, afraid that I might dissolve without returning to the source of souls, that I might be left as fragments of what once was a person in this gap between worlds.

"Yael!" I call. She looks up, stands, takes up the talisman, and once again begins to turn, the opposite way this time, looking clearly at me when her eyes pass the candles, her gaze certain and strong.

I hear her chant the sounds of my name, reversing their order, the voice returning from the front of her mouth to the back, closing into a hum, then into the voiceless hush. The sound repeats, slows, forming a lullaby of farewell. I feel my soul releasing its grasp on itself, on location, on time, feel myself forgetting, forgetting what it was that I was forgetting, forgetting my life, my name, my self, returning to the substance of souls from which we all emerge and return.

One last thought leaps from Yael to me across the border between the world of the living and the spacious timelessness where I—the specks of existence that still resonate together as fading identity—abide. She swears to me that she will remember this meeting, this moment, this soul for as long as she shall live.

And the fragments of my soul each pray, as I—we—they dissolve into the embrace of the void, that, when they return to new lives, combined with others as they may be, when they hear the story, hear whispered the tale of the prophet at the Well of Generations, that these souls might touch a memory of her powerful, gentle soul, and that, at least, remembering, they may smile.

For comments and discussion about the tale of Samuel and to hear the audio version, please visit http://www.thebookofvoices.com/Samuel

ELISHEVA (INTERLUDE 5)
אלישׁרבע

I awaken, my hands seeming sticky from the memory of blood. My body, my mind are clouded with the sense of being marked with blood, of having run through nightmare fields of fire and dirt and blood.

I look down at my robe and expect to see streaks and handprints of dirt, of blood. They are not there, but the sense, the memory is so strong that I see their absence as afterimages, as the ghost of what I might see were I to hold my hand up to the sun then look away.

But I am not out in the fields, nor in the sun. How long has it been since I have seen either? Though I miss them, it seems that, over time, I have grown to miss them less and less.

Over time, perhaps, I have lost the world in which I lived. At first, when my world disappeared, I must have been able to remember it. Then I could only remember that I had remembered it. Then I could only remember that I had remembered something without remembering what the thing that I had remembered was.

Now, the remembering of the remembering itself is gone. Now, I have only the memories of dreams, or perhaps only have dreams of memory. I have lost myself, found myself in this moment, in this room, and perhaps this present moment is all that I need.

Will I grow to forget that I had ever remembered anything? Angel, will I come once again to have an empty child's mind?

The angel looks up at me, sighs silently, and smiles. He does not give an answer, either yes or no.

Perhaps that is death: to cease to remember the sense of remembering. Or perhaps it is to remember all: to have the colors of sunlight and love run and blur into loss, into blood and dirt and fire, till all turn to brilliant white or to black or to neutral brown or grey. Then the soul might come to join all others for a moment out of time, forever, or perhaps until it pulls away again and begins another life of memory, another life of sunlight, blood, and fire.

Angel, what do you remember? Can you remember anything, everything, nothing?

Again, of course, he does not answer. But his smile slowly darkens, leaving first his eyes, then the corners of his mouth. The angel sighs, and looks downward once again.

THE BOOK OF SINGING
ספר האירוח

ASAPH

אָסָף

Asaph was a Levite, a member of the tribe of Israel that had also included Moses, Miriam, and Aaron. The Levites assisted the priests and were responside for the music in the rituals concerning sacrifices and, later, the Temple.

When David became king after the death of King Saul and Jonathan, he brought the Ark of the Covenant to Jerusalem. Asaph was among the Levites chosen to lead the music in the procession.

The Bible says:

> The Levites carried the ark of God with the poles on their shoulders, as Moses had commanded in accordance with the word of the Lord. David told the leaders of the Levites to appoint their fellow Levites as musicians to make a joyful sound with musical instruments: lyres, harps and cymbals. So the Levites appointed Heman son of Joel; from his relatives, Asaph son of Berekiah...
> *(1 Chronicles 15:16)*

He is credited with composing many of the Psalms that were not attributed to David.

Asaph sings late in his life, as he looks back on his call to song.

I am song, and my world is song.
Just as we have dedicated this temple to God,
I have dedicated my life
To song, with song, for song.

This song is a song of God.
   This song is a song of God's mystery.
   This song flows
   From my mouth,from my throat, from my lungs.

But it is not my song.
   This song flows into me from elsewhere, from God,
   And emerges as human song,
   A song of the people.
   I hear their thoughts and I sing them back as song:
   Praise song, healing song, a song of life.

Without song, I was nothing.
   With song, I am nothing but a conduit,
   A channel through which song can rush
   As water rushes through the once-dry river beds
   When we sing the songs of rain,
   The songs of rejuvenation,
   The songs of the cycles of joy.

Without song, I had no voice.
   All my words without song came as stammers,
   As Moses stammered without Aaron to give him speech,
   As Moses stammered without Miriam to give him song.

Without song, my words were silenced.
   Without song, I shied away from the other Levites.
   Without song, I believed that if I had no words,
   I had no voice.

Without song, I stood far away from the singers,
   Banged the great cymbal,
   Watched as the sacrifice flames rose to God.
   But my voice was silent,
   Without words, without song.

Without words, they thought me stupid, thought me damaged.
   Then the Teacher of Song came
   To teach us, to sing with us, to listen with us.

Moving among the Levites,
Starting with the most talented,
Ending with me,
She sang a phrase of song
And had each Levite
Sing that phrase of song back with her.

And when she came down to me,
　When she came to me to test me with song,
　I bowed my head, hid my face behind the great cymbals,
　Hid myself from the song, from the Teacher of Song.
　She sang a phrase of song at me.
　I did not respond.
　She sang the phrase of song again.
　I tried to whisper, to stammer, "No. Please."
　The other Levites jeered. She summoned them to silence.

Then she sang a different phrase of song,
　A beautiful song, a complex song,
　A song that repeated without repeating.

Then I felt her touch her fingers
　To each side of my bowed head,
　To my chest, to my throat, to my lips.

Then she touched her fingers to my closed eyes.
　My eyes opened,
　And her eyes looked deeply into my own,
　And she sang her phrase of song again.
　I still could not respond.

Then she sang the phrase once more,
　This time without words.
　My lips opened to sing,
　But in shame, in fear, I still found no song.

And she sang the phrase of song to me,
　Over and over,
　Sometimes without words,

Sometimes with different words,
Sometimes singing:

"This song can be your song.
   This song is your song.
   Sing along when you can.
   Remain silent when you must.
   Sing whatever song emerges
   From your heart, from your throat, from your lips.
   The song that you sing may not be the same song,
   But the song that you sing will be the right song."

Then she paused,
   Then she sang a single note, a simple note,
   A note of song that seemed to last forever.

And I opened my mouth and I breathed,
   And I opened my voice and I breathed a note,
   A tentative note, a timid note,
   Not the same note
   That the Teacher of Song was singing,
   But a note that blended with her song,
   Merged with her song, became beautiful.

Then the Teacher of Song sang two notes, repeating,
   And I sang two notes as she sang,
   Not the same notes,
   But notes of song that blended, merged,
   Became beautiful.

And she sang three and I sang three,
   And she sang five and I sang five,
   And she sang eight and I sang eight,
   And we flew into melodies,
   Long wordless streams of song,
   Simple yet complex,
   The same yet not the same,
   Each person's notes of song
   Crashing into the song of the other,

Pulling against the song of the other,
Yet blending to form something more beautiful
Than either stream of song alone.

Then she fell silent and I fell silent.
And as we breathed in the silence,
In this absence of song, blessed by song,
She began once again to sing,
A simple phrase of song, with simple words:
"What is your name? What is your name? What is your name?"

And I joined her in singing,
"What is your name? What is your name?"
But she touched her finger to my lips,
Pointed to herself, pointed to me, sang,
"My name is Shirah. What is your name?"

And with fear, close to silence,
I sang the words "My name… My name is Asaph…
Asaph… My name is Asaph…
My name is Asaph, son of Berechiah…
My name is Asaph…"

And in shock, in joy, I realized
That I was not stammering,
That my words were clear,
That everyone could understand
The words of my song.

And she sang, "Tell me where you are."
And she sang, "Tell me what you see."

And she sang a simple phrase again, without words,
And I sang along with her:
"I am in a room.
I am in a large room with many others.
I am in a large room, full of sound,
Singing here with my brothers, the Levites.
And I am seeing their faces,

And I am hearing their hearts,
And I sense in their breath
Their joys, their fears, their futures.
And I am here with our teacher,
With the Teacher of Song,
And I can hear her voice,
Can feel her love,
Can taste her presence, the presence of her song,
As a mist in the air, as eternal honey
on my tongue, in my throat, throughout my being.
And the song brings me joy,
And the song brings me life,
And the song is life,
And my life is nothing but song.
Sing the Lord a new song!"

And I sang that again, repeating but not repeating,
"Sing the Lord a new song!"
And I realized that the Teacher of Song had stopped singing,
That the Teacher of Song was listening to my song.

Then the Teacher of Song began to sing again:
"Listen! Sing! Listen! Sing!"
And she moved among the Levites,
Touching her fingers to their hearts, to their lips.
And each began to sing with me,
"Sing the Lord a new song!"
Not the same notes that I sang,
Not our usual trivial unison,
But a complicated tapestry of sound,
Each person singing his own note,
Each person singing the right note,
Each person singing a note
Made richer, made right by
The notes that each other person sang.

Then the Teacher of Song fell silent,
And I fell silent,
And one by one the Levites fell silent.

And the silence was rich, was warm,
Was subtle, was strong as the taste in the mouth
After one has swallowed fine wine.

And the Levites turned to me,
  And I tried to thank them,
  Tried to speak

But my words failed me without song,
  And I stammered and could not speak,
  Spitting out broken pieces of words
  Like seeds, like shattered teeth.

And I bowed my head,
  And I listened for the inevitable laughter

But the silence held us
  As we held the silence,
  As I cursed my self
  For my moment of song, of beauty,
  Now lost in this desert of speech.

Then I heard a shout from afar,
  A note, a word, sung by an unknown Levite,
  A voice calling, "Sing! Sing!"
  Once, again,
  Then another joined,
  Then two, three, five, eight,
  Uncountable voices,
  All singing different notes together,
  All calling out, "Sing! Sing!"

And I opened my mouth,
  And words flowed in song,
  From me, through me, around me,
  As I heard my song proclaim:

"Sing joyously to God, our strength,
  Raise a shout for the God of Jacob.
  Take up the song,

Sound the timbrel,
The melodious lyre and harp..."

And all those around me
    Sang to me,
    Sang around me,
    Sang with me,
    Sang the word "Sing!"
    Or sang my song,
    No two of us singing the same thing,
    But all the notes
    Blending, merging,
    Becoming beautiful.

I looked for the Teacher of Song,
    But she was gone,
    And our song carried us along without her,
    As it has carried us since that day,
    As it carries us now,
    Now that time has passed and I am grown,
    Now that I am married and have children who sing,
    Now that I am old and sit in the temple where I sing

As I still play the great cymbals,
    As I teach others to play the great cymbals,
    As I teach those who believe that they cannot sing
    That they should begin by playing the cymbals,
    That they should listen to the song around them,
    Listen to the song within themselves,
    Let themselves believe the song,
    Become the song,
    Be the song

And that someday,
    If only on the day that they leave this world,
    The song will come for them,
    The song will come to them,
    The song will come

To join with them, to envelop them,
To join them with the souls of all that live,
Or to join them with souls of all who no longer live,

And the first, the last, the best thing
That they will come to understand
Is that they are song,
Life is song,
God is song,

And the song goes on forever,
  Around us, within us, among us,
  Carried between us
  In the motions of the wind, the water, the earth,
  Passed in the words, the breath, the touch
  That moves between each person and the next,
  Carried in the scent of the incense,
  In the fires of sacrifice,
  In the prayers of each person to God,
  In the blessings that God returns.

As the song is sung, pronounced,
  Captured, frozen, melted, burned,
  Witnessed, dreamed, imagined, believed,

While even one of us is living, is singing,
  The song will be the world.
  The song will extend the world.
  The song will sustain the world.

We know that the song

Will never end.

For comments and discussion about the tale of Asaph
and to hear the audio version, please visit
http://www.thebookofvoices.com/Asaph

DAVID

414

David was the king of Israel after King Saul.

The Bible credits David with having written much of the Book of Psalms. He established the city of Jerusalem as the nation's capital, and brought the Ark of the Covenant there.

David had many wives and concubines, and had many children with them. He married his most famous wife, Bathsheba, after sending her first husband off to be killed.

The Bible says:

> In the course of time, Amnon son of David fell in love with Tamar, the beautiful sister of Absalom son of David. Amnon became so obsessed with his sister Tamar that he made himself ill...
>
> When the king came to see him, Amnon said to him, "I would like my sister Tamar to come and make some special bread in my sight, so I may eat from her hand."
>
> David sent word to Tamar at the palace: "Go to the house of your brother Amnon and prepare some food for him." So Tamar went to the house of her brother Amnon, who was lying down. She took some dough, kneaded it, made the bread in his sight and baked it. Then she took the pan and served him the bread, but he refused to eat.
>
> "Send everyone out of here," Amnon said. So everyone left him. Then Amnon said to Tamar, "Bring the food here into my bedroom so I may eat from your hand." And Tamar took the bread she had prepared and brought it to her brother Amnon in his bedroom. But when she took it to him to eat, he grabbed her and said, "Come to bed with me, my sister."
>
> "No, my brother!" she said to him. "Don't force me! Such a thing should not be done in Israel! Don't do this wicked thing...."

> But he refused to listen to her, and since he was stronger than she, he raped her....
>
> Tamar put ashes on her head and tore the ornate robe she was wearing. She put her hands on her head and went away, weeping aloud as she went.
>
> *(2 Samuel 13:1-2, 6-12, 14, 19)*

David speaks to the imagined spirit of his late beloved Jonathan, later that night.

The palace now is quiet. All my wives and daughters have gone off now, after a dinner where they all glared at me in sullen silence, saying the very least that they could without actively incurring my wrath, the wrath of the king. My sons have retreated to their houses, all feeling unwell after perhaps too boisterous a meal. All except Absalom: he joined the women in their silence, the whole time seated with his back to his half-brother, Amnon, the whole time keeping his sister, my youngest daughter, Tamar, carefully in his gentle gaze. Tamar, my tiny, beautiful, wounded Tamar, sat perfectly upright, staring straight ahead, silent as stone. Jonathan, you never would have guessed yesterday from her fragile poise, the sweetness of her smile (which none saw today and which we might never see again) and the clarity of her voice when we would hear her singing, laughing, and playing in the palace halls, how her screams, as she stumbled outside last night, would shake all who heard them and would reveal the cracks in this family, this royal house.

The screams echo in my mind as I sit here, alone, my head resting on the cool wood of my harp. I close my eyes, but I cannot banish the image of her as I found her outdoors, kneeling in the dirt, covering her face and hair with the dirt, clawing at her stained, ornamented robe, as if to both conceal herself further and tear it away. Flanked by my servants (always flanked by my servants), I knelt beside her and tried to put my arms around her, to comfort her in a father's embrace. But she looked up at me, looked in my eyes without seeing me, screamed louder, and ran into the women's quarters where even I refrain from going. I stood again, silent, not grasping what was happening, until Absalom came into the courtyard, face pale, with quiet fury in his eyes.

"Tamar?" I asked. He nodded.

"What happened?" I asked.

He said only "Amnon," then turned and went back into his room.

And Jonathan, as a father knows the heart of his sons even if he does not want to believe what he knows, as a father cares for his sons even when the son has done wrong, I knew all that had occurred.

My first impulse was anger, was to lash out against Amnon, to strike him down as I had ordered the deaths of others. But the fury was conflicted by sadness, confusion, and the dissonance between the love I felt both for Tamar and for Amnon. I stood, closed my eyes, asked God for guidance, and quietly sang to God and to myself one of my repeating, calming songs to lead myself to a silence from which I could act.

Amnon's door was locked, bolted, when I tried to open it. "Unlock this door," I bellowed, "this is the king." There was no response. My servants stepped forward to break the door down. I stopped them. "Amnon," I said more quietly, "this is your father. Please open the door." After a long pause, I heard his chair move, and footsteps toward the door.

When he opened the door, dressed still in his sleeping robe, his face showed little, as if all emotion had been locked away. He stepped backward and sat again as I entered. My servants followed, but I gestured for them to wait outside. I stepped around the broken teapot and heart cakes on the floor, stood silently in front of Amnon, then pulled another chair over and sat down facing him.

"Amnon," I said. "What happened?"

"What happened," he repeated flatly. "What did she tell you?" He said "she" with a trace of a sneer.

"She is not speaking," I replied. "What happened? When they told me you were ill and wanted her to make you some of her heart cakes. I sent her to you. And now you are sitting here with this affectless stare, your house looks like there was a battle in it, and your sister –"

"Half-sister. Not my sister."

"She is my daughter. You are my son. And she is covering herself in dirt and screaming."

He sneered again. "So she acts the madwoman well. She is a schemer and a liar. I hate her."

"You loved her. You have always been her favorite brother, playing with her, talking with her, sitting with her out in the trees..."

"And she was always scheming to get me. And she got me alone, in my bed, and she made her move on me, and when she got what she wanted, she acted as if I was a criminal, insane." He glared at me in silence, as if accusing me of something.

"Got what she wanted?" I said, keeping my voice low. "Amnon, she is a little girl. What could she want –"

"A little girl," he said. "She is a woman, or will be. And you have taught me how women are, and how they are not to be trusted, and how they are to be taken –"

"I have taught you no such thing."

"Not in words," he said, "though you have rarely been one to teach in words — you save them to use in your songs to seduce your followers, your audiences. But I have seen how you have been to your wives, our mothers. You take them if you want them. If they are married, their husbands die suddenly. If they are from elsewhere, they are captured, or used in political bargains. And when you see the next woman that you want, you forget them, banish them to the women's quarters, until you need to put them on display at state dinners, or summon them when your most recent wife isn't satisfying you."

I wanted to strike him. I refrained. "But your little sister –"

"Half-sister," he said again. "And that I was her half-brother didn't dissuade her. She has always been trying to get me, moving against me as she played, climbing across my back or hanging tightly to me as we walked together, as if she didn't know what that did to — what that does to any man –"

"But she didn't know!" I protested. "At her age –"

He ignored my words. "And now when I was ill, I asked her that she come to my house, that she cook her heart cakes with whatever witchcraft she uses so that they heal the sick. And she saw me in my bed, and worked her wiles, her witchery on me, singing and dancing and moving so seductively as she worked the dough and stuck the pitted dates within each and fried them for me. And then, when they were ready, she climbed up onto my bed, onto my lap, and snuggled up against me, and fed one to me with her beautiful little hands, looking straight into my eyes with her own brown eyes wide open, and then she kissed me, first on the tip of my nose, then on my lips, and I..." He paused, then hissed, "I hate her. I hate –"

He stopped. His eyes widened, then clenched shut. His hands came up, formed fists, pressed against his temples, as he curled downward. His head rested between his knees, as he shook, sobbing. Spasms through his body pushed him forward. His chair slid out from under him and he hit the ground heavily, his head protected by my foot from striking the floor. His breath came in voiceless gasps that gradually turned into keening sobs. "Father?" he finally said. "What happened? What have I done?"

"You know what really happened," I said quietly. "You know what you have done."

"Can you forgive me?" he asked.

"Forgiveness is not mine to give," I replied.

He looked up at me and tried to rise from the ground, but the arm on which he raised himself buckled and he fell back to the floor. I reached down to him. He grasped my hand in mine and rose more steadily, first onto his knees and then to his feet.

He reached for his cloak. "I must go to her. I must tell her how sorry –"

"No," I said. "You will not go to her. You will not speak to her again. As of this moment, she does not exist for you. I will not speak of this, but word has reached the women's quarters and cannot help but spread like fire in a dry vineyard. As king, all whispers in the court reach me. The way that you looked at Tamar, that you look at the young girls has been noticed, though none wanted to speak aloud of it, none wanted to believe that what they sensed was true. You are the son of the king, and under protection of the king, and no harm can come to you. But know that you must never be alone with any of the girls without another grown person who is not one of your servants present. If you ever are, or if we ever hear of anything like what happened tonight happening again, my protection may not be enough. And I cannot protect you from the wrath of the Lord. You must look within yourself and out to him, to atone and to steel yourself against further sin."

He nodded, and looked like he wanted to say something, but remained silent. I bent down, picked up the remaining heart cakes, brushed them off, placed them on the plate that lay beside them and, rising, handed the plate to my son. "You have been ill," I said. "Eat and sleep, if you can. We need you to be well."

He reached out and took the plate. I held onto it for a moment before letting go, then put my other hand on his shoulder and looked into his eyes. Neither of us had anything more to say. We held the gaze, then he lowered his head and bowed to me. I turned, opened the door, and left.

I went to sleep, returning to my house and settling into bed beside my most recent wife. No one said anything more about this. In the morning, everything seemed normal, though the noise of the palace sounded quieter, somber. The dinner for the heads of the tribes went on as planned; if they noticed the tension among us, none reacted. Since fame had spread of Tamar's magical cooking, my wives helped her make for our dessert those small cakes that she does so well.

And now the women are gone. They have headed off in a small caravan with our best drivers. Tamar is going to visit the magical women at the Well of Generations. She may stay there awhile to recover, perhaps to learn from them.

And I am here, Jonathan, alone with my harp and the silence and the memory of you. After all these years, I still long for you to be here, to share my sorrows and occasional joys, to listen to me and return sage words of understanding.

Amnon's words still thunder in my ears. Yes, I have desired women, taken women, and have not acted well to them when new women came along. But though I have always desired the touch of women, the bodies and shapes and scents of women, I have never loved one as they have loved me, as I loved only you. Neither have I desired men, or ever loved other men, but your heart and mine, from the day we both were born, from the day we met, until the day you died, were joined as one.

My soul is torn by the things that I have felt, the things that I have said, the things that I have done. And now I see what I have done and what I have been thrown back at me in the words and actions of my sons. I worry whether I have not given them enough attention, if I have given them too much attention, if I have been too harsh with them, if I am now showing one son too much compassion. And I wonder if I should have asked their mothers how they should be raised, and if it will be too late, when they return, to ask for their aid.

I feel my fingers starting to move against the strings of my harp, and hear my voice raised, as if by a will outside my own. They are playing, singing one of my own old songs that I thought I had forgotten: "Happy is he who is thoughtful of the wretched; in bad times may the Lord keep him from harm. May the Lord guard and preserve him; may he be thought happy in the land…"

And now my voice and hands have fallen silent. And I wrap my arms around my harp, as I wish I could wrap my arms around Tamar, around Amnon, around my kingdom, around the Lord, and, most dearly, around my memory of you. Then my hands drop to my sides, and I know that I am alone, alone, in my thoughts and memories, among all my dreams and all my people, at last, silently, alone.

For comments and discussion about the tale of David
and to hear the audio version, please visit
http://www.thebookofvoices.com/David

ZADOK

צדוק

Zadok was the High Priest, late in the reign of King David.

Two years after David's son Amnon raped his half-sister Tamar, her brother Absalom had Amnon killed. Because of his beauty and his skillful political maneuvering, Absalom became the people's favorite. Absalom traveled to Hebron and declared himself king.

King David and his supporters ed Jerusalem.

The Bible says:

> The whole countryside wept aloud as all the people passed by. The king also crossed the Kidron Valley, and all the people moved on toward the wilderness.
>
> Zadok was there, too, and all the Levites who were with him were carrying the ark of the covenant of God. They set down the ark of God, and Abiathar offered sacrifices until all the people had finished leaving the city.
>
> Then the king said to Zadok, "Take the ark of God back into the city. If I find favor in the Lord's eyes, he will bring me back and let me see it and his dwelling place again. But if he says, 'I am not pleased with you,' then I am ready; let him do to me whatever seems good to him. "...
>
> So Zadok and Abiathar took the ark of God back to Jerusalem and stayed there.
>
> But David continued up the Mount of Olives, weeping as he went; his head was covered and he was barefoot. All the people with him covered their heads too and were weeping as they went up.
>
> *(2 Samuel 15:23-26, 29-30)*

David's army eventually defeated Absalom's, and Absalom rode out to meet David.

Zadok speaks as he stands with the Ark, watching David and his supporters leave Jerusalem.

I am shivering with the cold from the wind, with the chill in my heart, standing alongside the ark on this hill at the city walls. The sun is lowering toward the horizon, toward twilight. As I look to the west, I can see hundreds, perhaps thousands of people streaming past me, out of my city, out of the gates of Jerusalem, out toward the valleys and caves where some will disperse and some will hide in the dark. All of them have covered their heads and bared their feet. All wear muted colors, forming a vague dim tapestry of the shades of their skin, of the shades of the earth. All try to look the same, in unity, in anonymity. Each wants to be counted, to be reckoned with the group, yet to be hidden, to avoid being singled out as a person with a face, with a name within the crowd.

But in this blur of people, one traveler still stands out, as if he is glowing with a different light. David, our king, is leaving his city, our city, on a path whose tracks are drawn by his tears and ours.

And I have been left behind — I, the king's most loyal follower and comrade, the keeper of the sacred place. Of all the people around him, he trusts me to safeguard the ark, so he has ordered me to stay behind, to be his ears within the city, to send him word of those who whisper of his fate. All the people of Jerusalem who have followed him are leaving, save my fellow chief priest, our sons, the ten concubines who care for his house, and me. I watch him go and feel sadness, feel loss, and (I must admit) feel a tinge of anger, of frustration that he has chosen not to keep me by his side.

This king has been even more of a father to me than he had been to his sons. And as the father has been to his sons, so the sons have been to the father. All have strayed from the word that he purported to teach, and have done as he has done. Word has drifted from his palace, perhaps changed in the telling, perhaps making the stories gentler than the truth, probably making them worse.

The charming Tamar is gone, off to study, we are told (though rumor links her teachers to the concubines of the palace, who suddenly arrived as a group). But there are whispers of a darker story, involving Amnon, her brother, who was to be king and who suddenly died. And deeper whispers say that Absalom grew quiet and furious when David did nothing to

Amnon, that he was the one who killed their brother, and that this caused him to consider his father unworthy of kingship and to declare himself king.

This cold wind from the north braces my skin, blows up sand and dead foliage that hisses and crackles, that strokes and strikes my face, threaten to cut into me. I step to the south, around the ark, taking refuge in its solidity as I have so often taken refuge in my faith in its god, in our god. Huddled against its outer wall, I hear the absence of the wind as the loudest of silences, my ears adjusting slowly now to twilight's sounds.

I sit in silence, in this silence, close my eyes, and pray for wisdom, for answers. I bring forth my senses of David and of Absalom and hold them both, together, in my heart. I know that each knows that things have gone wrong, that neither wants war between their people. There can be peace, if only after time apart. Neither wants the other dead. But they have spies and counselors and ministers, and each will maneuver to have the ear of either king. And these people may want war, and they may fight among themselves, and perhaps this kingdom will not hold, will split into its separate tribes again.

In this silence, in this dim light just short of darkness, I feel my presence drifting. The daylight world fades, and I find myself on the cusp of sleep, in the place where souls meet and trade their visions. Here, the ark is glowing. The wall on which I lean turns to sand, to dust, to mist, and I am drawn inside.

The cherubim carved on the innermost shrine have awakened, are alive, are singing to me. They step down from the carvings and embrace me in their arms, their wings. They are as unashamed of their nakedness as I am unconcerned by it. I look upward as they look down. Each kisses me on my forehead, and they draw my gaze deep into their eyes, now golden, now clear water, now a reflection of what is yet to be.

And I see the people of our kingdom fighting, the men of Judah against the men of Israel, there in the shade of the oaks, in the tangles of the terebinths, the turpentine trees, within the forest of Ephraim. Then the surviving soldiers fade away, and the forest is littered with the dead, perhaps ten thousand, perhaps twenty, their blood seeping into the ground, dripping over rocks, forming into streams, all flowing together as a single river that cries out in its confusion, in its pain.

The call of the blood of the joined people resonates in the blood of their kings, in the heart of David, in the soul of Absalom. And each knows suddenly that this war must end, that they must reach out to one another, and find a way to settle their battle as a matter, at last, between father and son.

I see Absalom, rising from his bed in the palace, late at night, going to his finest horses, then turning, finding a simple mule. He rides out of the palace, of the city, quietly, anonymously, down toward Machanaim, down to find his father's camp. In the night, in the moonlight, in the darkness before dawn, tears stream from his eyes as he admits to himself and to our god that he has done wrong, that events have gone wrong, that it is time to make things right.

And I see him as the sun rises, the breezes rising from the valley blowing his fine long hair outward, upward, as if it is a curtain, a canopy, a cape that flows behind and above him, its strands dark and brilliant against the green branches of the terebinth that he passes beyond and below —

Then the vision stops, and the physical world abruptly returns, with a pain that I think at first is metaphor but then recognize as real. Small stones are hitting me, hitting the ark, thrown from below. Shimei, the madman, the idiot, is throwing them, cursing and laughing as he lets them fly.

I turn and bellow with my strongest voice, "Stop! This is the ark of the Lord. Whatever you wish to fight is not here."

Shimei throws a last handful, howls with something like laughter, and runs back down the hill, to where the people are marching out of the city. I trust that they will keep him from doing further harm.

Now, in the last bit of daylight, I can still see the marchers streaming out of the city, over the hills. Even David is lost in the crowd for now, one of the multitude, crying and walking with the common people.

The wind has died down, the chill of its gusts replaced by the more steady chill of evening. I will wait for the full moon to rise enough to light our way, then call on my fellow chief priest and our sons to help me raise the ark again, so that we may carry it back to the city, to Jerusalem, to our home.

For comments and discussion about the tale of Zadok
and to hear the audio version, please visit
http://www.thebookofvoices.com/Zadok

THE SHULAMMITE

השולמית

The Shulammite was a young woman during the reign of King David's son Solomon. She is the main character in The Song of Songs. The term probably means that she came from the city of Shalem.

We know little about the Shulammite. The Bible does not mention her name, though legends tell of couple of different ones.

But in the Bible, she does say:

> Dark am I, yet lovely,
>   daughters of Jerusalem,
>   dark like the tents of Kedar,
>   like the tent curtains of Solomon.
>
> *(Song of Songs 1:5)*

According to some traditions, this suggests that she is of African descent.

The Shulammite speaks from early in her life, when she was a child visiting her aunt, the Queen of Sheba.

It's hot here. It's hot here, and it's always raining. It's hot here, and it's always raining, and the way people talk is strange. It's hot here and it's always raining, and I just forgot what the third thing was that I was complaining about. I'll have to start the game again, hopping my left foot this time and tossing the stones from my left hand to my right.

I wish my mother were here. I wish my mother were alive. I love my father (though he's back at home in our city, far from here) and I love my aunt, but it's not the same. And I don't get to spend much time with my aunt. She's so busy doing all the things that a queen does.

But the time that we do get to spend together is good, on these damp summer nights when the stars are full and all you hear are the waves and the insects. We sit together then, just quietly sitting, talking, up there on the palace roof, overlooking the sea, her guards close enough to protect us from everything, but not close enough to hear what we're saying.

One of the best things about my aunt is that she looks like me. Everybody here—well, almost everybody, except the ambassadors and traders from elsewhere—looks like me. I'm not a freak here. And I've gotten so tired of being a freak, of having people point at me and laugh at my skin, at my hair, of hearing little children scream, "Mama! Look at that girl! She's all black!"

My Aunt Makeda understands this. (I call her Aunt Makeda, though her official name is Bilqis, Queen Bilqis, just like me, since my mother named me for her.) She grew up in a foreign land, too, since her parents, my grand-parents, who I never met, were traders in Tyre. She learned to deal with the people who would laugh at her and be mean to her, and she grew up to be a grand woman, a powerful and beautiful woman with whom no one dares disagree. What she wants done, gets done. What she doesn't want, doesn't happen.

I've only argued with her once, when I first got here. It was a beautiful night, and I wanted to go down to the beach and play with the seashells in the moonlight. She told me it was late, and that I was to go to bed. "No!" I said. "I won't!"

The people around us gasped and suddenly got quiet. My aunt looked at me for a long time, then lowered her head and gave me a glare that was almost frightening, a glare that I had only ever seen before from my mother when she disagreed with my father. "Little Bilqis," she said, "come here," and I came over to her, almost as if her eyes had frozen me in place then grabbed me by the shoulders and dragged me forward.

When I got to her, she knelt in front of me to talk eye to eye. (And I saw a few people near her also kneeling or sitting on the ground. I found out later that they didn't think that it would be proper to have their heads higher than the queen's.) "Little Bilqis," she said, speaking softly so that only I could hear, "I can't have you disagreeing with me. For one thing, I am your aunt, and your father has said that you are to listen to me as you listen to him. For another, I am the queen, and it's my job to give orders that people obey. If you disobey, everyone will think that they can disobey, too, and the kingdom will fall apart. So I'm giving you a big responsibility in asking that you obey me. If you ever disagree with me, please speak to me in private, where no one else can hear us. I promise that I will listen to you—though you will still have to do what I decide. Do you understand your responsibility? Can you do that?"

I stood straight up, looked at her, bowed deeply, and said, as seriously as I could, "Yes, your majesty." She smiled and winked, kissed me on the forehead, and said, "Good! Now go to bed."

But she does take time, almost every night, to talk with me before I go to sleep. She asks me about how my day has been, and what I have seen. She says she likes hearing how things look to me, since I see things that grown-ups and people who are used to always being here in Sheba don't. And she asks me about things back home, and how things seem to my father and me.

Things back home are a bit crazy, though not as crazy as they have been. The tribe of Judah and the other tribes connected to them all seem to agree on who their king is right now, now that the old King David's sons seem to be done fighting and killing each other and throwing each other out of the city, Solomon is in charge. My father says that he's a good man, fair and wise. I can see that he's very handsome, and very, very rich.

Last night I asked my aunt if she thought that I might marry a king someday. "Are you sure that you would want to?" she asked.

I was surprised. "Well, you did," I said, "and you became a powerful queen."

"Yes, I did," she replied. "But things seem to work differently where you are. Solomon already has a lot of wives, and King David had even more. The wives don't seem to have much influence at all. Maybe Bathsheba does, but she's the mother of the current king, and even she had a very hard time at first. You don't have to marry someone to be important. You are lovely, and I know that you are going to grow up to be very beautiful. And you are very smart, and talented—I've seen the pictures that you draw, and heard the songs that you make up when singing to yourself. So you don't have to depend on anyone else to be important. And you shouldn't have to marry anyone just to live in the shadow of their importance."

"When you married the king here, did you love him?"

My aunt looked far off, across the waves of the sea, and sighed. "I thought I did. I convinced myself that I did. But no, not as much as I would have wanted. It was an official marriage, to tie together my parent's business and his kingdom, just like your parents married to connect the business and the city of Shalem. But he was a good man, and we decided that we would learn to love each other, and we did. It's been such a long time since he died, and I still miss him, like your father misses your mother, like I miss your mother, like you."

I slid closer to her on our chair and rested against her side. She shifted her arm (slowly, so that my head slid down to rest against her side) and put her arm around me. She looked down at me, then off into the distance, then down at me again.

"Little Bilqis," she said, almost sternly, "listen to me. I did marry for business, for politics, as did your mother, and both of us learned to love our husbands. But you should never have to marry for anything other than love. No one should ever force you to do anything that you don't feel in your heart is right."

She paused and hugged me tightly. "Bilqis, if anything should ever happen to you, if you ever need to get away from Shalem, you are to come right down here. I am the queen. I can protect you. And I'm always listening to hear how you are doing. Word can reach me down here in Sheba faster than you can imagine. If you are ever in such trouble that you cannot get away, my sisters in Shalem will know and will tell me, and I will come to help you myself. You are not alone. Do you understand that?"

I nodded my head, my cheek rubbing against the side of her dress.

"Let me hear you say it," my aunt said.

"I understand," I said.

"What do you understand?"

"I am not alone," I said. Then, letting myself slide into the understanding, as if I were sliding into a perfectly fitted robe, I said it again: "I am not alone."

"Good!" my aunt said, and smiled, warmly, her thoughts no longer such a distance away. "Now let's go eat something—I'll have my people bring up some of the goat's milk yogurt you like so much, and fresh bananas—then it's time for you to go to bed."

I love bananas. I love bananas and I love my aunt. Let's see, I think I was hopping on my left foot and tossing the stones from right to left. I love bananas and I love my aunt and I love the sound of the waves…

For comments and discussion about
the tale of The Shulammite
and to hear the audio version, please visit
http://www.thebookofvoices.com/TheShulammite

NATHAN

נתן

Nathan was a son of David and Bathsheba. The Bible only mentions him in genealogies:

> David reigned in Jerusalem thirty-three years, and these were the children born to him there: Shammua, Shobab, Nathan and Solomon. These four were by Bathsheba daughter of Ammiel.
> *(1 Chronicles 3:4,5)*

While he was the older brother of King Solomon, he was apparently passed over for the kingship. This gave him a distinct benefit: he wasn't killed by any of his brothers.

Absalom, the brother of Tamar, killed their half-brother Amnon.

Later, Absalom declared himself king. Just as in Zadok's vision, having forced his father David to flee Jerusalem, Absalom rode through the woods to attempt to reconcile with his father. Unfortunately, his magnificent long hair got tangled in the branches of a tree. One of David's men found him trapped there and, against David's orders, killed him.

When David was dying, he indicated that Solomon should be the next king. Another son, Adonijah, declared himself king, but Solomon had him killed.

And so on.

Some legends suggest that the Messiah would be a descendant of Nathan.

Nathan speaks late in his life, near his school at the Well of Generations.

Again, one of my brothers has killed another. Or perhaps he has had him killed. I no longer keep track of the details, or of how many brothers have died, or of how many brothers survive. Thanks to my father and his many women, I seem to have had an endlessly replenishing supply of brothers. As far as I know, we have only had one sister, and none of us have heard from her in many years. But brothers kept being born, and brothers keep dying. I try not to think about it much. I don't think about it much. I carry on.

That is my role in life: to carry on. Out here in this cool valley near the caves, far from Jerusalem, far from politics, far from that family, far from whatever might distract me from the work that I quietly do, I carry on.

I do have family here, a new family, a wife and children and this community that feels like family: the children whom I teach and have taught, and their parents and their children and their families whom I teach or will teach or have taught. In this small town, home to farmers, artisans, and those few tradesmen who wander off to sell things then return to their homes, to their families, almost everyone can read. I hope that I might be allowed some small pride in that.

My oldest brother, Daniel, brought the news. He always brings the news. We are now certain that he is the oldest brother, since Amnon, the other oldest, born at the same moment but to a different mother, died years ago, his death ordered by Absalom, who was killed by my cousin, Joab, who was killed on the orders of my little brother Solomon, who also just ordered the death of our brother Adonijah. I think it was Adonijah. I don't keep track. I don't think about it much.

Daniel looked great, as always. He never seems to age. He was already grown up by the time that I was born, and remains grown up, not aging. His hair should be white, since mine is going gray, his face more lined than mine is now, and he should be slowing down, not quite as able to run about with the playing children, moving, like me, more slowly now. Maybe it is that he has never bothered to marry and to have the responsibilities of a family. Maybe it is that no one knows how he spends his time, other than when he suddenly appears to one of us with news. But I don't begrudge him this. He has found some secret of youth. I am happy for him. I am happy to age, to serve as an example to my students of how to have a good life as one ages. When I die, I will have many mourners and people who will remember me well. That is sufficient. I carry on.

Big Nathan used to bring us news, when he was young enough to travel. Yes, Big Nathan. I'm Little Nathan, even though I am at least a hand's breadth taller than anyone I know. I've been Little Nathan since my father named me for Big Nathan, his best friend. Well, his best surviving friend; there was always Jonathan, the one with whom he was so close, but he rarely spoke of him. He just looked pained when, at the family events that I attended, one of my stepmothers, Jonathan's sister Michal, would bring him up, bitterly. My father always wanted to name a son after Jonathan, but Michal insisted that he could only name a son after her brother if the child were her son, too. They never had a son, as Michal often reminds us, also bitterly. Michal speaks of everything bitterly. I am glad that I live far from them.

So now, I am told, Solomon, my little brother, is king. I don't know why my father chose him, and I don't much care. He was chosen early, and raised to be king, taught all the little mannerisms that make one royal. I have a different destiny. Big Nathan told me this many times, and he was usually right about things that would happen. My destiny has little to do with me. It carries on through me. Big Nathan says that our people will carry on for a long time. At some point, inevitably, we will lose the kingship, will lose our land, and be sent to wander amongst other peoples. But eventually, we will come back together. A king will arise who will bring us together. And that king will be descended from my father, through me.

Big Nathan almost told me too much, once, when he was getting very old, when my first child was about to be born. "Little Nathan," he said, "it pleases me that you have married, that your wife is going to have a baby soon. Your children are important, since the house of David will continue through your son M—"

"Stop!" I shouted, startling him. I had never shouted at Big Nathan before.

"What?" he asked, blankly.

"Don't tell me the name of the son that will carry the line on!"

"Why not?"

"If I know which son it is (and now I know that it will be a son and not a daughter), I will be drawn to care more for that son, since I know that he is more important than the others. Or conversely, I might let him get into more trouble and into danger, since I know that he is destined to survive whatever happens, at least until he brings me the grandchild that will carry the line on after him. And, come to think of it, if I know the name, I would logically want to delay giving any of my children that name, knowing that

that might prolong my own life indefinitely, since I would have to stay alive at least until that child is conceived. As it is, I would be tempted to give none of my sons names that begin with the letter Mem, since you started to say the beginning of the name, beginning with that. And the right thing to do now, I suppose, will be to restrict myself to giving them all names that begin with Mem, so I won't be certain that any of them is not the one who will continue the line."

Big Nathan started to say something, stopped, gestured with a hand as if about to make a point, then dropped his hands to his sides and laughed, long and loud. "Brilliant!" he said. "I really must remember this and tell your brother Daniel. I would have thought that only he could come up with something that is both so convoluted and so perfectly logical."

I laughed, too, but knew that my future had been constrained just a little bit more, and that, once again, no one had suspected that I might be as smart, as skilled, as strong, as dutiful, or as good as one of my brothers. I was ignored and passed over yet again, valued only for my ability to breed children (and if fecundity were a creature's most valuable trait, we would be worshiping insects, though, come to think of it, they do worship the lord of the flies down in Ekron).

And it was because of this, because it was my destiny to have at least one child, not to be king, not to be involved with all the other dramatic affairs inherent in being in the royal family, that I moved out here as soon as I could, out away from the family, here in this small village by the caves. If I was going to raise children, it would be my duty to raise them well, to teach them well, so I approached the teachers here and asked them to teach me how to teach.

I began slowly, as an apprentice, working alongside one teacher and seeing what she did. I started teaching children myself, with her watching, with her correcting me and giving suggestions so that I could work better, could teach more effectively. Eventually I was able to teach children on my own. And, one by one, the grown-ups would come to me, the men admitting to me (as they would not embarrass themselves by admitting to a woman) that they could not read, and I started to teach them too, individually, in secret if they wished, in larger groups if they were open to that. And after a while, when I was established, I approached my father for help, and he decided to humor me by giving me money and resources to start a school. So we opened the Academy of the Caves.

Most of the other teachers are women. A few men have joined me, but most are too invested in doing what they consider proper men's work, running around in the heat and the rain chasing sheep and birds and harvesting crops. Maybe they think that they will never attract women if they stay here and do the quiet work.

I was afraid of this, too, I must admit. Though Big Nathan had assured me that I would have a family, I was too quiet, too shy with the other grown-ups, to imagine that I would somehow attract a wife. I thought that perhaps my father would choose one for me, though seeing the way that he treated the women in his life (even my mother, who some claimed was his favorite), I distrusted his ability to choose well.

But as I worked, over the years, I came to grow comfortable with the women with whom I worked. And there was one in particular, Aviva, with her lightning wit and her brown eyes that seemed to discern what was happening deep within people, with whom I got along especially well. She had come from the caves, from the community of women that began in generations past and were rumored to teach magic, to keep the magic in this world. Though further rumor had it that they had forsworn contact with men, some moved easily between the caves and the outer world, and many returned to the world of rain and sun and did have families of their own.

Though I had fallen in love before, in massive conflagrations of desire that quickly burned down to ashes of regret, I felt none of the same intensity with her. Being with her seemed somehow right, as if we were parts of the same machine that worked well together, each being there for the other exactly when needed. We spoke together easily, sat together easily, and taught as if we spoke with one voice, with one heart.

The other teachers, and even the children, noticed this even before we were aware, and began asking when we would be wed, even though I had not dared to ask her to marry me. Then, one time, she answered casually, "On the fifth day of the week after the next new moon," and I said, as if equally casually, "I will cancel the day's classes and let my father know."

My father, of course, could not attend and sent his most sincere regrets, since he was dealing with some sort of crisis involving a more important son. But Big Nathan and Daniel were there, and we had a pleasant ceremony and celebration on the school grounds. Many women whom we had not seen before emerged from the caves, though most remained clustered among themselves far from the center of the celebration. There was one unknown woman whom some said looked very much like me, though, with her wild eyes and long, curling hair, I thought that she looked much more like my brother Absalom. But by the time that I was able to tear myself away from the well-wishers and approach her, she was gone.

Of course, Aviva and I had children, all with names beginning with the letter Mem. Meshullam has grown to be a strong, worthy boy, and Meira a lovely girl who, we suspect, will continue with the teaching, perhaps running the school after we are gone. The twin boys, Mattatha and Melea, are as quiet as I am, seeming to share a peculiar language between them that only their mother can understand. We did lose one son as an infant, Menna, when the brief plague of rashes struck the nursery; while nothing can quite heal the loss of a son, that loss has made our remaining children even more dear.

I think that I have finished fathering sons, since Aviva and I are old, her black hair turned to the finest white and her time of bearing long past. But my children each have children, most recently Mattatha, who has named his newborn son for his lost brother at my request.

So I sit here, looking west, into the sunset, my beloved Aviva sitting, breathing gently beside me. The sky is red and a bit overcast, so the weather will probably be good. Daniel is already gone, apparently on a mission to Sepharad. He moves so quickly between places that it seems that he must step off our mortal plane entirely and step back in where he needs to be.

In the morning, I will arise and teach again. I continue to teach the children how to read. Aviva teaches them history. I can never keep track of history, can never summon the interest—all those judges, from Othniel to Ehud to Shamgar to Deborah and so on, through Eli and Samuel, then the kings, first Saul and then my father, well, with Ish-bosheth in between, or maybe not, then my brothers declaring themselves king one after another and killing each other over and over again, while I sit in this humble house out here by the caves, not wanting to be king, no, not at all, though it might be pleasant to be acknowledged by my family, for them to admit that, with all their fanfares and fighting, I am doing more to help our world continue than any of them will ever do.

Looking down, I see that my bare foot has idly been drawing figures in he sand, as if of its own will: first a picture of an ox and the letter Alef, then a picture of a house and the letter Bet. It all comes down to these. I teach the pictures. I teach the words. I teach the letters that form the words. The children learn to read. They grow up. They grow old. Their children learn to read. The words carry on. Life carries on. I carry on.

SOLOMON

שְׁלֹמֹה

Solomon was the youngest son of David and Bathsheba. He became king after David died, and grew to be extremely wealthy. He had hundreds of wives and concubines.

Though he was renowned for his wisdom and for building the Temple in Jerusalem, he was also known to be demanding and cruel to those who worked under him. He was easily led into sin, and allowed practices that contradicted God's laws.

Though Solomon was married so many times, it appears that he never really understood love. The Bible quotes him as saying:

"There are three things that are too amazing for me,
　　four that I do not understand:
the way of an eagle in the sky,
　　the way of a snake on a rock,
the way of a ship on the high seas,
　　and the way of a man with a young woman."
(Proverbs 30:18-19)

(The beginning of the chapter attributes the saying to one Agur ben Jakeh, but legens suggest that this was another of Solomon's many names.)

Abishag was a woman brought to the court of King David in David's last days. She slept chastely with him, in hope that her youthful powers would restore his vitality.

You may remember the Shulammite, who spoke as a child a few chapters ago. By the time she had grown into a woman, more hearts than she intended have been drawn to her.

Solomon speaks as Abishag magically looks into his mind and projects into it what she has seen in the heart of the Shulammite.

Abishag's eyes draw me deeply in, propel me down chasms of memory, engulf me in emotions that I had never guessed were there, suspend me in a maelstrom of feelings, of thoughts, of words. I suddenly understand the meaning of this love and the tragic mistake that I am making. No, it isn't Abishag's love that I am experiencing, nor another's love for me. It is the love in the heart of the woman that I am to marry tonight, that woman's love for another man.

I did love, I do so deeply love that woman, but I have never told her so. It has nothing to do with our wedding. Like all my other marriages, this marriage would serve to symbolize politics, not passion. A payment to a high official of a territory, a physical consummation with the official's daughter, and our nation's ties to that territory are sworn to be secure, at least as long as he and I live. Sometimes the daughter and I do indeed find passion (it has happened a few times, with a handful of my dozens of brides), but I have mostly had dutiful matings with my wives. Most have ended up in the house of wives, getting on with whatever it is that wives do all day, available for me at night, should I have tired of my most recent bride and decided to revisit an earlier one as chosen from my menu.

But this woman, ah, this Shulammite... (I suddenly realize that I don't actually know her name. I am not surprised, but then am surprised that I am not.) This one, this bride out of all my brides is different. I think of her, hear her voice in my mind, and the passion that I thought I had forgotten comes alive. I see her, picture the grace of her movements, her smile which could dispel the sorrows of the world, and I want to be with her. I feel her touch as she brushes past me while I complete negotiations at her father's house, and I feel as if the breath of life itself has whispered past me.

She is not in her father's house now, nor in mine, nor in the women's chamber, preparing for our wedding. She sits in a cold room in our prison, captured by the watchmen of the city as she tried to run, tried to escape to the hills of Lebanon.

None of my brides and none of my father's brides had ever run before, so the watchmen were unclear at to what to do. When they captured her, though she struggled, they tried to treat her with respect. Once she was secured, they summoned the Daughters of Jerusalem, who took her deposition and brought it to me.

It is not a common deposition, since the Shulammite, like most women not trained at my brother's school, cannot write or even read. Abishag, the last of my father's wives, worked her empathic magic on her, looking deep into her eyes, into her soul, drinking in all that she could about the woman and her flight. Now she is here, looking into my eyes, transmitting the woman's message, the depth of her feeling, the unknown history that caused her to run, to disobey my demands.

The figure of a man runs repeatedly through her mind, through her desires. He is handsome, strong. In her memory, I see them meeting in her father's house where he had labored for months, see them hiding out in a chamber, their embraces, their furtive lovemaking (and I notice, with unkingly blushes, that her beauty, her grace, is even greater than I had imagined, arousing me even more than I might have hoped), see their last meeting before I drafted him, among so many thousands of others, to go to Lebanon, to cut down the cedars that would form my temple.

And, as their souls have come so close, I see her own image, reflected in her heart as it appears in that man's eyes: lovely, so unusually dark (her mother, I am told, was a sister of the queen of Sheba), her gentle movements, like a fawn who has grown certain of movement, whose every step explodes with the joy of flesh moving within and against the motions of air, the blessings of rain, the pull of the earth.

And, ah, their voices! They rise in song, in her own song, the one she sang alone in her house, a room away from where I was meeting with her father. I listen within my own history, my own heart, and locate the moment that I first heard her sing her song as the exact moment that I fell in love with her. For all that I am my father's son, I have no music in me. I cannot sing. And hearing her voice singing her song brought forth all the longing within me, the desire to merge with this woman whose soul contained everything that I found missing from my own.

But now I know that that was only half the song: I now hear in this reflection of her memory a song for two, a sacred duet. Their voices merge, diverge. His voice coils around hers like a serpent around an Asherah tree, like her body wraps around his in those images that accompany the song. Their words strike deep into me, engraving their messages with joy, with love, with the eternal covenant of their love: "Set me as a seal upon your heart, as a seal upon your arm..."

My own heart bursts with love, with the greatest desire for her, reaches out toward the emanations of her heart—but it does not reach her, does not connect with her. I know that her love, her joy, is with him alone. I call from within myself, shout within the silence that I love her, that I can make her love me. But the demand, the plea is silence within silence, the scream of a child who cannot have what he demands.

"But I love her!" my heart cries out again.

Then I hear Abishag's voice, a whisper within my own mind. "What is love?"

"I want to be with her, her flesh, her soul, her song! I demand to be with her!"

"Yes," Abishag's voice murmurs within me, "and then what? You are the king, and certainly can order this marriage, this mating, can order her flesh to cleave unto yours for a night, or for as many nights as you wish. But what of her heart?"

"It can come with time. In time, as a favored wife of the king, she can forget that man."

"Can she? Would she?" Abishag asks. "Listen within her heart, and see if they can ever be truly parted."

And I listen farther, hear the words, the songs within her heart, within her beloved's heart, her songs to him, about him, his songs to and about her, what they cry out to the watchmen, to the Daughters of Jerusalem, to those who guard our streets and our bodies, to those who minister to our souls and our hearts. I look for glimpses of the future, and see her joy in dreaming of being with him.

And I turn within the memory and look upon her more probable future, of her life as a wife of the king, an object of my love, bedecked in jewels, a prize caught in my palace, called to sing her songs as one might call upon a jester, upon a court magician, upon a kitchen maid to bring us their wonders. And in the depths of her soul I taste nothing but bitterness, sadness, longing for what could have been, a life of looking out upon the palace grounds and wondering if any man that she sees might be him, could be him, could be the man to whom she swore her love, whom she dreams will return and take her away.

"What is love?" Abishag asks, demands again. "What do you wish for her in loving her?"

"I wish..." I pause and look within myself for an answer. "I love her, and so I desire to be with her, and desire that she will live in joy for the rest of her days."

"And can you have both?"

"I... I fear that I cannot."

"Which desire is stronger?"

I look into the balances, weighing the cry of my flesh, my mind, my soul, against the evidence of her body, her dreams, and her song. I cry out, seeing that my love is futile, that she cannot be happy with me. "What would my father do?" I ask.

"You are not your father," she replies. "You can be better than your father."

And she sends another flash of memory within me, captured from my father when Abishag was first summoned to minister to him, when she was brought by my brother Daniel from the women of the caves to be with my father as he died, to lie beside him and calm his heart, his soul, his memory.

Through my father's eyes, I see my mother, young, beautiful, bathing on the roof, embracing her first husband, Uriah. I see my father summoning her to his chambers, taking her, then sending Uriah off to die so that he can have her for all time.

Then I look through his aged eyes, at the last grand dinner that he called before he was taken ill, before he died, and I see his wives arrayed before him, in the order of the dates on which he took them: from Michal, the old woman, daughter of the previous king, and on through the newest, some barely of age to be women, most briefly used and filed away in his archive of wives while he pursued his lust, his supposed love. In the eyes of each of them, I see the same dull sadness, mixed with bitterness for some, with resignation for others, but without any remnant of love for him or from him.

And I see Abishag there with my father on his deathbed, looking into his heart, placing one hand upon his chest, one upon his right hand, her head upon his shoulder, hear him whisper, with his final breath, the name of the only person that he ever really loved.

"Which desire is stronger?" she says again. And I hear the words again of the Shulammite's song: "Love is fiercer than death, passion as mighty as the grave... If a man offered all his riches for love, he would be laughed to scorn."

And I feel the sad decision forming within my heart. "Yes, I can be better."

Abishag closes her eyes, and I close mine. As the connection between us fades, I realize that the words, the songs of the Shulammite and her love still reverberate within me.

"What is your will, my king?" she asks, this time aloud.

"Dress the Shulammite in her wedding dress, and bring her to the women's chamber. Summon from Lebanon the man of whom she dreams, not as a prisoner but as an honored guest. Bring her father the bride-price on which we had agreed, and we will sign our treaty papers. And when her beloved arrives, he... they..." My voice stops, cracks, as a last explosion of my love for her, of the loss of glorious possibility erupts from within me. "When he arrives, we will announce and celebrate their marriage, with full ceremony. Promote him within the leadership of the Temple building project, with pay that will support them in the life that they desire."

Abishag places her hand against my chest, nods, smiles, and leaves.

I look up as she passes through the doorway, and see my mother standing, listening. "Jedidiah..." she says, calling me by my childhood name. She looks like she is going to say more, as I see many emotions drift within her gaze. Then, silently, she walks up to me, places her hands gently on the sides of my head, rises on her toes, and kisses me on the forehead. We embrace for a long moment, then she, too, leaves me there, alone.

I sit at my desk, listening to the echoes within me of the songs of the Shulammite and her beloved. Almost without thinking, I reach for a fresh scroll, my ink, and my pen, and begin to create a wedding present for the betrothed, a record of the words that have burst from and joined their hearts. "The Song of Songs," I write at the top, then, breathing deeply, start to transcribe the first of the poems:

Kiss me with the kisses of your mouth,
for your love is more delightful than wine...

For comments and discussion about the tale of Solomon
and to hear the audio version, please visit
http://www.thebookofvoices.com/Solomon

Elisheva (Interlude 6)

אלישֶׁוע

I awaken to an unexpected sensation, an unexpected sound. I listen: a human voice is singing, somewhere in this space. I inhale, and the sound stops, though its reverberations hang in this room for the briefest of moments before they completely fade away. I exhale, and the sound begins again, then stops short as I gasp in realization: the sound is my own voice, which I have not heard for so long a time that I no longer recognize it. The sound is thin yet strong, the pitch steady though it vibrates, trembles, perhaps because of my age.

I listen to the resonance of the note within the room, within my memory, within myself. Tentatively, gingerly, I change the note, sliding its pitch upward. The sound weakens as it strays from its start. I return to that pitch, sliding downward this time. Again it weakens, fades. Again I return.

This note, this pitch holds some special magic. I drop to silence, then, when the silence has washed the remaining sound from the room, start again, singing more powerfully now. I listen for the magic, and more glimmerings of memory arrive: The spell of sound is not cast by the summoning of powers from another plane but by the earthly blessings of mathematics, of architecture. This room, just like, if I recall, all rooms within this hive of spaces, has been constructed to fortify this note. When one of us here would sing the note, it would ring out not only in the room in which she sang but in the rooms nearby. And others would hear and sing the note with her, each in her own space, an embrace of voices that would tell her without words, "We are with you. You do not need to feel alone. We are here."

I pause again, and hear the resonance of memories of voices, of those who must have been my sisters, been my friends. And in the gaps between my breaths I hear another voice, the most powerful, the most clear: Aspaklarya, always Aspaklarya.

Her voice was not the loudest of ours, as I remember it. The pure color of her voice did not cut through the other sounds. But her perfect memory captured everything that she had heard. She could match her singing to the memories of the note as it had rung most true within the rooms, blessing and blessed by their walls, their air.

The present sound, my own unfamiliar voice, is broken by an unvoiced gasp, a keening, a moan. Here on the soft stone, I roll onto my side. My arms and legs pull inward, as if I could contract into a single point, as if my body could come to fill the sudden breach within my soul, within my heart. In this broken silence, I am weeping, wracked with pain, with emptiness, loneliness. I hear my mouth whisper a cycle of sounds. Breath, tongue, palate, teeth conspire again and again to bring forth her name: Aspaklarya. Aspaklarya.

I cover my face with my hands and see her image drifting there, in the colorless glow of afterimages that float before us when we close our eyes in lighted rooms. I see her there, my sister, my mirror, and in the reversal of the light I suddenly know how she complemented me, completed me: she could sing with a voice of perfect beauty where I could not sing at all; where I could remember nothing, she could remember everything that she had ever known. And suddenly I see the pain in the image of her eyes, and know how I reflected her, completed her: "You lost your words because you could not remember," her image whispers. "I lost mine because I could not forget."

There, on the stone, I reach forward, my hand pressing out into the emptiness, into the space that her image appears to fill. I feel my hand taken, cupped in another's hand. Then yet another hand covers mine, the two hands holding mine gently, warmly.

For a moment I let myself believe that all that has happened was a dream, that my sisters have never left, that Aspaklarya is still here. But then I realize that the hands that hold mine are larger, rougher, cooler than hers. With one more sob, I open my eyes and see my angel, kneeling before me, his face close to mine.

Angel, can you take me back? Must I have this memory, more painful than forgetting?

He says nothing, can say nothing, but can see what I remember, what I wish to remember, what I wish not to remember.

Angel, can you bring back the sound of my sisters, that note that sounded within our souls?

He releases my hand and touches my lips, touches his ears.

Do you wish me to sing, me to create that sound?

He nods. I open my mouth and bring forth a note. But it is the wrong note, and though I slide the pitches up and back, wider, wildly, I cannot find the sacred note.

Again he touches my lips, this time returning me to silence. Then he closes his eyes and rests one hand over his heart.

After a long moment, long enough for my breath to pause in silence, he lowers his hand. In his palm I see an amulet, the holy image of a hand that is both left and right, attached to a glowing thread.

He takes the end of the string in his other hand and, standing, swings the amulet above his head. It makes a high whistling, humming sound as it circles above us. Gradually, as it swings, the thread becomes longer. The sound of its circling becomes richer, deeper, until – yes! – it reaches the resonance of the room and sounds that magic note.

He once again touches my lips and draws out my voice. I am singing, yes, I am singing, that sound, that note, that resonance of comfort, of community, of joy that had surrounded me for so long.

But the sound is no longer quite as pure, quite as beautiful. It holds an emptiness, a hollowness, the subtracted echo of the hole within me that Aspaklarya's presence once had filled. Now that I have remembered her, I am no longer able to forget, and the presence of the joy overwhelms the memory of joy.

Angel, I thank you for giving this to me. But can you now take it away?

The angel touches one hand to my head, one hand to my shoulder. I am fading, relaxing, unfolding, shifting so that once again I lie on my back, silent on this bed of soft stone.

Speak to me, my angel says.

I can feel my pain drift away, feel my sense of my self drift away. My body stiffens, and I can feel my face taking on expressions that are not my own.

Speak to me, my angel says. And I feel a last flicker of familiar strangeness as another voice comes forward, emerging from my own.

THE BOOK OF STRUGGLING

ספר המאבק

JEROBOAM

יָרָבְעָם

Jeroboam was the first king of the independent Kingdom of Israel.

Solomon dealt harshly with the workers in his kingdom. When his son Rehoboam became king after Solomon's death, the people of Israel asked him to deal with them less harshly. Jeroboam, a rebel leader who had fled to Egypt during Solomon's reign, returned to lead the attempted negotiations.

But Rehoboam ignored the advice of his elders. Instead of lightening the people's load, he followed the advice of his friends, who told him to say:

> "My little finger is thicker than my father's waist. My father laid on you a heavy yoke; I will make it even heavier. My father scourged you with whips; I will scourge you with scorpions.'"
> *(2 Chronicles 10:10-11)*

(And I suspect that what is translated as "waist" here was a euphemism for another part of his body.)

The ten northern tribes of Israel seceded from the united kingdom and formed the Kingdom of Israel. As the Bible says:

> When all the Israelites heard that Jeroboam had returned, they sent and called him to the assembly and made him king over all Israel. Only the tribe of Judah remained loyal to the house of David.
> *(1 Kings 12:20)*

Jeroboam established temples in other cities within Israel, so that the people would not have to go to Jerusalem, which was within Judah, to worship. He allowed methods of worship that were banned from Solomon's Temple.

| Jeroboam speaks to the people at his coronation. |

My friends, priests, fellow leaders, people of the city of Shechem, and citizens of the united tribes of the renewed nation of Israel: With both humility and pride, I joyfully accept my coronation as king. With humility, since you have chosen me, a workman from the lowest of families, for this highest of honors; with pride, since with this act the people have come together to throw off the yoke of tyranny and corruption, to return this nation to the role that the prophets of its god have foretold.

Yes, I have indeed come from the lowest of the people. The rumors of my parentage are true. My mother was indeed a harlot and died as a leper. I never knew my father. Like so many others, I suffered in the streets until I was arrested for stealing bread and was thrown into Solomon's prison.

But in that prison, I decided to better myself, to learn. And I quickly learned how buildings were built, and, more importantly, began to learn how communities are built. I listened to my fellow prisoners, and I found that the blind, harsh rules of the taskmasters had them working against each other rather than to help one another. I listened and I worked to understand them, and I was able to come to the taskmasters with a plan that improved both our effectiveness and our lives and working conditions.

At the end of my sentence, I was asked to stay on, and went to work as a bondsman building Solomon's houses, first building the walls themselves and then, more importantly, building coalitions and trust among the workers, and building understanding between the workers and the taskmasters.

And I rose to be a taskmaster myself, and a leader of taskmasters. But I never forgot my roots among the lowest of the people, and I continued to walk among the workers and to listen to them, to hear their voices. And I got to see not only the splendors that the workers under Solomon created but also the darkness that lurked beneath the hammered gold: for each chair of the finest cedar at each splendid table in his palaces, a family sat in the dust, eating what crumbs they could afford; for each sacrifice that soared to heaven from his temples, a workman was laid in the earth, broken, sickened, defeated by the deathly conditions that he was forced to endure.

And in working on those palaces and temples, I came to hear an inner voice. Some have said that the Lord spoke to me. If so, it is as the god of Israel speaks to all of us. To me, it came in the voice of a simple worker, laboring in the fields. And what he said to me was so clear, so true, that I knew that it was the course that I must follow. And it is this course that has led me here to this fateful night.

People of Israel: Too long have we suffered under the hands of kings who speak of God but oppress mankind. Like our ancestors in old Egypt, so many generations ago that we have forgotten its evil pharaoh's name, the common man is crushed under the burden of building structures for the rich. But we have learned once again to have a voice. We have learned once again to cry out to our god. And we have learned, perhaps for the first time, how to organize ourselves to speak to the people in power, how to make our voices heard.

People of Israel: We have learned that creating families of kings puts us back into the hands of oppressors. When we first asked for a common leadership, when we asked for a ruler to represent all the tribes a hundred years ago, Saul rose to be our leader, a good man, a man of the people, valiant and truthful.

But then David arose: unbidden, charismatic, alluring. And he charmed an army into usurping the leadership of the nation, into overthrowing Saul, defeating the people's leader, and installing himself as king for life.

Yes, David was in many ways a great man and did many beautiful and wonderful things. Under David, the arts of the people of Israel flourished as they never had before, with music, poetry, architecture, all exploding into view, into a golden age of worship and of beauty.

But for all that beauty, under all that gold, a price was paid: we lost our own voices, failed to remain a vibrant people, and fell into a repetition and emulation of David's work. And with all that richness came an increasing poverty, a growing chasm, wide as the Sea of Reeds, between the glistening extravagance of the ruling families and the abject dirt in which the workers had been forced to survive.

And David's riches led to corruption, and his corruption led to oppression and destruction. His own family erupted into wars between themselves, battles between factions, the roots of which we may never know. And his sons began killing one another and sowing disaster among his people.

Of those, only Solomon survived. And he became king, though the people never chose him. Never before had the leadership of Israel been handed down by sheer heredity, and never has it been true that the son of even a good king would necessarily be good himself.

And yes, Solomon, too, did some great things. He was renowned by all the other nations, with a reputation as a wise man, and a talent for getting great buildings built, creating alliances with the rich of other nations, and accumulating wealth for his kingdom.

And so it may have seemed to those who saw him from afar, to those who arrived in caravans, who were shown only the great palaces, and were kept away from the common people. But we, the people of Israel, knew what lay beneath the glory. For we were the ones that he enslaved, the ones that he forced to work in conditions of horror, that he placed under the heaviest of yokes and whipped when we could not meet his demands, could not meet his insane deadlines with the meager resources that we were allowed.

I came to learn of these things as I worked in his houses, eventually leading the workers from the tribes of the sons of Joseph. But when I came to speak to Solomon of these things, when I finally gained an audience, he responded not with wisdom but with rage, and declared that I was to be killed for daring to represent a voice that disagreed with his.

So I had to leave. I went south to Egypt, under its good king and more peaceful people. And I studied there, and I thought and I wrote and I learned, I hope, how to be a more effective leader. I always kept the people of Israel at the forefront of my thoughts. I wrote my scrolls of suggestions as to how things could be better here, and was gratified to hear that they were copied and that they were passed, hand to hand, in the darkness, among those of you who could read them, and even learned and passed by word of mouth among those of you who could not yet read.

And now Solomon is gone. But he has been replaced by his son. And while we thought that the plight of the people was as dire as it could ever be, we have discovered that the new king, Rehoboam, is even worse. When I returned from Egypt under our moment of amnesty, in that moment when we thought that a reconciliation might be possible between the people and those who claimed to rule over us, I went with a committee of the tribes to meet with the new king, to present our demands.

And this new king did claim to listen, but he did so with less than half a heart. He stalled, he maneuvered, he delayed, and finally, when he could not delay any longer, gave us his answer: in addition to using a lurid metaphor that I will not repeat, especially in the presence of our dear children who have gathered here with us tonight, he said, and I quote: "My father burdened you with a heavy yoke. I will make the yoke heavier. My father chastised you with whips. I will chastise you with scorpions."

So we left. And we have gathered together, and we have spoken, and we have listened to the people. And we have heard your voice, and your voice has been carried on the winds to all the corners of Israel, and has brought us together on this solemn and wonderful day.

People of Israel: as of this day, we declare that we are our own, independent, sovereign nation. We do not need the sons of David. We do not need Jerusalem. We, the people of Israel, now and forever declare ourselves to be the sovereign nation of Israel. We have our own voice. We have our own leaders (and, yes, if you insist on calling us kings, we will humbly accept that title, never forgetting that we are still the most common of people).

And Israel will have its own temples: I declare today that, by consent of the people, we have begun construction on new temples, north and south, in the beautiful cities of Dan and Bethel. The temples will be dedicated to the god of Israel—but those who worship their gods in other ways will not be locked out. As we did in the days of Moses (though then, too, some leaders did not understand), we are erecting calves of gold in each space, to welcome those who call their gods by other names, so that all might see that the paths of all humanity are united. As Moses said, "Listen, Israel, the Lord is our God and his name is one"—but it is only one. We believe that our god, with all his faces, has ears to hear those who worship under any name.

And the worship in these temples will be open to all the people. While we respect the good work done by the men of the tribe of Levi over the generations, we declare that the care of the temple, the offering of prayer, and the offering of sacrifices must be open to all men, regardless of whom their parents happened to be.

People of Israel, from Dan to Bethel, and (yes, even to our brothers down in the tribe of Judah who have not yet chosen to join us), from the eastern desert on west to the great sea: I welcome this coronation with humility and with pride. Whether we last a thousand years, or whether the voice of the people demands continual change, this government, this leadership solemnly swears to listen, to lead, to report, to represent, to honor, respect, obey, inspire, and be inspired by you, to strive to evoke the best in each of us in service to that which is best for all of us, in the name of the Lord God of Israel, under all his many faces and names.

People of Israel: let us celebrate our nation, our freedom, and our sacred voice. May our voices, may your voice ring out joyously throughout the world, throughout the years, to all people, to all the visions of God. In the name of the god of Israel, let us rejoice. Let us listen. Let us sing.

For comments and discussion about the tale of Jeroboam
and to hear the audio version, please visit
http://www.thebookofvoices.com/Jeroboam

ASA

אַסָא

Asa was the great-grandson of Solomon and a king of Judah. He worked to restore the worship of one God. but met with resistance within his own family.

The Bible says:

> King Asa also deposed his mother Maacah from her position as queen mother, because she had made a repulsive image for the worship of Asherah. Asa cut it down, broke it up and burned it in the Kidron Valley. Although he did not remove the high places from Israel, Asa's heart was fully committed to the Lord all his life."
>
> *(2 Chronicles 15:16-17)*

(Actually, the translation that I'm using here says that Maacah was his grandmother, rather than his mother. The terms here are vague, and the genealogy is confused. Several other translations say that she was his mother. And, for that matter, there's no agreement as to what the 'repulsive image' was. This is the only time that that Hebrew word appears in the Bible. In contemporary Hebrew, it is now used to mean 'monster.')

Asa speaks on the day after these events.

And so my mother is gone. Still alive, still well, but gone from the palace, from her place of authority. She has slipped away under the silent gaze of the moon to a place where she will be hidden, safe from capture, safe from harm, safe from me.

She took few belongings, but left even fewer. I knew that she had been paring down what she owned, giving clothing to my sisters and donating trinkets to be displayed in the public palace galleries. Still, I was unprepared for how spare her quarters had become.

My knock on her cypress wood door sounded far more hollow than it had before. When my mother opened the door and I stepped into her receiving room, I saw that the Medean tapestries that had lined the walls and the back of the door were down, rolled neatly and stacked near the fireplace on the south wall.

We stood for a while in silence. Finally, she raised a hand, its near-translucent skin making it seem smaller and more frail without its jewels, and gestured at the space behind me. "No guards?" she asked.

"For you or for me?"

"Either." She smiled. "Both. So are you here to kill me or to arrest me?"

"Which would you prefer?"

She closed her eyes and looked up to the right, feigning deep thought. "I am old," she said, "but not yet ready to be dead."

"And it looks like you have been preparing to leave."

She shrugged. "It is time for me to retire."

"And you couldn't have done so quietly?"

"What have you ever known me to do quietly?"

"That... thing you erected—"

"I think 'erected' is precisely the wrong word," she said under her breath.

"That thing you... built," I said. "Quite impressive in its own way. Disgusting, but impressive. To have put it up in a single night—I don't know whether I should execute your architects or hire them."

"If I believed that your court would ever actually hire a female architect," she replied, "I would gladly recommend them to you and would stay around to see what you'd ask them to design. But it would probably be more towers for war and to worship that god of your fathers."

"As opposed to this structure for..."

"For the god of your mothers, of course. So did you get to see it in the daylight?"

"No, it is down already. My workmen are also efficient."

"Well, Asherah has always been more partial to moonlight than to the sun. I didn't expect it would last. But those who built it and saw it at night will remember it." She laughed, then sang, "A time to build up, a time to break down, a time to kill, a time to heal..."

I smiled. "Did Solomon have a song for everything?"

"If not him, then his father. You should learn to sing sometimes, Asa. You might learn to relax."

"I don't get to relax," I said. "I am the king."

"Yes," she replied. "So I've noticed."

We stood again silently. I shifted my weight to the other foot and heard my sandal scuff against the floor, now wood where there had been carpet. The sound joined the hollow reverberation that had been our voices.

I looked down and up again. My mother was still looking directly at me.

"So when will I be arrested?"

"The order will go out tomorrow at dawn."

"And if I'm not here to arrest?"

"Then we will announce that you have been banished."

She nodded. "Thank you."

"Do you have somewhere to go?"

"I have friends. And over the years, the architects have created a hidden place. I can live there comfortably. Perhaps I too will relax. Perhaps I will teach."

"Mother, your teaching is the problem."

"No." She crossed her arms and glared. "It is only a problem because you have declared it to be a problem, you and that invisible, unnamed, arrogant god of your fathers' and yours. Asherah is happy to share the world with other gods. Only your god insists on being the only god in the world."

"It isn't that he insists. It is simply the truth."

"It is the truth because the king says that it is?"

"The king says that it is the truth because it is."

She smiled and shook her head. "Stubborn as always. Well, I guess you got that from me."

"You taught me well."

"At least the things that you chose to learn."

There was silence again. This time, both of us stood still.

"Asa, may I ask you one favor?"

"As the king or as your son?"

"Both. Either. Whichever will be more effective. Asa, you have destroyed almost everything that my people have built for worship. The altars and the buildings are gone. But the high places that you have cleared, the places that are sacred to me and to my mothers, can you leave them clear? We will not build further structures on them ourselves. Can you do the same? There are too few places where one can go on a cloudless night and be alone with the moon."

I frowned. "I can't condone gatherings to worship other gods."

"I'm not asking you to condone them. Just leave the spaces clear."

"Yes, I can do that. But the trees that you had planted for worship—"

"You can leave them or cut them down if you wish. They are symbols, not Asherah herself. Every tree is Asherah, or can be, if people choose to see her within them. Will you cut down all the trees in the world, tear up their roots, and dig up their seeds so that none can grow again? And if you do, what will keep the mountains from sliding down when your god has a tantrum and unleashes another of his storms?"

I stomped my foot. "My god does not have tantrums!"

"But the king still does."

I glared at her. Then she grinned and laughed, the echoes of the laughter ringing both harsh and warm in the hollow room. And after a moment I found myself laughing too.

Then the laughter faded, and the silence returned, fuller this time, until no sound echoed but that of our breathing.

"Asa," she said again.

"I guess this is the end," I said. "You will be gone tonight?"

She nodded.

"The king will be relieved," I said. "But your son will miss you."

"I'm sure that if one of us ever really needs the other, word will get through, and something can be arranged. You will not know which people will know where I am, but word will get through."

I nodded back. "And I am sure that every single time that I make a grammatical error in a speech, I will hear your corrections in my mind."

We both smiled. Then she stepped forward, rose up on her toes, placed her hands on either side of my head, and kissed me on my cheek. I put my arms around her, and held her tightly to me, my chin resting beside the top of her head. I felt myself shaking slightly, and realized that she was shaking, too.

I stepped backward and took her hands in mine. I stood awkwardly, feeling as if I should be saying one more thing, but could not bring myself to remember what that one thing might be.

I let go of her hands and turned. Reaching down, I opened the door and stepped quickly through it, my left foot knocking askew one of the sandals that she had lined up along the wall inside.

I closed the door and stood outside in the quiet morning, looking around, listening, smelling the scent of the burning wood as the remains of my mother's structure smoldered on the banks of the Kidron.

I stepped away from the house, then, instinctively, turned back again. Opening the door a hand's breath, I reached in and down, and lined the sandals up properly. Then I stood, closed the door again, glanced one more time at the house, and walked away.

ZIMRI

זמרי

Zimri proclaimed himself king of Israel after betraying and murdering the previous king. His kingship didn't last long.

The Bible says:

> In the twenty-seventh year of Asa king of Judah, Zimri reigned in Tirzah seven days. The army was encamped near Gibbethon, a Philistine town. When the Israelites in the camp heard that Zimri had plotted against the king and murdered him, they proclaimed Omri, the commander of the army, king over Israel that very day there in the camp. Then Omri and all the Israelites with him withdrew from Gibbethon and laid siege to Tirzah. When Zimri saw that the city was taken, he went into the citadel of the royal palace and set the palace on fire around him. So he died...
>
> As for the other events of Zimri's reign, and the rebellion he carried out, are they not written in the book of the annals of the kings of Israel?
>
> *(1 Kings 16:15-18, 20)*

Unfortunately, the Book of the Annals of the Kings of Israel no longer exists, so most of the other details of his reign have been lost.

Zimri speaks in his last moments, as the castle burns around him.

I am the king of nothing. This castle is mine, this crown, this goblet. But all this, all my actions, my risks, my sacrifices are worth nothing. This castle is empty, silent; this crown feels like lead, feels like thorns; this goblet, filled with the strongest liquor, tastes of poison, tastes of rust. And the words of the prophet, the words of our god ring like mockery as they echo in my soul.

The prophet said that the king must die, and I slew him. The prophet said that all the men who surrounded the king must die, and I had them slain: all the men from within his family, all the men who imagined him their friend were slain by the order of the Lord.

And where is my honor, where is my glory? This people who claim that they love the Lord, who claim to follow his words, have turned against the one who did what he desired. While I have taken my rightful place as king, they have crowned another, have followed his commands against me, have stolen this army that should be mine, have taken this city, have surrounded this castle, have set their arrows, their spears, their catapults to destroy the one that they should reward.

I have called out to the Lord from these depths, from this abyss of betrayal. I hear only wind, only mocking silence. The mob shouts outside my door, but no words, no wisdom, no flashes of insight tell me how to turn these people back to the path of righteousness.

I have nothing, nothing but this room, these draperies, this fine strong liquor which burns within me as this castle is beginning to burn. I have surrounded myself with its casks and am drinking, drinking, feeling the strength of these draughts bring me a blessed lack of feeling.

This castle is burning, and I will burn within it. I who burned with passion for the Lord will burn in this fire, will burn for the Lord. If the Lord will not listen to my prayers, perhaps he will listen to my flames, to my sacrifice. I will die with the taste of this fine drink on my lips, my last sensation before my final stupor, before I relinquish my will, before I challenge this god to prove that he is a true god, to prove that he cares about his people. I challenge this god to take me from these flames, to take me to a realm where those who do his bidding are treated properly, treated as the heroes that they are.

Yes, let all of Israel know that I was a hero. Let all of Israel say that I was a martyr, that I performed the will of the Lord, that I reigned to further the glory of the Lord, that I sacrificed myself so that this king, this castle, this holy moment will not have been defiled by those who refuse to honor his name.

Let history show, as it shows for all kings, the truth of what I did, what I became, what I believed. For are not all our acts written forever in the book of the chronicles of the kings of Israel?

For comments and discussion about the tale of Asa
and to hear the audio version, please visit
http://www.thebookofvoices.com/Asa

OBADIAH

עבדיה

Obadiah was an administrator in the court of King Ahab, who took power twelve years after the death of Zimri. Ahab's wife, Jezebel, began to systematically wipe out the prophets of Israel's God.

The Bible says:

> Obadiah, [Ahab's] ... palace administrator ... was a devout believer in the Lord. While Jezebel was killing off the Lord's prophets, Obadiah had taken a hundred prophets and hidden them in two caves, fifty in each, and had supplied them with food and water.
>
> *(1 Kings 18:3-4)*

The Bible contains a brief Book of Obadiah which contains prophecies of the fall of an oppressive Edom, though at that point in history, Edom was a vassal state to Israel. According to some myths, Obadiah was a convert from Edom.

Obadiah speaks late at night, after hiding the prophets.

The noise in here is incredible. Fifty prophets (well, they call themselves prophets, but they just sound to me like shouters) are milling about this small cave, all arguing about what is going to happen. It was hard getting them to move quietly to the cave, but we hope they will be safe here from my boss, King Ahab, and his crazy wife Jezebel. Now that there's no need for silence (much as I might wish for it again), they're making up for it by shouting even more loudly than before.

Everyone agrees that things are bad now and are about to get worse, but there's no consensus as to what will happen after that. Some say that Israel and Judah are doomed. Some say that things will get better quickly, some that they will get better after a long period of troubles, and some that they will only get better at the end of time, whenever that is. But each of them is absolutely certain that God has shown the true future to him (or her — most of the women and a few of the men have gone off to the caves with Deborah, but some of the women have stayed with me) and that the ones who disagree are idiots, infiltrators, or insane.

Someone approaches from behind me as I look down over this ledge at the prophets milling below. The shuffling of small bare feet, a scent of lilacs, then a gentle hand on my shoulder — without looking, I know that Adina is here.

"How are you doing?" she asks.

"Tired," I say, "and hoping that this works and is worth it, How are you?"

"Reasonably well," she says. "I was able to find a chamber in which I could sit in silence for a while. It helped. I'll have to show you where it is."

"Thank you. So now we just wait?"

She steps beside me and also leans on the ledge. "We wait. A few days at most. Tomorrow Elijah confronts the prophets of Baal. When he wins, we'll need to lay low for a little while, then our prophets can filter quietly back out into the populace."

"Quietly? Can this mob ever do anything quietly?"

She smiles. "Each on his own can be quiet. Together, they just seem to get each other agitated. But I've found some busy work to keep them occupied. My friends have gotten some scrolls from the days of the Judges that might benefit from interpretation. They're old enough and ambiguous enough that the crowd will likely consider them deeply important."

"Will they keep shouting?"

"There will be some moments of quiet contemplation. But on the whole, there's little to be done about the shouting."

"I hate to ask, but what if Elijah doesn't win? I mean, I know that God is on our side, but I still worry."

"Appropriate worry is good," she says, "as long as it doesn't overwhelm you. But I have a backup plan."

"You always seem to have a backup plan."

"It's my nature. I worry, too, but then I look for solutions."

"And what is your solution?"

"If needed, we'll move everybody to my sisters' caves — quietly, very quietly, maybe only a few at a time. From there, we'll be able to relocate them into safer places and times."

"You make it sound simple."

"These things are rarely simple, but they usually are possible."

An even louder uproar rises above the general din. Two prophets have gone beyond arguing and are now punching and shoving each other. Two others, seeing the fight, run to them. Each grabs one and drags him to a fall wall. They then return to where they had been before intervening and continue their own bellowing argument.

"When you were young, did you ever imagine that you would be involved in anything like this?" Adina asks.

"Me? No, nothing like this at all. I thought I'd grow up to be a boring shepherd off in Edom, like the rest of my family. Then I followed my brother to Jerusalem, came to believe the word of God, got a job in the palace, and now here I am."

"I wouldn't have believed this either when I was young," she says.

I start to laugh, then clap my hand over my mouth. "I'm sorry," I say.

"It's so hard to imagine that I was young?"

"It's — well, you have always been the same age since we met decades ago, so I've never thought of you ever being another age. You were young once?"

"I was. Even those of us among the Sisters had to have been born some-time and to have grown to our present ages. Some age more than others. For some it depends on how much time they spend out in the world, though others who never leave age anyway. But I was, indeed, a child, a few hundred years from now, before I came to join the Sisters."

"What was life like — or what will life be like — then? Or are you not allowed to tell me?"

"I can say that Israel still existed. We were ruled by others, but there was a Temple and we still prayed to our God. Most of us kept to ourselves, but others were involved in political struggles that I didn't get to see much or understand. I was a young girl, after all, in a small village, and I didn't get to see much before I went to join the Sisters."

"It's good to hear that we have a future. So are the shouters down there right?"

"None is entirely right. None is entirely wrong. Only God can see all of time (and frankly, I sometimes wonder if God knows how to handle the perfect information that he has). Each of us gets to see some glimpses of what will be. Some are better attuned to the information, much as some of us have better hearing or a sharper sense of smell."

"Even me?"

"Even you," she says. "I can tell you this: a scroll survives into the future, with prophecies written under your name."

"Mine? I'm not a prophet."

"What is a prophet? Just someone who has a sense of the future and communicates it to others. Most people who see what is to be are never heard because they never tell anyone. The ones who are known are those to get the word to others. We usually don't find the quiet ones."

I point at the crowd below. "Hence, the shouters."

"Yes, the shouters."

We stand for a while, quietly watching the people below. Clusters of people form and dissipate as prophets move from one argument to another. On a table along the edge of the cave farthest from the entrance, a seemingly endless supply of simple bread and water fills a basket and a pitcher, no matter how many people eat and drink.

"So," I say, "in this scroll of mine, what do I say?"

"I honestly don't know," Adina says. "I was tempted to read it when I was assigned to come here to work with you, but was advised against it — not that there's necessarily a problem with what's in it, but things are easier when we can't divulge too much."

"Oh."

At the edges of the crowd, toward the walls of the cave, I see that some of the prophets are beginning to lie down to sleep, wrapping their robes around themselves and placing their packs as pillows under their heads. This doesn't seem to limit the noise much, but I suppose that some people can sleep through anything.

"Somehow," I say after a long moment, "I can't picture myself as a prophet or imagine what I might say."

"Don't worry about it too much. When the time comes, you'll know what to say. For now, you're being far more helpful with what you're already doing. No one else, after all, seems to be able to talk to both Ahab and Elijah."

"Though perhaps things might be better off if they hadn't communicated."

"Perhaps," she says. "but we can't know this for sure."

"Until after tomorrow," I say.

"Yes, until at least after tomorrow."

A bellowing voice suddenly bursts from the noise of the crowd. "Thus says the Lord!" One of the older prophets has leapt up onto the table. "You are all liars — a generation of liars and — Oh!" The old man is falling, having stepped and slid in a puddle where the pitcher of water had spilled.

Other prophets catch him and pass them over their heads toward the south wall, where, gently but unceremoniously, they set him down. He resumes his shouting, but his voice again blends into the blur of argument.

Several armed men — friends of mine, men whom I trust — have come in from guarding the entrance to the cave. Others are wearily picking up their swords and shields and heading out to replace them. It is midnight, and too few of the prophets are tired. The shouting here may never end.

It's going to be a long night.

AHAB

ℵℵℵℵ

Ahab was the king of Israel in the time of the prophets Obadiah and Elijah..

Early in his reign, he married Jezebel, the daughter of the king of Tyre. Like most such marriages, it started as a strictly political arrangement. But Ahab came to love Jezebel and adopted her ways. He supported the worship of her god Baal and the goddess Asherah.

The prophet Elijah spoke against Ahab, and set up a showdown between Ahab's gods and the one God of Israel.

The Bible says:

> So Ahab sent word throughout all Israel and assembled the prophets on Mount Carmel. Elijah went before the people and said, "How long will you waver between two opinions? If the Lord is God, follow him; but if Baal is God, follow him."
> But the people said nothing.
> Then Elijah said to them, "I am the only one of the Lord's prophets left, but Baal has four hundred and fifty prophets. Get two bulls for us. Let Baal's prophets choose one for themselves, and let them cut it into pieces and put it on the wood but not set fire to it. I will prepare the other bull and put it on the wood but not set fire to it. Then you call on the name of your god, and I will call on the name of the Lord. The god who answers by fire —he is God."
>
> *(1 Kings 18:20-24)*

Ahab speaks during the night before the contest.

Jezebel cries when I hold her, late at night. She trembles and whispers, even as she sleeps. In the language of Tyre, the language that I learned when I found that I loved her, not long after we were wed, I hear her words repeating in a fearful, panicked stream: "My god is dying."

I try to do what I can to comfort her, calm her, appease her, but she feels each challenge to her god as if she herself has been confronted, as if each challenge to her god has been a whip biting into her skin. In all other lands, the people have welcomed the gods of new arrivals as gifts, welcomed the building of shrines as embassies, as bonds between lands whose gods could share the world. Only here do the followers of the nation's god, the god of my fathers, shout and threaten other gods, in the supposed voice of a deity so arrogant that he claims that only he exists.

Jezebel loves her god. When, at the moment that she was no longer a child, the necessary business of royalty tore her from her land, from her family, from the people that she loved, she clung zealously to the memory of the god of her land. Her ferocity, her anger when she lashes out against the people who deny her god, comes from this love, from this desire to protect him as she believes that he protects her. In my love for her, I cannot fight her rages. I have done what I can to protect whom I can. When she moved to purge the prophets of my fathers' god, I saved those that I could, had my servant take them to the hidden schools where they could safely live and learn.

But still she cries and lashes out. As each person loses belief in her god and moves to the god of my fathers, she feels a piece of the soul of her god being cut away. She fears that when people no longer believe in her god, he will disappear.

Before her purge, the prophets of my fathers' god had moved out into the land, had come to the people, family to family, flock to flock. For each small group they worked tiny miracles, little stunts that seemed to prove the power of their god. They prayed to their god and jugs of water were filled. They sacrificed a dove and wild fowl came to rest by the altar, to feed the family for a week.

And the prophets taunted the believers in Jezebel's god, demanding miracles, claiming that he could not be a true god if he could not be called upon for miracles. Jezebel cried at these attacks but could not respond in kind. Her god, she says, is not a god of miracles. He protects his cities, protects his people in quiet ways. That the winds continue to blow, that the sun continues to rise and set, that the seasons pass in a consistent order is a sign that her god continues to work for his people, that he is staving off the beasts of chaos that would scramble the world, that would turn the oceans to deserts of salt and the mountains to plains of dust.

Now I hold Jezebel as she sleeps. I hear her murmur, see the path of her tears on her face in this full moon's light. From our window, I can hear the keepers of the city sweeping the temple grounds. The moon casts distorted shadows of the Nechushtan and Asherah, from the temple yard to where the prophets of Jezebel's god will gather in the morning. They will travel from there to Mount Carmel to meet Elijah, prophet of my fathers' god, and debate the powers of each of their gods.

Jezebel shook when she learned of this. She demanded that Elijah die the moment that we see him, but I have granted him amnesty through the time of this debate. She screamed that her god is in pain from this doubt, from this challenge, that she must destroy those who would deny him, that she must protect her god.

But I am the king of all the people. I must be fair. Little harm can come of this meeting. The prophets will meet in full view of the people, will speak of the powers of each of their gods, will do what they can to convince the people to follow their gods. And then they will leave, and all will be as before.

Still Jezebel trembles in fear for her god, needing to protect her god, needing to show her love for him. I, too, tremble. I need to do the right thing for my people, to act from my royal love for my people, but still to act from and feel my almost overwhelming love for Jezebel, this need to protect her as I protect my people from her.

I watch the edges of the sky above the hills past my window, the whisper of dawn as it colors the sky with its glow. I wonder which god is controlling the sun, whether it might be either god, whether it might be both or neither, and whether I can know the answer or if I should care.

But I pray, as I lie awake stroking my Jezebel's hair, to whichever god controls all this, whichever god will act or show himself tonight or at any future time. I pray that that god will be gentle with this difficult people, that that god will act not out of anger but out of love.

For comments and discussion about the tale of Ahab
and to hear the audio version, please visit
http://www.thebookofvoices.com/Ahab

ELIJAH

אליהו

Elijah was a prophet in the time of King Ahab. Little is known of his background.

The Bible tells his story in a series of disjointed and often magical anecdotes.

Toward the end of his career, he was told to pick the shepherd Elisha to be his successor as a prophet. Elisha was with him as he was taken to heaven in a chariot of fire.

The Bible says:

> When the Lord was about to take Elijah up to heaven in a whirlwind, Elijah and Elisha were on their way from Gilgal.
>
> The company of the prophets at Bethel came out to Elisha and asked, "Do you know that the Lord is going to take your master from you today?"
>
> "Yes, I know," Elisha replied, "so be quiet."...
>
> Elijah said to Elisha, "Tell me, what can I do for you before I am taken from you?"
>
> "Let me inherit a double portion of your spirit," Elisha replied.
>
> "You have asked a difficult thing," Elijah said, "yet if you see me when I am taken from you, it will be yours—otherwise, it will not."
>
> As they were walking along and talking together, suddenly a chariot of fire and horses of fire appeared and separated the two of them, and Elijah went up to heaven in a whirlwind. Elisha saw this and cried out, "My father! My father! The chariots and horsemen of Israel!" And Elisha saw him no more...
>
> *(2 Kings 2:1,3,9-11)*

Legends say that Elijah appeared at various times in history, long before and after his recorded lifetime. He was said to be the same person as the priest Pinchas during the Israelite's time in the desert, John the Baptist in Christian tradition, and a large number of other mysterious figures in stories from later times. Jewish tradition says that he will reappear to signal the start of the Messianic Age at the end of time.

Elijah speaks as the chariot takes him and he discovers who he really is.

In this whirlwind, time explodes. Identity returns. A sudden loss of forgetting, and I know why I am here.

I drop into history from somewhere else, as fruit drops onto random earth when time and weather tear it from the tree. I land without a name, without a past, a mission made flesh, cursed with the confusion of the newborn, without a mother's care, blessed with just enough language to say what the Lord demands that I must say.

As I enter this whirlwind, my memory starts, recoils from the events that it now puts in order. The awakening this time: in Gilead, naked, frightened, in the corner of a field, the settlers demanding, "What is your name? Why are you here?" A name? The struggle to remember what a name might be. The shout from my lips of what I have been brought here to say: "My god is the Lord!" They hear that as my name, assume that is my name, so my name becomes what they repeat: Elijah.

Ends. Beginnings. A slashed scroll, a palimpsest of a life with flashes of purpose amid discontinuity. Now I am in Gilead, given a robe and leather belt;

a breath later, I stand before the king and am surprised to hear myself tell him that the Lord has declared that there will be a drought;

stepping back, turning, I am no longer in the palace, now running through forest, toward the Jordan, hiding by a brook, huddled, no sense of why I am still alive, still here, no sense of what to do;

after a little time or a long time I am starving, until the sound of ravens stabs my ears, but I know that they are friends, gathering around me, bringing me morsels of bread and meat, feeding me as they would feed their young, dropping food into my mouth as I lay there;

I turn my head, and the brook from which I have drunk is dry, and I have exhausted the kindness of the ravens;

again I am running, weak, afraid, but I must get to Tsarfat, to a widow in Tsarfat who I know will feed me;

the widow and her son are about to eat their final meal, about to die, but I know (how do I know?) that if they feed me, the food and water will grow and sustain them much longer;

then the widow is weeping and the child appears to have died, until I lay him on my bed and lie down with him, and I breathe into his mouth and he revives, and the widow is drawn to believe in my god

(and I see her looking at me with seems to be affection, though I am ugly, in every life ugly, though I am cursed with the permanent gaze of a madman, and I see the three of us together, and I wonder if this is what love is like, if this is what being in a family is like);

and again I am torn away and torn away, shouting at kings and bargaining with demons, performing tricks that lead to worship of my god and that slaughter those who follow other gods;

and again I am running and hiding and crying: in the moments when I do not have to perform as a prophet, I am lost, despairing, with no idea of who I am or why I should continue to live, until again the still small voice resounds in my head, sends me running again, tells me that I must pursue another mission in another town;

and I run. And I shout. And I preach. And my prophecy is fulfilled. And I run. And I hide. And I despair. And the voices whisper. And I am running. Repeating. Beginning. Ending.

But now when I am running I am not alone, for I am with Elisha, my daring Elisha, devoted, dogged Elisha. He was never born to be a prophet, never housed by Obadiah, never hidden with the daughters of Jephthah. But when I threw my cloak in the air, it chose to fall on him. I ran to him and wrapped the cloak around him and around myself, and I saw in his eyes a beckoning emptiness that reflected, absorbed, returned, corrected and fulfilled the emptiness in mine. So he kissed his family farewell, slew his flock to feed us, and learned to be a prophet (though for all his conviction, he still weeps when delivering the Lord's harsher decrees).

When the voice told me, today at dawn, that this would be my last day among the people, I felt my presence fracturing in space. Suddenly I was in Gilgal, suddenly in Bethel, suddenly in Jericho, now suddenly at the bank of the Jordan. But through all the discontinuities, Elisha has been with me, never thrown by the disruptions, never despairing of following me, always by my side.

Now that I have again thrown down my mantle and have crossed the river in its wake, he has crossed along with me. I feel myself dissolving, losing my contact with this world, with the orders of time, yet his presence, his will keeps me here.

I look into his eyes; they probe mine with a fervor and tenacity that anchors me to them, that will not allow me to leave. I cry out to him, "What must I do for you before you can let me go?"

"Let a double portion of your spirit stay with me," he says. "Let me be your heir, so that I may continue your work."

I do not know how to do this, or what a double portion of spirit might be. "The power," I say, "is already in your eyes. If you can let go, can see me off without regret, then it will be so, but the longer you keep me here, the more shattering and difficult my departure will become. More of my spirit will be lost."

Elisha is nodding, releasing his soul's grasp on mine. I feel myself loosed from the demands of this world. I feel my soul announce that I am ready to go.

The world is blurring, swirling around me. The last portions of my self are flying out of the whirlwind, joining with Elisha. Releasing his claim, he has become open to receive what he could not actively take. I hear his voice calling out to me from outside my storm, from within his sudden vision—"My father! My father! The chariots of Israel and its horsemen!"—and the whirlwind takes on the image of a chariot and horses of fire. I feel myself rising with them, not up from this world but out of it, out of time, out of any sense that any place is far away or near.

I am resolving into my higher self. My mantle falls from my back, drifting out of the storm toward Elisha, as four broad wings emerge from my back. I see myself as I truly am, distributed among worlds, among histories, dropped into lives where the Lord needs me, to teach, to cajole, to convince, to lead the souls of people and others closer to truly seeing each other and seeing the Lord.

And I know that each time I will again feel trapped in the shards of reality, not knowing who I am or why I exist. Each time I will be redeemed, I will survive. People will tell stories of my appearances, calling me Pinchas,

Jochanan, the mysterious beggar, the visitor from the Lord, the invisible traveler who samples their wine. And some may even glimpse me in my true body, outside of matter, and may call me by my real name, Sandalphon.

Some may not realize that they saw me at all, except that there was an odd person at the edge of their vision in a moment when the world opened up for them and caused them to change their way, in an epiphany, perhaps unconscious, that led them to do an unexpected moment's kindness or to be better to another or to themselves.

But for now, I am fading into the fire, joyous, renewed. My moment here is ended. I know who I was. I know who I am. And my chariot is here.

For comments and discussion about the tale of Elijah and to hear the audio version, please visit http://www.thebookofvoices.com/Elijah

ELISHEVA (INTERLUDE 7)

אלישׂבֿעׂ

I awaken to the sound of quiet weeping. I pause my breath and listen: what I hear is not the sound of my own tears, nor is it the sound of memory.

My angel stands before me, his back turned, his white wings sinking downward, the fine feathers just out of my reach. I roll to my left side, press my hand against the stone, and rise until I am sitting. Sliding off my bed so that, at first shakily and then solidly, I stand, I take one step forward. Brushing gently past the feathers of the leading edge of his right wing, I lay one hand on his pale, muscled arm.

The angel's broad left hand comes up and enfolds my hand within it, covering it completely, clasping it to his right arm. He turns his face toward me. His pale cheeks glisten with tears.

Our eyes meet. Then his eyes close, and I hear a voice echo within my mind: "Sandalphon," it says, "Sandalphon."

The voice reverberates as if in a larger room than the one in which we stand. As the sound of the portions of the name that have already been voiced fades away, portions yet to come fade up from silence to their full sounding. "Sandalphon," the voice repeats. The word rushes toward and away from us. "Sandalphon."

With my free hand, I point first toward him, questioning, then to myself.

"No," the voice says, "the name is neither mine nor yours."

I look up, startled. "Yes," the voice, the voice of my angel, says from within my mind. "I have a voice, though the words have worn away. I have moved through space, through time, throughout this world and throughout many of the planes and worlds which our God has blessed with life. I have spoken so many words, sung so many songs, that the words have

230

slid past song into silence. Other angels have traveled like me, traveled with me. But only Sandalphon..."

He pauses, and the sound within my mind fades to silence. The angel's breast rises and falls in a breathless semblance of a sigh before words again emerge.

"All you children of Eve live simple lives. Your souls form and you are born. You live within a single plane, move through time in a single immutable direction, then die within a single definable moment.

"As for us, the angels... As our God said of himself, we are what we are. We will be what we will be. In the moment before this world's creation, God spoke a single word and we were there. We remain at least until the end of this physical world. All that we will ever know, all that we have ever known, we know now. And all things past and future that we remember, we can never forget.

"Yes, in moments of great emotion we can lose track of our memories, lose track of our missions. But the memories, past and future, always return.

"My heart holds all the joy that I have seen, each star born, each sprouting flower, each of you that I have seen fall in love or rejoice in the achievements of your children. But I have also seen all the creatures of a world die in slow agony as a flood drowns their land, or perish in sudden terror as their exploding sun devours all that they have known. And I have seen people destroying each other's lives: with words, with commands, with acts; with stones, swords, and catapults; in pits where the living are crushed and smothered with dirt, in halls of prayer locked and set ablaze, in buildings created for the sole purpose of pouring in lethal vapors and pulling out bodies. All this I have seen; all this I can never forget.

"But Sandalphon... only Sandalphon has received a singular blessing, though he feels it at times like a curse. He alone has been able to step down to your world, take the form of a child of Eve, forget for each of his brief lifetimes that he is indeed an angel. He alone experiences the blessing of not-knowing, the relative peace of forgetting all that he had seen, then is thrust into the moment that he describes as wondrous, in which the memories of his forgotten eternity flood back in as he returns to angelic form.

"I had managed... I had been able not to forget Sandalphon, but to press my knowledge of him back into the roar of other memories. But now, to have heard his voice, to have heard him speak through your voice... I am reminded of what I am, of all that I could never be.

"I have known that this moment would happen, known, as fact but not yet as feeling, that I would be standing here now, crying now. Perhaps we retain the knowledge of all that happens, all that will happen, as lists of events, as information. But the wisdom of understanding happens only in those moments in which experience triggers emotion. From this, even angels learn. But in moments of learning, as in moments of growth, something breaks so that something new can be born. And I must be gaining wisdom now, since my existence now feels broken."

I listen for more of his words, but the sound inside my head has gone silent, gradually replaced by the noise of my own emotion.

I stand in silence with my angel for a moment, for a seeming eternity. His hand relaxes its hold on mine and drops to his side.

Stepping forward, turning to stand before him, I see that his eyes are closed, his head lowered. I reach up to rest my hand on the fine feathers atop his head, then trace the contours of his face as my hand comes down to caress his tear-dampened cheek.

I step further forward, and rest my own cheek against his chest. The pristine linen of his robe does not disguise the strength of the body beneath it. I reach up and wrap my arms around him, my hands barely meeting beneath the point from which his wings extend. His arms rise to wrap gently around me, his great hands joined behind my heart. I am sure that he can feel my heart beating, my breath flowing quietly in and out, as his never can, never has, never will.

I look upward and see his deep violet eyes looking down at me. Speak to me, they say. Who are you? Where are you now?

I listen for the voice of another to course up from within me, but no voice arrives. I have nothing to say, my eyes respond to his. For the moment, I am merely Elisheva. And I am here. And that is enough.

A silent torrent of emotions pass between his eyes and mine. His head lowers, and I wonder for an instance if we will kiss.

But my angel slowly releases his hold on me, unclasping his hands and stepping back. My hands drop away from him. We stand, separated, in silence, for another eternal moment. Then he takes one more step backward, and is gone.

THE BOOK OF DISSOLVING
ספר הטמורות

HAZEL

ㄣㅅㅇ

Hazael was a king of Aram, which included some of what is now Syria.

There is archaeological evidence of his existence, including one inscription that refers to him as "Hazael, son of a Nobody."

The Bible says:

> Elisha went to Damascus, and Ben-Hadad king of Aram was ill. When the king was told, "The man of God has come all the way up here," he said to Hazael, "Take a gift with you and go to meet the man of God. Consult the Lord through him; ask him, 'Will I recover from this illness?'"
>
> Hazael went to meet Elisha, taking with him as a gift forty camel-loads of all the finest wares of Damascus. He went in and stood before him, and said, "Your son Ben-Hadad king of Aram has sent me to ask, 'Will I recover from this illness?'"
>
> Elisha answered, "Go and say to him, 'You will certainly recover.' Nevertheless, the Lord has revealed to me that he will in fact die." He stared at him with a fixed gaze until Hazael was embarrassed. Then the man of God began to weep.
>
> "Why is my lord weeping?" asked Hazael.
>
> "Because I know the harm you will do to the Israelites," he answered. "You will set fire to their fortified places, kill their young men with the sword, dash their little children to the ground, and rip open their pregnant women."
>
> Hazael said, "How could your servant, a mere dog, accomplish such a feat?"
>
> "The Lord has shown me that you will become king of Aram," answered Elisha.
>
> Then Hazael left Elisha and returned to his master. When Ben-Hadad asked, "What did Elisha say to you?" Hazael replied,

> "He told me that you would certainly recover." But the next day
> he took a thick cloth, soaked it in water and spread it over the
> king's face, so that he died. Then Hazael succeeded him as king.
>
> *(2 Kings 8:7-15 NIV)*

Some writers suggest that, by capturing Judea and putting it under his protection (after the usual massive killing and the like), he kept it from getting overrun by the Assyrians, who would have been even worse.

Hazael speaks as he faces the weeping prophet.

This prophet is weeping. He has told me joyous news, the news that I want to hear. But this prophet is weeping.

I have come here, to this tent at the edge of our city, to greet the prophet, to bring him gifts and get his blessing. But the gifts that I have been forced to bring are what is left of my legacy, the riches that were not destroyed or taken as personal booty by those who captured my father's kingdom, who took me as a child and left me without a family, without a family name. They call me Hazael, son of Nobody. And no one dares even whisper to me my family's original name.

Here I am, standing in this tent on this plain of dust, with the ragged, drunken dregs of the king's household behind me. It is a caravan of fools, sent both to greet and to silently mock this prophet.

When I asked him, as I had been ordered, if my ailing king would recover from his illness, the prophet looked down and mumbled. Did he say that the king would recover? That he would not recover? That part of the answer was murmured, unclear. But then he cleared his throat, looked up at me, and said, not loudly but unmistakably: "But he will surely die."

And then he looked in my eyes, a long look that grew from calm to surprise to fear to anger to a mere deep sadness. Silently, he began to weep.

I asked him why he wept. He said nothing. And then he raised his arms, at first pointing both arms at me and then spreading them wide, encompassing me, this room, my caravan outside, and the rest of the world that surrounded us.

Our eyes met and locked into each other's gaze. His eyes drew me forward, from my careful position near the door, forward toward him and into his arms, into his embrace. He wrapped his arms around me as I wrapped mine around him.

"Why do you weep?" I whispered. He said nothing, but held me more closely and kissed my cheek. Compelled but not understanding, I kissed his cheek in return. His tears flowed from his face onto my lips and then, as I opened my mouth to ask again, onto my tongue.

The tears, sweet and bitter, burned my tongue. The fire spread within me through my mouth, up to my eyes, to my brain, and down through my throat to my stomach, my blood, my heart, my lungs, my hands, my feet, to all the tortured organs of my body, of my soul.

I slid downward from this prophet's grasp onto my knees, my hands, my side, until I lay gasping like a wounded dog at his feet. Images of horror that I knew to be visions raced behind my eyes like memories of the future: buildings set on fire, young men slashed apart with swords, women disemboweled, children dashed upon the rocks.

I cried out to this prophet, "Who will do this evil to my people?"

And this prophet answered through his tears, "This evil will be done not to your people but to mine. The one who will do it is you."

I looked up at him as he spoke, but all that I could see were his hands, first moving with his voice, then stable, then clenched, then waving across the spectrum between belief and despair.

"How can I prevent these things?"

"You cannot prevent them," he said, "and you must not. These evils prevent a greater evil: as you fight us, and secure our lands as your own, your own strength will grow, and you will keep from us the armies of a greater empire, who would destroy us so utterly that no one at all would survive."

"But how can I live, knowing that I am evil, knowing that I will do these things?"

This prophet looked down at me again, and his eyes again grew gentle. "None of us are entirely evil. None are entirely free from evil. But you can be spared a life of this knowledge. Take my hand and arise."

I reached up and took his outstretched hand, then rolled to my knees and rose to my feet.

"Bring me a cup," he said.

I looked inside the small satchel of initial gifts that I had brought into the tent with me and pulled out a golden chalice. I gazed at it for a long moment before handing it to him.

"This cup is not just a gift from your king," he said.

"No," I replied. "It had belonged to my family, whoever they were, before he took them. I have been ordered to surrender all these riches to you."

He took a flask from the table to his left, and poured wine from it into the chalice. "Drink of this, the wine of forgetfulness, tinged with the water that the Phoenicians had brought from the river Lethe, from Boeotia. The visions will quickly fade."

I took the wine and drank. The chill inverted fire of the wine sent a shivering coldness along the paths that had been forged within me by his tears.

He took the chalice back from me. "Take the rest of your riches home with you," he said. "I have no need of them. I will keep this chalice alone."

And he looked deeply at me, within me. And as I stand here within the tent, as if emerging from a dream, he stares at me still, his tears abating as he steps back away from me. "Please repeat what I have told you," he asks gently, like a teacher.

"The king may recover from his illness. But he soon will die. Did you say more? I have a sense that you had said more that I did not understand."

"There is much that you have to do. It will happen as I have seen. You cannot know the story. But know that someday this chalice will return to you. And on that day you will understand, and the story will end."

As I look into his eyes, I seem to remember an embrace, or perhaps just the desire for an embrace, and taste the sharp memory of a flavor on my tongue, sweet and bitter but tempered by wine. He attempts a smile, but again tears escape his eyes. He steps again away and turns his back on me, on the door, on the people I have brought with me, the people that my mind suddenly calls my army.

I step outside the tent and look to the west. The setting sun glints off the gold and silver that we have brought, that I know that we will hide away. And I realize that these people that I have brought hate the king as I do, and that we are well placed to destroy the leaders of the court in a single night when we return.

The memory of the sad warmth within the tent is departing. I am left with a cold joy within my heart. I cannot know what the future will bring beyond what can be done right now. But what I must do now is clear.

It no longer matters that I do not know who I was, that I do not know my family name. What matters is who I will be.

Tonight, they call me the son of Nobody.

But tomorrow they will call me king.

For comments and discussion about the tale of Hazael and to hear the audio version, please visit http://www.thebookofvoices.com/Hazael

JEHU

אֵיהוא

Jehu was a general in the army of Israel, engaged in the battle against Hazael. He became king after a sort of hit-and-run anointment.

The Bible says:

> The prophet Elisha summoned a man from the company of the prophets and said to him, "Tuck your cloak into your belt, take this flask of olive oil with you and go to Ramoth Gilead. When you get there, look for Jehu son of Jehoshaphat, the son of Nimshi. Go to him, get him away from his companions and take him into an inner room. Then take the flask and pour the oil on his head and declare, 'This is what the Lord says: I anoint you king over Israel.' Then open the door and run; don't delay!"
>
> *(2 Kings 9:1-3)*

Jehu speaks on the day that he becomes king.

I act. I don't think. I don't feel. I act. I move forward by God's command, true as my arrows, powerful as my chariot, clear as a reflection from my shining sword.

I never asked to be king. But when the Lord gives you a command, you follow it or you die.

So there I was, sitting in my tent in Ramoth-Gilead with the other commanders, telling stories of our war against Hazael and the Arameans, talking about the battles that we have won and the battles that we should have won.

Suddenly, there's someone standing in the doorway. He's gotten past the guards somehow. He says he has a message for the commander. Of course, we're all commanders there.

"Which commander do you want?" I ask.

He stares directly at me and points. "You," he says. "Alone."

I look carefully at him and past him. It looks like he isn't with anybody. He's unarmed, carrying only a flask. "What's in there?" I ask.

He says, "Oil."

"Pour some out on your hand," I say.

He does. It doesn't burn him.

I tell the others that I'll be right back. We go off into the next room together.

"What?" I ask flatly when we're alone.

He lifts the flask of oil and pours some onto my head. It's warmer than I expected, and the warmth seems to seep into my skull and travel down my body. I'm more awake, more alert than I've been ever before.

"Listen to me," the man says. His voice sounds like it's both echoing off the mountains and coming from inside my head. "By command of the Lord God of Israel, you are now king. You will strike down the ruling house, the house of Ahab, his wife and everyone that follows him. This is the word of the Lord."

Then he is gone, and I am alone, shaking, sweating, excited. I've never been one to listen to gods or think much about them. But right then I know in my gut that this all is true, that this god is to be followed, that I am now king, that the destruction of this house is my holy duty.

I step back into the main room. "What did he want?" the others ask.

"Nothing important," I say. "He's a madman."

They can tell I'm lying. "What did he say?" they ask again.

I shrug, try to play it lightly. I chuckle and say "Oh, he just made me king of Israel."

And then I look at them, and somehow they know it's true. They all run outside and start yelling, "Jehu is king!"

I run after them. "Be quiet!" I say. "We need to handle this carefully. There are some things I need to do before everyone finds out."

They stop shouting and kneel before me. "Get up," I say. "We need to get started. First we need to quarantine the camp, so no one who has heard you gets out."

"We will do that," they say. And I head off alone, riding in my chariot to Jezreel.

I know that the kings of both Israel and Judah are there. Joram of Israel has been wounded in the last battle against Hazael, and Ahaziah of Judah is visiting him. I come riding up toward the tower.

Of course, the lookout sees me. I get close and a horseman heads out to meet me. "Is all well?" he yells.

"It's not going to be well for you unless you get behind me," I yell back.

He looks confused, tries to figure out what I mean. Then he gets close enough to see me. Something in my face, I guess, tells him that I'm serious. So he gets behind me, and doesn't head back.

When that horseman doesn't return, another comes riding out. Again, this one yells, "Is all well?" and again I yell back, "It's not going to be well for you unless you get behind me." And this one, too, gets a good look at me and gets out of the way.

At this point, I guess, they know it's me. (After all, nobody in the world can drive a chariot like I do.) So King Joram himself, who I guess hadn't been wounded all that badly after all, comes out riding towards me. And he sees me and calls, "Is all well, Jehu?"

And I hear myself yelling back, "How can all be well as long as your mother Jezebel is carrying on with her harlotries and sorceries?" I'm as surprised as he is, since I've never talked like that before.

He gets a good look at me, then spins his chariot around and heads back to the castle. Just as I hear him yelling, "Treason, Ahaziah!" a single arrow flies out of my bow—which I don't even remember preparing—and hits him right in the middle of the back, going through his heart and out the other side. He falls over dead, his hand still raised from signaling to the tower. I tell my servant to take Joram's chariot and dump the body out in the field of Naboth, and head off.

By this time, Ahaziah knows there's trouble, and he tries to get away from the tower. I see him fleeing, and, again with one arrow, shoot him down.

So now I head off to Jezreel to deal with the queen. Jezebel's still there, and, I guess, doesn't know that anything's happened to her son. They see my chariot coming, and she dresses up to greet me, figuring, I think, that I'm heading in to report a victory. She comes out along the parapet and waves at me. I hear myself yell "Throw her down!", and sure enough, a couple of eunuchs, without hesitating, grab her and throw her over the edge. She's probably dead the moment she hits the ground.

Some people are riding horses past the tower right then, and she gets trampled. There's blood everywhere. I've seen some gory battles, but this is really bad. She deserved it, for all the things she's done, but it's still awful.

I try not to think about it. I go in, take over, and have the servants bring me some dinner. I'm sitting there eating (and it's some very good roasted lamb—Jezebel brought harlotry and evil into the palace, but she also hired some really good cooks), and I keep picturing her body, with her royal robes, trampled in the mud and the blood. I'm getting a bit remorseful, and find myself thinking that even if she was evil, she was also the daughter of a king, and deserves some sort of proper burial.

So I send my men out to retrieve the body. All they come back with is a small box. The dogs on the grounds have run to the body and completely devoured it. All that's left are her skull, her feet, and what we think was the skin of her hands. I look at it, and the remorse goes away. If this is the way that the Lord wants it, that's the way it is. He wants the evil completely destroyed.

I tell the men to just dump the remains out by the dung heap. Then I sit back and finish my dinner.

So here I am. Last night, I slept in a tent. Tonight, I sleep in the castle. Last night, I was just another commander. Tonight I am king.

All this is as it should be. From the moment that the oil hit my head, I've felt a sudden rightness in the world. God wants me to be king. I am king. God wants me to lead. I lead. God wants me to kill. I kill. Dozens, perhaps hundreds more must die to clean up the land. So be it. I will clean up the land. Maybe people will say that I am a monster. If so, I am a monster of God.

I feel the good dinner digesting in my stomach as I lie here on the royal linens, preparing to sleep. I open my mouth to laugh and instead belch loudly. The belch blends with the laughter that follows it and echoes about the royal bedchamber.

I don't know what my next step is, but something will strike me in the morning. I don't have to think about it, don't have to feel. I just have to act. And I will have a lot to do.

For comments and discussion about the tale of Jehu
and to hear the audio version, please visit
http://www.thebookofvoices.com/Jehu

JONAH

ﬠﬡﬡﬥ

Jonah was a prophet in the time of the Kings. He was called by God to go to Nineveh and prophesy the city's destruction, but repeatedly resisted the call.

The Bible says:

> The word of the Lord came to Jonah son of Amittai: "Go to the great city of Nineveh and preach against it, because its wickedness has come up before me."
> But Jonah ran away from the Lord...
>
> *(Jonah 1:1-3)*

He kept trying not to go to Nineveh, but his travels took him there.

Famously, he went part of the way in the belly of a large fish or a whale.

Jonah was surprised that the people of Nineveh actually did repent their ways and were spared. His story ends with him rather annoyed at God for this and God somewhat annoyed at him.

Jonah speaks soon after first getting the call to go to Nineveh.

The call has come to me in the night, in an instant, a compulsion echoing from inside, waking me up with the knowledge that I must go to Nineveh. I have never been there, have never been to a city larger than my tiny town, never been more than a day's journey from the house where I was born, never even gone on pilgrimage to the temple in Jerusalem where I have meant to go so many times.

And now I must go to Nineveh. I have tried not to go, tried to ignore the call, tried to continue as if I have a normal life. But every moment that I spend in evading the call feels like an eternity with my eyes on fire. Every second of delay pulls a fine golden noose around my heart. It threatens, if I wait too long, to strangle my soul, to slice my soul away from my self and leave me falling forever into the abyss of what could have been.

I try to be pleasant with friends. I try to be cordial to my customers as I sell them the sandals that I had formed so carefully in my shop. Before the call, I had made each sandal fit each individual foot perfectly, as if they were blessings, as if they were wings to carry each person on his own particular pilgrimage. But now I have to fight the desire to cut and shape each sandal quickly rather than well, to thrust the finished sandals at the customers and grunt when I take their barter or their coins, rather than to listen to them and gently touch the expressive contours of their feet to sense their wishes and their needs.

And now my own feet shuffle nervously, trying to drag me to the ocean, to the west, to take me toward my destiny. I dream of Nineveh. My tongue and lips and larynx murmur the name of Nineveh without consulting with my mind. The landscape of my imaginings is only that of Nineveh, of the sights and smells of this city that I have never seen.

This is all that I truly know of the place: it is a city of unfettered evil, a city of slavery, of murder, of pain and cruelty, of people casually maimed as others cut away their satchels or their shoes. Few from my village have gone to Nineveh, and even fewer have returned. Those who return all fear to speak of the city. Their eyes grow wide and fill with tears as they try to remember and try not to remember the horrors that they have seen.

I close my eyes and pause my breath, and I see Nineveh, I hear Nineveh. Within it I hear the echo of my future voice crying out, telling them to repent, telling them that if they do not repent their city will be destroyed in forty days. In response there is silence. I hear nothing that tells me whether they will laugh at me, whether I will be mocked or attacked or injured or killed, whether the arrogant absurdity of the message that I hear myself bring will rain down wrath and destruction upon me and upon those whom I love back at home.

My mind, my heart, my soul all demand that I stay in my home, that I hide from this call to go to Nineveh. But I cannot hide from this compulsion. It screams at me from within the depths of my self, an invader from another realm, perhaps from the realm of my god, that will not let me rest until I go. As I stand and try to move to act against it, it throws me to the floor and shows me new visions, visions that can only end if I give in or if I die.

Enough, then. I surrender to this impossible will. I will take with me my food, my bag of small scrolls, a second robe and my sturdiest sandals, and I will proceed farther than I have ever gone, to the shores of the sea, to the port of Jaffa. There I will ask my soul again what I must do. If I must, I will go on to Nineveh. If I must, I will say what I seem fated to say. I will face the destiny that awaits beyond the silence at the edge of my dreams.

But I pray that this all will end. I pray that I will find that this has all been a nightmare within a nightmare, that I will rise from the floor and see the sun rise to the east, and I will know that I have survived some strange inner test that my soul has created to torment and strengthen itself.

And I will sit quietly, here in the shade of my kikayon tree, huddled silently, never to travel, never to speak out, my eyes to the ground, as I work the strong leather of the sandals, listening to the footsteps and voices of the people of my town, answering only to the eloquence of the feet of those whom I serve.

For comments and discussion about the tale of Jonah and to hear the audio version, please visit http://www.thebookofvoices.com/Jonah

HEZEKIAH

חזקיהו

Hezekiah was a king of Judah, several generations after Jehu reigned in is Israel. He was known for his moves to restore the worship of the one God and to remove the places and icons of worship to other gods. Archaeological records also document his struggles with the Assyrians for control of the kingdom.

Hezekiah's mother may have been from a priestly family. If so, he would have grown up familiar with both the life of the kings and the environment of the Temple.

Many centuries earlier, while the Israelites were wandering in the desert, God told Moses to create a brass serpent.

The Bible says:

> The Lord said to Moses, "Make a snake and put it up on a pole; anyone who is bitten can look at it and live." So Moses made a bronze snake and put it up on a pole. Then when anyone was bitten by a snake and looked at the bronze snake, they lived.
> *(Numbers 21:8-9)*

Apparently, the people took the serpent with them. By the time of Hezekiah, it had been set up in the Temple court and worshiped by the people. Next to it was a pole or tree dedicated to the goddess Asherah.

Once Hezekiah became king:

> He removed the high places, smashed the sacred stones and cut down the Asherah poles. He broke into pieces the bronze snake Moses had made, for up to that time the Israelites had been burning incense to it. (It was called Nechushtan.)
> *(2 Kings 18:3)*

247

(The name Nechushtan comes from the Hebrew word for serpent, *nachash*, and the word for brass, *nechoshet*).

Hezekiah tore them down to restore the Temple to be solely for the one God.

Hezekiah speaks as he goes out to cut the icons down.

I have approached them slowly, with reverence, with regret: Nechushtan and Asherah, the healing brass serpent and the life-giving tree. Each is an object of ultimate beauty. Each must be destroyed.

Each is ancient, sacred: the serpent Nechushtan, formed by Moses in a single night on orders from the Lord, so that those who gazed upon it might be healed; the tree Asherah, grown from the seeds of the tree of the knowledge of good and evil, the only things that our mother Eve could take from the garden.

Each has stood in the courtyard of the temple for two hundred years, though our people carried the serpent and the seeds for much longer. In the years that they have stood here, they have intertwined, the branches of Asherah growing to slide between and wrap around the coils of Nechushtan, the tree's roots extended to embrace the broad base of the serpent.

Each had been created merely as a symbol, an icon, a sign, speaking silently of our one true God, who alone gives life and alone brings healing. But the meanings shifted as the generations passed, from symbol to allegory to myth and finally to being seen as gods themselves, a mother goddess and a serpent god of healing. The people approach them in the courtyard and stop before they ever get to the true temple, praying that these two fantasies can answer them and help them, ignoring and forgetting the invisible god that they can not see or touch, but who alone can do these things for those who still believe in him.

Here, the absence of the dim new moon's light shapes their shadow, the darkness in which I stand. I am here. I am not here. My heart, soul, and mind are hovering, distant, divided: my mind is committed, my heart conflicted and breaking, and my soul lost in the chasm between the love of beauty and the love of God. They watch my body decide what I must do.

I touch Asherah's bark. I smell, taste the last of its flowers, its fruit. I bask in its beauty, as we bask in the beauty, the tenderness, the loving kindness of the Lord. But I know, as my people seem not to know, that Asherah is not the Lord.

I stroke Nechushtan's skin. I hear the deep ringing of air within brass in response to my caress, watch the shimmering of the new moon's reflection as the vibrations of brass and air react to the movements of my hands. I resonate with its power, as we resonate with the healing power, the glory, the authority of the Lord. But I remember, as my people have forgotten, that Nechushtan is not the Lord.

I listen, within the ringing of Nechushtan, for the voice, coming up through the ages, of Moses, our leader, our teacher, he who crafted the serpent at the command of the Lord. I ask if we will lose our memory of Moses with the loss of Nechushtan, the last physical vestige of what he had done.

A whisper returns in the breath of the wind through the leaves of Asherah, as a modulation within the ringing of Nechushtan:

"My memory remains in my teaching, in the work of my words, not the work of my hands. Though my body is lost, my grave invisible on the heights of Mount Nebo, and though this last relic might not stand by morning, my legacy stands in the words of the Lord, as inscribed in the stones (also never seen by any but the High Priest) that I carried down Mount Sinai: that he alone is our God, that there shall be no graven images of him, that we must honor his sacred names, must honor the Sabbath, our parents, life, commitment, and people's connections to each other, their homes, and what their homes contain. And yes, that people cannot have idols.

"And the Lord has now learned that even if the idol is made by his command, the people will worship it instead of him. They will place their faith in objects and images, rather than in his spirit which is around us, is within us, and cannot be imagined to be locked within one object, within one place."

I take one last step up to the Asherah, to the Nechushtan. I embrace them both, my arms barely reaching across their breadth, my head bowed, weeping, nestled in the space where they meet. My tears run down the brass, the wood, leaving cleansing streaks of water that gather in a pool by their base, by their roots.

Then I step back three steps and let out one long cry, as if my voice has been possessed by the call of the ram's horn, as if my sorrow at the end of all this beauty might cause the heavens to open, might cause the hearts of all the people to change in an instant, and might reverse the stern decree.

In the shadow, the ghost of a vision appears: the image of a child, an echo of myself when I was young, when I did not yet know that I would be king, that I would have to shoulder the burdens of a people, that I would have to make harsh decisions and live with consequence, uncertainty, and regret.

The memory of the child sits in the comforting shade, sure that this is a place of safety, of security. The child draws letters with his fingers on the ground before the tree and the serpent. Then he rises, again admiring the towering icons, the greatest art made by nature and the greatest art made by the hands of man. He dances in the shadow, arms raised, eyes closed, open to the Lord, to beauty, to the joys that he expects that the world might bring. Then, with a gust of the breeze of the present day that returns my attention to my cold facts and responsibilities, the child disappears.

Now, as my long breath ends, as the reverberations of my cry cease to vibrate the wood, the brass, I stand and listen to the infinite silence of my surroundings, the pained silence within my heart, my soul, my mind, and the stark silence of the Lord, as I am left, at last, to watch my body choose what I must do. I pause, look upward one more time, then mutter a curse, whisper a prayer, and raise my ax.

For comments and discussion about the tale of Hezekiah and to hear the audio version, please visit http://www.thebookofvoices.com/Hezekiah

JEREMIAH

יִרְמְיָהוּ

Jeremiah was a prophet in Judah, several more generations after the reign of Hezekiah. He came from a family of priests.

The description of Jeremiah's call to prophecy is more wrenching than most. He says:

> "You deceived me, Lord, and I was deceived;
>> you overpowered me and prevailed.
> I am ridiculed all day long;
>> everyone mocks me."
>
> *(Jeremiah 20:7)*

Different translations give widely differing views of those lines. In his book *The Prophets*, the great Rabbi Abraham Heschel, noting parallel uses of the same verbs elsewhere, gives the most shocking interpretation: "O Lord, Thou hast seduced me and I am seduced; Thou hast raped me and I am overcome…"

His visions tended to be quite grim. It seems that he could never see any object as what it simply was. Instead, everything was overlaid with other images and imbued with deep, often catastrophic meanings.

He would see multiple possible futures, most of which would serve as warnings of troubles to come. In the prophecies in his own book of the Bible as well as those in the book of Lamentations, he had repeated visions of the destruction of Jerusalem and the country as a whole.

Jeremiah also speaks particularly harshly of women. Whether as real people or as metaphors, the mentions fixate on harlots and adulterers, with further repeated references to "anguish, like a woman in labor."

251

Jeremiah speaks here at the age of thirteen, when he has just experienced his painful call to prophecy.

Voices, hands, the shuffling of feet and the scent of people are guiding me as I move along these halls. I see so much that I am blind. I look at an almond branch and see the word of the Lord written in flame. I look at a boiling pot and see a cloud of evil swarming toward us from the north.

I did not ask for this vision, for these visions. When I dove into the glory of the Lord, I was immersed in its waves, in its flames, not thinking, not knowing what I would find. Now I feel what flows from the heart of the Lord more strongly than I feel what flows from my own heart. What pleases the Lord I feel as more joy than this body can stand. What angers the Lord I feel as inconsolable rage that makes me scream, makes me lash out, makes me berate and attack whoever surrounds me. When I feel an evil action happening, if only the gust of a breeze from a young person pushing past an old man walking slowly ahead of him, I feel an urge to strike that person down, to shriek at him the litany of punishment that he will endure if he does not change his ways. When I sense a passing gentleness, if only that of a person saying hello to another lonely person on the street, my heart erupts in such overwhelming joy that I can hardly walk.

I was angry, lost, and lonely when I stumbled into this vision. As so often before, I was in Jerusalem. My family of priests traveled there from Anathoth three times a year for the festivals. And as so often before, my mother had disappeared from our camp, reappearing late at night, once again disheveled, once again drunk, once again (as I heard my father bellow) smelling of strange men and of the incense offered to Ashtoreth, the supposed queen of heaven. And as so often before, I heard my mother and father shouting and heard the shattering of pots, the breaking of furniture.

But this time, now that thirteen years had passed since I was born, I had been allowed to go with the adult priests during the day to help them offer the sacrifices at the temple. I studied the path, memorized each footstep that led me there, recorded each action that we made in slaughtering and burning the animals upon the altars. I spoke to the animals to calm them before they were led to slaughter, offering my gratitude that they were helping to bring us closer to the Lord, hiding my envy that the smoke from their bodies would reach the Lord sooner and more effectively than I could.

Late that night, when I heard my parents fighting, when the illusion of my comfortable life, my happy family finally dissolved and I was left with the image of a miserable future in a house of destruction and strife, I slipped out of our camp and ran toward the temple mount. I do not remember what I saw, what I heard, what textures my feet encountered as I ran. All that I recall is the pain that propelled me, the desire to no longer see this world, to no longer be alone in it, that pulled me toward the temple, toward the holiest of the holy. I screamed aloud to the Lord that I wanted to explode beyond this body, beyond this world, to see his creation through his eyes and feel it with his heart, to sacrifice myself on the altar of his wisdom and be one with the greater world as he knew it must be.

Then suddenly I felt the world disappear from around me, felt my soul being pulled away from me in some direction that I could not name. A blinding, bitter, acrid, sharp-cornered howl contorted my senses, and suddenly I was confronted, consumed by the heart of the Lord. In that timeless moment, I realized that God, too, was angry, lonely, dismayed that people would not listen to him, needing a person, a vessel through which he could pour his words. I opened my soul to him and he invaded it, making connections across the walls between souls, across the walls of time.

Then I was suddenly back in the city, running and stumbling, trying not to collide with things that were there, trying not to flinch from colliding with things that were not yet there. A panoply of future Jerusalems appeared in my path, all visible at once. Those most likely to happen were shown most clearly. Those that would happen soon were closest to me. Less probable futures or those more distant in time appeared more hazy, farther away.

The clearest futures of this city all howled of destruction and smelled of death. Icons, symbols embedded within the visions no longer meant to me what the objects once did; all were overladen with metaphors and meanings that glowed more clearly than the mundane objects themselves. The people that I saw were not simple people but many-bodied, many-armed specters, displaying in apparent flesh all their thoughts and desires, all the things that they might think, feel, and do in an infinite tree of futures.

I ran up to a couple walking in the night and tried to tell them of the futures that they bore, the evils that they would create if they did not change their ways. But the words that I heard emerge from my mouth were scrambled, unintelligible, as I tried to say many sentences at once. They tore away from me, frightened, leaving trails of where they might have been and where they might go in their wake. As I spun about trying to determine which image of them to follow, I felt the ground slide from under my feet, felt all the noise turn to merciful darkness, to blessed silence.

Then, in the silence, I felt hands touching me, lifting me, ten hands or more, gentle, careful, carrying me from that place. I felt myself being placed in a wagon, heard a slow mule pulling the wagon a long way, away from the temple, out of Jerusalem, across parched steep hills and into a quiet valley. Time passed, and I awoke in a cool room, perhaps underground. When I opened my eyes, I saw hazes of people standing around me, visions (far less clear by now) of these lives and futures of the people who were actually there. They spoke to me, but I heard their soft voices as a blur of all the things that they might have said. Only their touch was clear: Ten hands placed atop my head, on my brow, on my heart, chest, arms, legs, and loins, drawing lines of power between them, channeling the chaos within my body, my soul, into the pattern of a jeweled tree.

The people spoke in unison, their words, spoken together, now clear against the echoes of what had not been said. "You are safe," they said. "You are in pain, for you have touched God, and God has touched you too closely. You will always bear this connection, but we can help you ease the pain. Listen to us, learn from us, and we will guide you in the ways of the prophet." Then they stepped away and left me to fall into a sleep deeper than I had felt in years.

And so they talked to me, and so they taught me, and I learned their secrets from their voices, from their hands. I only ever saw the face of one, an ancient woman, when her cowl slid off her head as she reached down to touch my forehead. "Who are you?" I asked. "Who are you all?"

"I have lost my name," she replied. "I am only known to history as the daughter of my father. I have taught them, and we are teaching you what I have been taught. You, we, are prophets, and that is as much a burden as a gift. But you are learning to direct your gifts so that others may learn of God." Then she adjusted her cowl so that it again covered her face, touched her fingers to my ears and her thumbs to my eyes, and I again fell into a learning trance.

I do not know how long I have been here. I know that I am taller, my voice deeper, with far more hair than when I arrived. I still see the baffling visions, speak in a babbling stream. But they tell me that after one more journey, I will be ready to leave.

And so the voices, the hands, the sounds and scents of my teachers are now guiding me down a long hallway from the room in which I have lived. I can hear the reverberations at the end of the hall grow nearer, and I can tell that I am at a pool of water in a massive room. "Farewell, Jeremiah," the voices are saying. "Honor us with your work."

The hands have removed my robe and are guiding me forward. In a burst of panic, I can feel my feet go over a ledge and try to grab their balance on rushing air. I am falling, farther, farther, hitting the surface of the pool and sinking farther still, thrashing and gasping as the water of the Well of Generations fills my mouth, my lungs. My world has turned to black.

Reaching out to God to save me, I can feel his presence, as I did at the temple, but moving in reverse. I hear not words but knowledge, wisdom, flowing from the Lord. And I know that I will live, and I know that I will carry his words and visions for him.

And I also know that he is sorry for how he reached out to me, that he now knows that the human soul cannot handle so direct a touch, that he has learned not to contact a person in that way again. And I can feel, as though written in my skin, his solemn promise: that though I will see visions of horrors, though I will see people doing evil and will continue to feel his pain as they miss the mark of what they could achieve, still things will turn out well, and we will emerge into a world of light at the end of days.

But now his direct presence is fading. I am again in the pool, gasping, near drowning, but rising steadily within it, through the surface and up to the air. I feel a fresh breeze entering my nostrils, my mouth, returning me to life. Lying on my back. floating in the water, I am calm.

Slowly opening my eyes, looking upward, I can see a ceiling hewn from rock, with an opening through which rain can enter the pool. But no rain is entering now, just the warmth, the light of the sun. I can see the light as it really is most clearly, with the spectres of what might be seen as a dimmer echo, further than the real light.

I drift to the edge of the pool and climb out of it. I am alone. As I stand in the shaft of light that shines down from above, my body dries in its warmth. I slowly put my robe back on. Turning, entering the hallway, I can see an open door that leads to the outside.

I look around at this place where I have been, and call out, looking and listening for any people, for my teachers. No one is here.

I walk up a long path and find myself on a road, where signs point the way to Jerusalem. I stop people and ask how I might get there. I can now speak to people without babbling, can see them as they actually are, no longer confused by the alternate lives and trails that I still see emanate from them.

It is once again the day before the feast of Shavuot. Pilgrims are once again heading to the temple. I do not see my family among them. I do not care to see them.

I accept a ride into Jerusalem in a small wagon at the back of a herd of sheep. I speak to the sheep gently, thanking them for their efforts, my soul reaching out to them in resonance with their upcoming sacrifice.

But I will be leaving them, going not to the temple but to the palace. A hard night is now approaching, and I know what work I have to do.

JEHOIAKIM

יהויקים

Jehoiakim was a king of Judah during the life of Jeremiah. He had little authority of his own, but acted as a vassal for other empires who had power over Judah. He was put into power by Egypt, but switched his loyalty to Babylon when that empire took over.

Jehoiakim had little patience for prophets of doom. He had at least one prophet killed. Jeremiah survived his Jehoiakim's reign, but the king didn't care for what he preached:

As the Bible says, he had one of his underlings read to him from scrolls of Jeremiah's prophecies that the scribe Baruch had been reading to the people.

> It was the ninth month and the king was sitting in the winter apartment, with a fire burning in the fire pot in front of him. Whenever Jehudi had read three or four columns of the scroll, the king cut them off with a scribe's knife and threw them into the fire pot, until the entire scroll was burned in the fire.
>
> *(Jeremiah 36:22-23)*

Jehoiakim speaks as he trashes Jeremiah's scrolls.

Another prophet. Another scroll. Another alarmist. A litany of complaint.

A wind from the south. A wind from the north. Trees bend. Fruit falls. Leaves fall. The trees still stand.

Egypt invades. Babylon invades. We pay fealty to whoever rules us. I change my name, if that is wanted. I change my loyalty, if that is needed. I remain here. My small palace stands.

Gods come in with the winds. Gods are forgotten with the seasons. The names change. The sacrifices change. Moral absolutes drift and change as the scents of their sacrifices dissolve in the breeze. People remain. I remain.

The gold from the useless temple has been well invested. It ensures our protection under the mantle of Babylon. Our lazy youth are drafted to work in their palaces. Someday they will return as proper citizens. We are healthy. We are safe.

And yet these prophets complain, complain. They shout that what we do is somehow evil. They speak of doom at the hands of our benefactors. They shout of supposed destiny. We have no destiny. They claim that a god that no one has seen is angry. We see no acts of gods. Men rule men. Men serve men. Leave the gods in the stories of children. Let men be men.

The prophets appear with new books of supposed history, twisted to undermine their kings. They claim that these scrolls are the echoes of greater scrolls, kept invisibly, eternally. They say that we must listen to them or there will be famines and destruction. There will be famines and destruction, nonetheless. But for the moment we are happy. For the moment we are well.

They come to Jerusalem three times a year. They think that they have seen the world. They have seen nothing. I have been to Egypt. I have been to Babylon. I have seen all the greatness in this world. These cities hold more glories that can be pictured in a peasant's dream.

And now this scroll. This complaint. This parchment whine. This prophet thinks that his words will change hearts. They will change nothing.

Let these leaves be useful. Let them clean my knife. Let them sharpen my blade. They can bring no light. Let them bring needed heat.

Let these words shred. Let them burn.

For comments and discussion about the tale of Jehoiakim and to hear the audio version, please visit http://www.thebookofvoices.com/Jehoiakim

Pharaoh Hophra

𐤐𐤓𐤏𐤄 𐤇𐤐𐤓𐤏

Hophra was the king of Egypt toward the end of Jeremiah's life. Writers in other languages called him Apries or Wahibre.

He was not one of the more successful Pharaohs. He failed in his attempt to defeat the Greeks in Libya, and had to be smuggled back home. When the Babylonians took Jerusalem, he tried to fight them and lost. He did manage to harbor some of the Jews, including Jeremiah, though Jeremiah correctly prophesied Hophra's eventual death:

> "This is what the Lord says: 'I am going to deliver Pharaoh Hophra king of Egypt into the hands of his enemies who want to kill him, just as I gave Zedekiah king of Judah into the hands of Nebuchadnezzar king of Babylon, the enemy who wanted to kill him.'"
>
> *(Jeremiah 44:30)*

Hophra's trusted general Ahmose eventually rebelled against him and declared himself Pharaoh. Hophra was killed, possibly in battle with Ahmose's forces, but Ahmose made sure to give him a respectful burial.

Hophra speaks on a peaceful night, as he steps out of his palace.

I am kneeling by the water, summoned from my sleep by the full moon, by its light from above, by the light of its reflection in the water, in the river below. I have slipped from my bed, careful not to awaken whichever wife it is whose sleeping breath has brushed my face like an echo of the river's breeze, and crept out of the royal house, almost silent, almost awake, almost alone. I have put on a simple robe, simple sandals, and almost, as

259

usual, put a crown on my head. But tonight I wish to be only a man, called from my bed to the light, the water, the arms and embrace of this present moon, this swollen river.

They say that my power alone makes the Nile river fertile, brings the river to life. But the breeze, as it whispers through the reeds, through the rushes, as it makes the face of the moon dance and explode into shimmering hieroglyphs on the face of the water, as it makes the reflection of my own face now distort into grotesque and magical caricatures of itself as I kneel and bend down ever closer to the water, speaks of the deeper truth: that only by the power, the blessing, the love of this river am I here, am I alive.

I was born to be king. I was raised to be king. It was not a choice but a destiny, they told me. I am, my father was, my firstborn will be incarnations of the falcon god, fated, bred, and blessed to wear the brilliant crowns: red and white for the upper and lower river; for when we ride into battle, a brilliant blue.

But each time that I rode proudly into battle, I retreated in secrecy, in shame. That I failed in battling Babylonia was allowable. That I could not lead us into effective combat against Greece could be understood. But when I could not even defend Judah from its attackers, scurrying back in disgrace, camouflaged, like my chariot, under the haughty stars and mocking moon, I knew that I could no longer lead these wars. My general, Ahmose, runs the armies for me. I remain here, as if tethered to the palace, seeing to ceremony, to the dutiful couplings that seek to extend the dynasty, to the myriad of supposedly critical details designed to keep me from getting too usefully involved in the actual work of governing.

I kneel here by the water, my clothes neatly by my side, and breathe in slowly, listening to the whispers and sighs of the river. I let the scents and sounds expand and fill me, enveloping and silencing all rational thought, all worries and dreams of my supposedly real life. I catalog these senses deep in my memory, next to the memories of so many similar nights, merging them with these impressions to create a new reality within me to replace this netherworld of gold leaf and shadow, goat's hair beards and ill fitting crowns in which my body finds itself.

I have found my escape within, into this night-born world, so many times before. When my hooded chariot carried me home from hopeless battles, I curled up on its floor, hidden, embraced by the nondescript cloak thrown on top of me. I opened my mind, my heart to my memories of the river, let them fill me, let them welcome me into a world of comfort, until I no longer smelled the stench of combat, until I no longer heard the cries, the screams, the moans of the wounded and of those who counted and carried off the dead.

I kneel ever closer to the water, see the rippled reflection of my face grow larger within it, hear the water lap against the reeds, the stones, its voices broken into the infinite pitches of a curtain of dripping bells. I smell the air changing from the fertile green pungency of the rushes, the reeds, to the musty clear scents of the living water itself. My arms, my thighs propel me forward, forearms and knees still stable on the ground. My face approaches, meets its reflection, until the tip of my nose meets its nose, my lips touch its lips, my eyes, still open, meet its eyes. I slide forward, further forward, until my shoulders touch the water, my head submerged. In its not quite darkness, its not quite silence, the water has welcomed me into its embrace, into its love.

I raise my arms and immerse myself further still, tilting forward as my weight presses my knees into the damp earth. I submerge my head further into the love of the river, not thinking of breathing, further forward until my knees begin to slide backward, until my waist touches the ground, my feet rise into the air, and my body begins a final descent into the waiting water.

But then my descent stops and I feel myself pulled backward, out of the embrace of the water, into the dank air of the world outside its grasp. Firm, gentle hands have taken hold of my feet, then of my waist, then finally, with a strong arm reaching around me from behind, of my chest. My head comes up above the water as it went in (though I do not see the matching reflections of the way out, my rapid emergence having disturbed the water so much that all I see is glimpses of the color of my skin against the colors of the rushes, the sky, the moon). Coming up to rest again on my knees, I tilt my head back onto the solid shoulder that I know will be there, as I shake and cry with the shock of my emergence from the water, from the river's embrace.

For I am not alone. I am never alone. Hemwahibre, my constant servant, has been silently by my side, watching, listening for my needs. He keeps his distance, appearing when I want him, when I need him, often before I know of the need.

I close my eyes, feel his breathing calm against my skin, feel my own breath synchronizing to his breath, my pulse to his pulse. "So you have saved me again," I whisper.

"I have saved you again as I must," he replies, his voice as quiet as mine.

"Even if I command you not to," I say.

"Yes. That is the one command that I can not obey."

We have had this conversation before, and will have it again. It will never change. All he knows is to be my servant. He even has no name of his own, only the title that incorporates my name, sworn to me, my servant for life. He was born to one of the women of the palace (we do not know whom) in the same hour that I was born, and taken to be raised with me, to be dedicated to my life, to my care. He expects to die in the hour that I die, to be buried with me, unless he dies earlier, defending me from harm or obeying my most trivial requests; my commands are more valuable to him than his own life.

He takes the hanging sleeve of his robe and moves it over my hair, my face, drying them, removing the water of life, the water of my beloved river from them. The only water remaining on my face is that of my tears. I rest there for a long time as he kneels with me, my head on his shoulder, my back against his chest, one of his arms holding me, centering me, as the other moves around me, drying me and swatting away the river's flies, his scent mixing with the fragrance of the river, of the rushes, the touch of his skin, of his moving hand, strong and soothing as the breezes, as the yielding, supporting earth.

I do not know how much time passes as I listen to his breathing, to the breeze, to the rushing of the river. What thoughts I have, what words I have, drift and flow like the soul of the river, swirling in whorls of image and meaning, chaining and blending with other thoughts that emerge, unbidden, in my mind from nowhere, in streams, in channels and cycles, until they dissolve and disperse into the trails of other forgotten dreams.

When I open my eyes again, the moon is much lower in the sky. "I love this river," I say.

"Yes," he replies.

"Does the river love me?"

"If that is your desire. You are the master of the rising and falling of the river."

"Would the river love me if I were not its master?"

"If that would be your will."

"Would anyone love me if I were not their master?"

"You are loved," he replies. "You have the love of the people, the love of your court, the love of many gods."

"Though not the love of the armies," I say.

"Armies do not march on love," he replies.

We are quiet again for a long time, until we see the faintest hint of dawn appear before us. "It is time to go home," he says. "It would be good for you to be back in your bed when your queen awakens."

I try to picture the face of the wife that I have been with tonight, but all that comes to mind is the shimmering of the face of the moon on the river. "Which queen is that?" I ask.

He utters a name, long, complex, and not entirely familiar. "That is one of my wives?"

"She is."

"And does she love me?"

"She is your queen. It is time to return to her. Come. The river will always be here." He places his free hand at my elbow, and powerfully, easily, lifts me to standing. He holds my robe, open, behind me, and I slide into it, fasten its belt, and step into the sandals that rest by my feet.

We turn, away from the river and back toward the palace. There, I know, a prepared bath, a warmed clean robe, and a bed with a sleeping wife already await.

We walk. The sounds of the river, of the breeze through the rushes, mix with songs of the first of the morning's insects and birds. As they move through the space around me, behind me, I still hear their whispers forming into my name, calling me back, promising me the eternal love of the river.

I know with a peaceful clarity that one day, somehow, perhaps when I have sent my servant off on an impossible task from which he cannot quickly return, I will be able to answer the call of the river. On that night, I will leave a wife asleep in my bed, leave dressed in simple clothes, and go to the banks of this beloved river. I will kneel in the rushes, prostrate myself, and eyes open, slide into the river's embrace. Then I will let its voice envelop me, take me, consume me. And I will drift north, into eternity, north, past the workings of man and the images of gods, north into the waiting ocean, into the waves, beneath the waters, into the salt and water and sand for which the river itself yearns and which it worships, north into the seas of silence, where I will find love, where I will find my hope, where I will find my home.

For comments and discussion about
the tale of Pharaoh Hophra
and to hear the audio version, please visit
http://www.thebookofvoices.com/PharaohHophra

ZEDEKIAH

צדקיהו

Zedekiah was the last of the kings of Judah, reigning during the
me of Jeremiah.

The Babylonians captured the nation of Judah and the city of
Jerusalem.

When Jerusalem was destroyed, Zedekiah and his men fled. The
Babylonians captured him and brought him to their king, Nebuchadnezzar. There, as the Bible says:

> ...the king of Babylon slaughtered the sons of Zedekiah before
> his eyes and also killed all the nobles of Judah. Then he put out
> Zedekiah's eyes and bound him with bronze shackles to take
> him to Babylon.
>
> *(Jeremiah 39:6-7)*

Jeremiah prophesied that Zedekiah would die peacefully which
wouldn't seem to go along with this. But what he says here suggests that he did.

Zedekiah speaks from prison, a long time after he was blinded,
having found peace.

This morsel is lamb, cooked in a mint yogurt, I believe, with a hint of
cardamom. As usual, it is only a single bite, as small as the last segment
of my thumb. Still, chewing as gently as I can, I can hold it in my mouth for
a hundred heartbeats, savoring its texture, its flavor, memorizing it, until
it dissolves and drifts down my throat to give my stomach a hint of its joy.

The rest of the day's meal, as always: a loaf of bread, a bowl of lentils (still
warm, this time, with sufficient salt), and a jar with enough water to last the
day. The morsel was tucked under the bread, as it often is. The tiny gifts do

not appear every day, but often enough that the anticipation is worthwhile, and that the experience of that day's morsel or, if there was not one that day, the most recent, is fresh enough in memory to recall and relive throughout the day and into the night. Perhaps they are scraps retrieved from the king's table, perhaps from a peasant's, as one might toss a scrap to a dog. I don't mind. I am satisfied. I am thankful. I am unashamed.

The bucket in which the meal arrived sits a few steps away from me on the ground, a rope leading slackly upward from its handle to the place above from which it comes. My waste bucket sits at the far end of the space, a distance roughly twice my height away, its cover fortunately secure. Once a day (or at least once in each of my cycles of sleeping and waking—I have no sense anymore of what a day is), each rises to the top then, a while later, is lowered again, the waste bucket having been emptied, the meal bucket (in which I have placed the emptied plates and jar) containing the next meal. It took me a while to learn the rhythms and protocols of my captivity. If I would fail to put the emptied bread plate, lentil plate, or jar in the meal bucket, no new one would be returned. Fortunately, the rules for the waste bucket were less ambiguous, once I discovered, in my blinded explorations, that it was there and what it was for.

There is little else here: a stone bench, a knife, and some robes that have accumulated over time. I sleep on the bench, and sit on it while awake. It is not secured to the floor, and is just light enough that I can push it across the floor or lift one end. I move it when I feel like changing my space or for exercise. I also try to lift it with my hands or with my legs to keep my body strong.

The knife, like the bench, was here when I arrived. I have never encountered, or even spoken to, another person while I have been here, so it is of no use as a weapon. I use it to cut the bread and to trim my hair and beard. When it gets dull, I sharpen it on the edge of the bench. I remain surprised that it is here at all. Perhaps they hope that I will injure or kill myself. Perhaps they trust that I won't.

The robes appear at random, a long time passing between them. When the first new one appeared, I sent the old one back up with the food tray, but it returned to me unchanged. So as they accumulate, I use them when I sleep. Two, folded up, lie under my head. I spread the third across the bench as a sheet, and use the fourth as a blanket.

I do not understand why I have not been killed, or why I have received what few mercies arrive. Perhaps it is some form of professional courtesy, king to former king. Perhaps another king has arisen. And perhaps someone in a position to make a difference has taken pity on me (I am no longer too proud to benefit from pity), or is repaying some kindness that I had done (though that is unlikely, since kindness was not among my more noted attributes as king).

The morsel continues to dissolve as I chew, over the now forty-nine, fifty, fifty-one heartbeats since I began. Its juices comfort and awaken every point on my tongue. Its fibers detach, drift apart, decompose into bearers of beauty against my teeth, tongue, throat.

I still remember the years when I had taken such food for granted: the years that I spent on the grounds of this very compound in Babylon as the guest of a king, then the years as king, after my brother and his idiot son were gone and I was free to run the kingdom as it should be run. Perhaps I gambled poorly. Perhaps I backed the wrong empire. The cost that my family paid were great; I know that I was, I am, I am to be the last of the kings.

So here in this pit I live what I have left of a life. I sleep. I awaken. I eat. I sleep again. I feel almost as if I am an orphaned child: the basics of sustenance come from someone and somewhere unknown, according to rules that I slowly learn to follow. I have no family, no friends, no kingdom, no gods, other, perhaps, than the mysterious beings who raise and lower the buckets and allow me (or condemn me) to live.

There is no sound, other than my own motions, my own heartbeats, my own breathing, and the clanking and whispering of the buckets and ropes. Without eyes, I see nothing. Still, the world of my inner eyes is rich, is busy. As I look about, I see palaces, fields, oceans, memories of my former life, as vivid as if they were real, more vivid than my reality would be were I to see it. I listen within the visions, and hear with my inner ears the sounds of song, of wind, of fire.

I sit still, ignoring the roughness of my robe against my skin, the hardness of the stone on which I perch. These images rise, congeal, overwhelm my senses and take me off to where I was, who I was. I let them carry me, rejoicing, comforted by memory, by imagination.

Sometimes they take me to the garden where I played as a child, where my caretakers sheltered me against all that was outside, where I met the other children who became my friends as we played, who also became leaders, also became kings, who may now be rulers of empires, or may be living in a pit like mine, or might not be living at all. And I see them sitting still with me, sometimes children as they were, sometimes grown, alone together in considering who we could have been, who we have become.

Sometimes I arise and dance with them to music in my head, to what I have remembered from the playgrounds and banquet halls so many years ago. I do not know if anyone can see me, do not care: if this is madness, it is a blessed madness, a madness for which I would thank my God or gods, if I ever had believed in gods.

Then I return to the silence, the darkness, the textures, the scents, the tastes of my world as it is now. I feel a chill, feel myself shiver slightly, feel an itching in my side. I taste the last of the morsel of lamb, now dissolved, disappearing, digesting. And I hold that flavor on my tongue, in my mind, as I lie down, on the robes, under the robes, and hope that sleep will take me back, back to memory, back to innocence, back to the madness of dreams.

For comments and discussion about the tale of Zedekiah and to hear the audio version, please visit http://www.thebookofvoices.com/Zedekiah

SERAIAH

אֵרָיוֹה

Seraiah was the last High Priest of the first Temple in Jerusalem.

The Babylonians captured and destroyed the city of Jerusalem in the year 586 BCE.

The Bible says:

> The commander of the guard took as prisoners Seraiah the chief priest, Zephaniah the priest next in rank and the three doorkeepers... and brought them to the king of Babylon at Riblah... There at Riblah, in the land of Hamath, the king had them executed.
>
> *(2 Kings 25:18-21)*

The Temple contained the original Ark of the Covenant in a central room, the Holy of Holies. Only the High Priest could enter that room, and even he could only enter on one day each year, the fast of Yom Kippur.

Seraiah speaks as he enters the burning temple to try to rescue the Ark.

Fire—all around me—fire—wings of fire—tongues of fire—apparitions of angels and demons of fire. I rush through fire—through rooms of fire—halls of fire—through paths and patterns made unfamiliar by fire—until I pass through fire to the secret room—the home of God—the holy hall that only I can know—

Here at its border—the edge of this secret room that only I can cross—there are no markings—all gold and brass that had been here has been taken—all curtains burned by fire—all wooden forms consumed by fire—and yet I know that this is the edge—know it as clearly as if I were standing at the edge of a lake of fire—standing at the edge of the physical world. Only I can enter—only the high priest—and only on one day of the year—two months and one day away—I can sense the date's approach—as clear and as far away as a storm of fire across the ocean—and I can only enter when prepared by prayer—when cleansed and anointed by the other priests—all gone—or by the Levites—all gone—all taken or dead—

And today I am unclean—unclean—having run through filth—having carried the dead—and I cannot enter—cannot cross this final wall of fire—yet I must. The word of God—the very stones on which God himself carved his words—carved with fire—with black fire on white fire—are here—and I must save them—must save them from unholy fire—strange fire—from fire that might burn them—might release them into the hands of the unclean—those even more unclean than I—into the hands of Babylon—of those who speak with spite what words of our God they know—as jokes—as curses—with hearts of the unclean—tongues of the unclean—tongues of the serpents who spit venom—the poison that kills—that burns like fire—

God—you who saved my fathers—I cross this line—the one that you ordered us not to cross—to save what we have of you—I cross this line—disobey you to honor you—I—distant son of Aaron—knowing what happened to the sons of Aaron. If I live, I live for you—if I die, I die for you—the merciful and compassionate—who determines who shall live—who shall die—who by water—who by this fire—

I cross this line—walk with fear—without fear—through the wall of fire—eyes closed—then speak the most secret name of God—the most secret name that I know—open my eyes—

And there is silence. Here, there is no fire. Expecting to feel the smoldering wood of the floor, my feet, amazed, feel damp grass. On my head, on my body, soft rain falls. I look around me, and see that I am in a meadow, a paradise.

"Have I died?" I say, and am surprised to hear my voice clearly, not drowned out by the sounds of fire, of roaring flames and buildings collapsing in fire.

In front of me, I see a small cube. The mighty cherubim are seated upon it. I am comforted and again surprised. The cherubim, forged from our finest metals, should not be here. All the ornaments of the temple had been given over to the Babylonians, in an attempt at appeasement, to avoid the destruction of which our prophets had warned. "No, not the statues." I hear two voices, male and female, in unison, speaking these words. "We really are here."

I look up, and see the cherubim are now standing, wings outspread, one hand of each on the shoulder of the other. "How?" I say. "I had never seen you alive in the temple. Are we still in the temple?"

"No. And yes," they say. "The temple on earth is gone, is burned. This is the greater temple, the temple that no man can destroy."

"And the tablets? Have they been saved?"

The cherubim part and step to the sides. There, on the ground, between them, sits a cabinet, not the ark with which I (and only I) am familiar, but a small, clear box, protected from the rain by their outstretched wings. I cannot see its walls, save for the way that the image of what lies beyond them is bent by the light passing through.

And there, in the cabinet, are the tablets of stone with their sacred writing, the two complete tablets sitting among the rubble of the stones that Moses broke. They are tilted at an implausible angle, resting against the ark's now invisible walls.

"What will happen to them?" I ask. "Do they stay with us, with the priests, with the people of Israel?"

"No," the cherubim say. "They will remain here, in the safest of places, in the Garden of Eden, until the temple is rebuilt, until the Eternal Flame returns to light our way back to Jerusalem."

"But how can we live? How can we survive without the tablets? The children of Israel are dispersing. The temple is burning. Where will we find what we need to keep us whole? How will we find and worship our God?"

"Did you ever wonder how Abraham worshiped?" they ask in return. "Or Moses before the tablets appeared to him? Remember that there have not always been priests or a temple. Remember that all that exists on your world is temporary. When you had many people in one place, it helped you to have a temple. Now the people are leaving the land. Many, though not all, will return. And all need to be able to worship the Lord."

"But without a temple, what do we have now?"

"What you have always had, what only living, mortal people have had. When it was time for the first people to leave this green place, God blessed them with words, with the power to speak, with the power to give names to the things and ideas of your world. You now have these words, and with them you can carry the tablets within you, as you always have."

"What words are these?" I ask. "All words? Any words?"

"All words are sacred, yes, and any. But most particularly, you must remember these."

The cherubim bend down to human height. Each whispers a sentence in my ear. Not the same sentence; in this lone moment each speaks different words.

As I hear the sentences, each in one ear, they combine in my mind. In their combination, their collision, their clash and their harmony, I find that together they have contain all knowledge, everything that I have ever known.

They stand again, as one, the edges of their wings brushing my shoulders as they pass. They wait, silently, as I recover from hearing their words.

After a while, they speak again, as one. "We must leave you now. You must leave us. This world must fade for you. You must return to your own."

They gesture around themselves. In the distance, beyond the almost infinite green, fire is rushing toward us, contracting toward us, the flames of my own destroyed world pushing in toward this sacred place where we stand.

"Will I survive this fire?" I call out. "How will I live? Where will I live?"

"You will live a bit longer," they said. "And though you will be martyred, you will die quickly, with honor, without pain. But you must tell these words to all whom you meet. All to whom you tell them will live to tell them to more people, and those people will tell them to even more. Over time, all Israel will hear these words, and perhaps all mankind. And in these words, you will find life."

I look around, and see that the green around me is almost gone. The flames are rushing toward me, the furnace that had been the temple returning to bring me to certain death.

I fall at the feet of the cherubim, try to grasp at the tips of their wings. But the softness within my grasp dissolves like dreams, dissolves like smoke. "Please—do not leave—do not make me leave! How can I live without the presence of God?"

"The presence of God is all around you, is within you," they say together, their voices now faded, now obscured like light beyond smoke. "It always has been there. Look, listen, open all your senses to the world outside yourself, within yourself, and you will find that you are in the presence of God."

I look up and see the fire rushing toward me, surrounding me. The roar of the flame merges with the rush of the mighty wings of the cherubim. They are ascending, drifting upward toward the sky, out of our shared reality. I see them get quickly smaller, more swiftly than mere distance would imply. Their voices ring out, almost inaudible in the noise, but clear within me. "You must speak our words to all that you see. But now—stand—and prepare to run!"

And all around me—the green world gone—flames rush to me, engulf me—I stand—I run in the arbitrary direction that I am facing—through walls of fire—past pillars of fire—and am not consumed—surrounded, protected by steam—drenched with the gentle rain of Eden—not blinded—not burning.

And then screaming—I hear screaming—crying—from before me—to my right—by my feet. I look down—into a pocket of the absence of flame—a space beside, below an altar, where the flames have not reached. There—surrounded by fire—protected from fire—two children huddle—a boy and a girl—trapped—terrified—alone. I reach down—through flame—into the pocket of air—scoop them up—one under each arm—protected by the dampness of my robes. Again I run—through the temple—what remains of the temple—out of the temple—out of the fire—out to the open air beyond the reach of fire.

I set them down on the ground. They are stunned—no longer crying—terrified into silence. "Are you an angel?" the boy asks.

"No," I say, "but angels sent me to save you."

"What do we do now?" the girl asks.

"Someone will find you. You will be safe," I say—surprised that I know that—not knowing how I know that.

They nod, but do not move. "I need you—the angels need you—God needs you to do something. Are you willing?" I ask.

Again they nod.

"I will tell you each one sentence. You must say it to everyone that you meet. Tell them that this is what God needs them to know."

I kneel down—embrace the boy—whisper in his ear the sentence that the male cherub gave me: "Listen, Israel: The Lord our God is the one God."

The boy closes his eyes—looks like he is thinking—hard—then repeats the sentence back to me: "Listen, Israel: The Lord our God is the one God."

I kiss him on the forehead—relax the embrace—shift over to the girl—take her in my arms—whisper in her ear the sentence from the female cherub: "Don't do to anyone else what you would want him not to do to you."

She furrows her brow—cocks her head—looks at me—says, "That's all? That's simple!"

I smile—look her deeply in the eyes—say, "Yes, you can still believe that it is"—kiss her, too, on the forehead—let go—stand up—say to them, "Now run together back to the other people. You will be safe. And tell them what I have said—what the angels have said—what God has said."

They turn from me—look back at me—look ahead—join hands—then run off—to where other people still live—to where they can tell their sentences to the other people—where the sentences will combine in the people's hearts—where from the simplicity of the combined ideas will rise the complexity that will sustain their lives—

I look at them—see them run off—around the fire—past the fire—until they are obscured by the fire—by the smoke—until I can no longer see them—

I know that I have work to do—know that I do not have long—know that soon I will be captured—soon I will die—but that there will be time before then—all the time the world needs—time to spread these words—to those who will survive me—who will spread the words to the heart of the world—

Then I turn—face back into the fire—hear further voices calling faintly—calling from inside the fire—and I run back in—to save them—to save the people—to help God save the people—to help the people preserve the memory—the glory—the beauty—around us—within us—all that exists—all that is all—all that is the presence of God.

For comments and discussion about the tale of Seraiah and to hear the audio version, please visit http://www.thebookofvoices.com/Seraiah

EZEKIEL

ᐟᑎᏡᑭᏡ

Ezekiel was a prophet in the days when the kingdom, Judah was conquered by Babylonia. Born in Judah, he was among the exiles who were forced to leave. He lived the rest of his life by the rivers of Babylon, on the banks of the Chebar canal.

God forced Ezekiel into bizarre performances to communicate his prophecies. For example, the Bible says that God gave him this command:

> "Now, son of man, take a block of clay, put it in front of you and draw the city of Jerusalem on it. Then lay siege to it: Erect siege works against it, build a ramp up to it, set up camps against it and put battering rams around it. Then take an iron pan, place it as an iron wall between you and the city and turn your face toward it. It will be under siege, and you shall besiege it. This will be a sign to the people of Israel.
>
> Then lie on your left side and put the sin of the people of Israel upon yourself. You are to bear their sin for the number of days you lie on your side. I have assigned you the same number of days as the years of their sin. So for 390 days you will bear the sin of the people of Israel."
>
> *(Ezekiel 4:1-5)*

Many of Ezekiel's visions have become popular images. In one, he saw a wheel in the sky with the heads of an eagle, a lion, an ox, and a man. In another, he saw a valley of dry bones return to life.

Ezekiel speaks from the banks of the Chebar.

I am soft stone, yes, a heap of dust that only God's word can animate, dust that returns to dust when God's will is done. The animal sense of

275

my body drags me from my sleeping mat to a table and then to the rain barrel as I awaken, feed myself, clean myself. The dogs of the street that I once befriended bring me their scraps to eat. The rats and the rain carry away my waste. I sit in silent stupor, waiting for God's word, fearing God's word. When he needs me to dance for him, he puts visions in my head, causes me to demean myself, to rant like an idiot in the eyes of the people. Then I sit again, speechless, broken, cowed. I do not complain. There is nothing left within me that knows how to complain.

I have no father. I have many fathers. My mother, when asked, could not remember who my father had been, or perhaps did not care. When she dumped me at the temple gates, she insisted that he was a priest, since so many of the men who came to her were of the caste of priests. They declared that I was a priest, too. When they asked what to say my father's name was, she said, "He is the son of *buzi*—the son of my shame." So Ezekiel the priest, son of Buzi, was what I became.

I do not know which of those women was my mother, whether she is alive or dead, whether she was left behind in Jerusalem or came with us here to Babylon, to the banks of the Chebar. But I do know my anger when I see any of them, see them luring our men into their false temples, into their beds, taking from our men each time a bit of their money, a bit of their seed, a bit of their souls, leaving in each of them an emptiness, a hollowness, a disease in their hearts that spreads by conversation, spreads by scent.

The priests took me in, yes, and raised me with those whom they knew to be their own. But I was never truly one of them, always the last in line, the last of the chosen, the runt of the litter. Had I been a rodent, I would have been eaten immediately when I was born. All seemed to know, though none ever mentioned aloud, that I was close to untouchable, the bastard son of a harlot and a sinning priest. I failed at my studies, failed at physical activities, failed at all my social endeavors. The boys, the girls, all shunned me, all but one, but the cruelty of fate and law kept her away.

I had my own inner life, yes, a world of monsters and angels that hid inside my head, whispering and laughing and playing with and for me, in secret languages, with secret fire. But I knew that that was inside me, knew that it was less real, knew that though it could warn and comfort me, it never could protect me from the human shadows of real life.

We were ruled by so-called kings in Judah, weak shadows of their ancestors, of the mighty rulers who made us a people. When the invaders came to take our land, the supposed king shrugged and gave us up. Our world died, not with any sudden collapse but by a gradual dissolving. The vermin of Babylon chewed at our culture and drained us of all that made us more than just another people.

And now our people sit here on the banks of the Chebar. I took the long walk when I was twelve, exiled from Jerusalem with the rest of the now-useless priests. No longer fed by sacrifices, we would sit and wait for people to bring us sustenance, telling ourselves stories of how things were, of how things would be when we would return, berating the people on whose charity we had to depend, telling them that they were at fault for angering our god, for causing this exile in which we had suspended our lives.

And still the women followed, these parasites upon parasites, these harlots, who would open themselves to anyone who would give them some fresh-caught fish, who would leave a few farsin at the foot of the beds as they pulled their robes of shame back on and slithered out of the tents. I would glare at the women, never going to them, seeing them as they were, as seething bags of corruption who infected our men with their wiles, with their lies. I was not tempted, though my resistance to temptation was rarely tried: when their eyes would dare to meet mine, even they would skitter away like insects into the night.

And yes, I do love, did once love a girl, my lovely Drorit, my flightless bird. Her fair skin, her bright red hair told all who gazed upon her that she was alien, was to be feared, was no doubt a witch. Her parentage was also unknown, her future as uncertain as her past.

I was eleven when I met her. She was nine. When I would sit in the dust at the edges of the fields, gazing into the shadows as the other children played, she would also often be sitting, also watching. Gradually I noticed that everyday she seemed to sit a little closer to me. Gradually, I moved closer to her. Finally, after who knows how many months, how many days, we reached each other, reached out to each other, took each other's hand. We sat silently in the corners, in the dust, her head resting sometimes on my shoulder, my head sometimes resting on hers. We spoke once, exchanging names. Then there was nothing more to say, nothing more to do, but to meet, to sit together, to hold each other's hands, to gaze into the shadows, alone, together, in silence.

And then the invaders came, as they did so often, separated a group of us, seemingly at random, and ordered us to leave Jerusalem, to make the long walk to Babylon, to this camp here by the waters. I thought of running, of hiding within the city, but when I saw that all the men around me were resigned to leaving, my will drained away and I joined the trudging pack. We gathered in the fields where the other children had played. I looked for Drorit in the crowds, in the corners, in the shadows, but she was gone, safe, I hoped, with whoever might look after her.

Then we walked, made the long walk from Jerusalem to the heart of Babylon, in the sodden cold of winter, so many weeks – though we lost count of how many, since they never let us stop, not even for the sabbath. Some died. Most survived. Some were dumped from the group earlier, some later. We were left at the camp at the Chebar canal, without guards, without guidance, a sad pack of people, stranded in a valley and ignored by the world.

Here we have sat for many years. Something of a city, of a society has rebuilt itself, has grown, without a temple, with some people trying to repeat the words of our history in lieu of sacrifices, and some mocking as arrogant their attempts to sing the Lord's songs in this foreign land. Again I sat in dust, in the corners, doing what small tasks I was ordered to do by the other former priests, speaking only to the animals who shared my place near the gutters, closing my eyes to the outside world when I could and running within myself with the monsters and angels who had been with me since before I could speak. Often, over the years, I imagined that I could sense a soft hand held in mine, the scent of fine, freshly washed hair from a small head as it rested against my shoulder.

Then, some weeks ago (how many weeks?) a new group of our former countrymen were dumped in our camp, people held by the cruelest of the invaders and used to their will, then cast out like garbage onto our dunghill of a supposed town. Many were crippled, many insane, all defeated by horrors of which none of them would speak. I was assigned to work with them, cleaning the sleeping mats and collecting the chamber pots from the ones who could not bring themselves to move.

And there, among the women, those who shrieked and those who whimpered, those who tore all clothing from their bodies and those who wrapped themselves in infinite layers of whatever coarse fabric they could find, I saw a small woman huddled in a corner, in the dust, staring at shadows. A cry emerged from within her shabby robe, and I saw that she was cradling a baby, with the palest of skin and bright red hair.

I reached down to touch the baby, to brush a leaf from where it had landed on the baby's face. The woman's hand shot up from within her robes and clutched my wrist, holding my hand away from the baby, her jagged nails digging into my skin. I pulled my hand loose and, stepping back, knocked her cowl away from where it hid her face—and I saw that she, too, had the same red hair, the same fair skin. She turned to look at me and our eyes met. Then her hand reached up, and I held it in mine.

"Drorit?" I said. "You are alive?" To the first question, she nodded. To the second, she shrugged.

"Is the baby yours?"

She nodded.

"Where is your husband?"

Her eyes widened. Tears formed.

"You have no husband?"

She bowed her head.

"The invaders—did they—"

She pulled her hand from mine and placed it over my mouth, silencing me.

I did not think, did not need to think. I knelt by her side. "This baby will have a father. You will have a husband. Arise. We will marry. Now."

And we arose, and we embraced, and I took her by the hand and led her to the home of the eldest priest of the town. We entered, and I told him that we wished to marry.

"So..." he said slowly, "you have found someone who would marry you."

"Yes," I said, almost proudly.

"This one?" he said. "This one with the child?"

"Yes," I said.

"She is a widow?"

I looked towards her. She looked down and shook her head.

"Then, no," he said.

"No?"

"It is the law," he said. "You are still a priest." He closed his eyes, moved his head as if scanning an invisible scroll, then chanted: "They shall not take a woman that is a harlot, or profaned; neither shall they take a woman put away from her husband; for he is holy unto his God."

"Then I resign my priesthood," I said.

"You cannot," he replied. "That is the law." He opened his eyes and glared at me. "Did you want anything else?"

I stood in silence, stunned. Then I slowly turned and looked at Drorit.

And she screamed, long and loud, a howl rising from the depths of her bowels up beyond her voice's highest reach to where only the dogs could hear her pain, the cry of a heart exploding, the cry of a soul being ripped by the talons of eagles, by the teeth of lions, by the horns of oxen, by the harshest words of man. Then she ran from the house, clutching her baby, down the dirt road, toward the edge of the camp, until her screams could no longer be heard in the distance.

I turned and looked back, mutely, at the chief priest. "Now," he said, "it is not good for any man, even you, not to be married. I know of a woman who will marry you."

He took me to the daughter of the cemetery keeper, the sickly, sullen, stumbling, stupid, hairy woman that no other man would have. With all choice, it seemed, torn from my life, I married her, grunting through the ceremony some time later, ignoring the half-hearted, mocking good wishes from the other priests who happened to be around, trudging back with her through the winter mud to the tent that would be our home.

After the sun set, she lit a candle in our tent, shrugged her robe onto the floor, and lay there on the bed, naked, large, and hideous, her doughy flesh seeming as if it could consume me, destroy me, as if she would burst into putrefaction if I would ever touch her.

The monsters and angels from within my mind leapt forth and told me to run with them. And as if in an instant I was far away, lying naked on the banks of the Chebar. The creatures hovered above me, outside of me, burst out into the real world, each turning and guarding a wheel with which they would crush anyone who would threaten me.

Then a glow emerged from between them, a radiance like burning amber, like a rainbow from a storm, and I knew that it was the presence of the Lord. And a hand emerged from the radiance and thrust toward me a scroll. It ordered me to eat it, and it tasted like honey, like love, like all the good things that had been missing from my life.

But then the scroll began to glow within me, to burn like fire. I felt my very self being seared away from my body. The Lord ordered me to shout the words that I had eaten, to go and berate my people, to tell them that they, too, must do what he would order, or all would be destroyed, all would die.

The great hand grabbed me by the neck and threw me onto mountains, into valleys. It gave me orders to enact performances before the people, to act out symbols that few would understand. God told me to lay siege to toy cities, and I did as I was told. He told me to bind myself with cords and lie on my side in the street for hundreds of days, and I did. He told me to eat bread baked on a fire fuleed with human excrement; in his mercy, though, he changed that order and allowed me to merely use a cow's excrement instead.

Now I am standing in the street, eating the bread of filth and screaming at my people. This screaming is all the speech that I have. I have no words for myself anymore.

I hear the shocked mumblings of the people around me, hear everything that they say about me, the disgust they feel about me, know that they do not understand the message that God intends my performance to convey. I know that my life as it was, my world has ended. My sickly wife will soon be dying, and the Lord has ordered me not to mourn. I will not mourn.

My last thoughts of anything like joy are of my Drorit, my beloved Drorit, my tiny, wounded, defeated Drorit. For I have heard whispers that she, at least, has escaped. When she ran from the city, the wise women found her, comforted her, spirited her back into Judah, into the hidden caves where they hide and where they keep the Eternal Flame, where she can revive, can heal, can remember, unlike me, what it means to be alive, to be human.

For now I am nothing but God's mouthpiece, God's machine. My mind is that of an animal, running in circles on a leash, obeying commands. My body is excrement, fed on excrement. My soul has burned, rotten, decayed. There is nothing human left within me. I am the ash, the dregs, the indigestible refuse that remains after all that was human is gone.

I am human no longer. I am Ezekiel no longer. I have no name. Call me only "Son of Man."

For comments and discussion about the tale of Ezekiel
and to hear the audio version, please visit
http://www.thebookofvoices.com/Ezekiel

ELISHEVA (INTERLUDE 8)
אלישׁרבצע

I awaken to silence, to the stillness of the air, to the weight of the knowledge that I am alone. Though I remain in this place where I have lived for all of the life that I can remember, my friends, my sisters are gone. Alone, here in my home, I am lost, in exile.

The space that this silence leaves within my mind gradually fills with memory, pouring into me as if from an external stream. My mind fills with the sound of voices, the memories of people swirling about, my sisters in a dance of organization, as each gathers belongings, supplies, memories. Many form into groups and move together or move apart. In the middle of this I sit, unmoving, silent.

What moment is this? Through the tear in the fabric of my forgetting, I recognize it as the last of my memories of my days in community here. The Sisters of Sarah are preparing to leave.

I sit alone, though Aspaklarya frequently flutters by, touching her hand to my shoulder, listening to my breath to see that I am still present, still alive.

Around me, plans are made, suggestions are given, groups form and dissolve. Each of us has looked out into the world and discovered a heart-felt destination. Methods are discussed, developed, tested.

Some of the sisters will remain in the present time at the moment of the closing of this place. Some will step into the relative past, some to the relative future. Some will stay close to Judea, to Jerusalem. Others will move farther away. One group will move east to where the rivers meet, where Eve and Adam first emerged from the garden. Another group speaks excitedly about traveling far to the west, to a place that they know as the Island of Apples.

But persistent whispers surround me: "What of Elisheva? Where will Elisheva go?" And occasionally the voice of one of our elders is heard: "Elisheva will go where Elisheva will go. She will not be alone."

But now I am indeed alone, my sisters gone, my angel disappeared. I rise as always, move my lips in automatic prayer as always, but I feel the pressure of my solitude. Am I a captive here? I have no better place to go. This room, now, is my entire world. Does the rest of the world exist now? Does this room still exist within the path of time? I do not know. I cannot tell. I do not know whether it matters, or whether I should care if it does.

I lower my cup into the stream at the edge of my room. The slight splash brings another flow of memory: another large room, in which all my sisters have gathered. All stand there, dressed in their simplest white robes. One by one, they step through a doorway into the next room, from which emerge the sounds of water, moving, shifting, rising, and subsiding. It is the ritual bath, formed from the walls and living waters of Miriam's well, the Well of Generations, in which we have immersed ourselves for meditation, for purification, for a reminder of how richly the waters of life flow around us and within us.

As always, each who enters does so without adornment. At the top of the ramp that leads to the floor of the pool, each removes her robe and lays it to one side. Then each walks into the pool, continuing forward until she is completely engulfed by its water.

Though the bath is only large enough to hold one person at a time, none walk back out into the room. From there, each travels, to other places in the world, to other points of time. Each emerges from water, rises from water, from wells or streams, rivers, baths or fountains, alone or with sisters.

I sit alone, silent, as my sisters leave. Each of them knows her own destiny, knows the place and time to which she is called. I have no destiny, other than to remain here.

Finally, only three of us remain. Aspaklarya kneels on the floor before me, her hands holding mine. Miriam, the one who has always been here, stands beside us. Her skin and hair, whiter than salt, seem to glow when seen against the dark wood of the ceiling and walls.

We three hold the silence for the longest of moments. Then Miriam crouches beside us and places her hand on Aspaklarya's arm. "It is time for you to go," she says.

Aspaklarya turns toward her then back toward me. Touching my cheek with her trembling hand, feeling me nod, she cries, "Don't ask me to leave you, to go back now that I've been following you!" I know the words, the voice, as those of Ruth. "Where you go, I go. Where you stay, I stay. Your people are my people; your God, my God. Where you die, I will die, and there we will be buried."

Miriam stands and reaches down to Aspaklarya. "It is time for you to go," she says again. "You have your own destiny. But you can see that Elisheva will not be alone."

I realize that there are no longer three of us here but four. Looking down to my left, I see a pair of feet: pale (though not as pale as Miriam), powerful, shod in perfect sandals as black as the straps of phylacteries. Muscled calves lead up under a robe of purest linen (yes, as pale as Miriam). I look up and see strong hands on outstretched arms emerging from the sleeves and, rising from his back, between the shoulders, wings.

This is not the first angel that I have seen, nor the largest, but is the most beautiful. Flashes pass through my mind, and I wonder if these are memory. It seems as if the angel has always been here with me, will always be here.

"Yes, this is your guardian," Miriam says. Not for the first time, I wonder if she has heard my thoughts. "He will stay with you, now that we must go." She raises her arms and reaches forward. The angel takes her hands, which now seem so small, in his. Their eyes meet, and I can sense the torrents of information, of feelings, passing between them.

Their hands unclasp, and each reaches down to each of us. We reach up and take their hands. We rise: I come up unsteadily, depending on each of the hands for support; Aspaklarya stands with eternal grace, as if her body were as drawn to the sky as to the earth.

It is the time for farewells. Aspaklarya and I step forward, nearer each other, and embrace, each of us resting her head on the shoulder of the other. Her hands meet behind my heart, as my hands meet behind hers.

The angel and Miriam again reach out, and I feel their hands resting atop my hands on Aspaklarya's back and atop her hands on mine.

"Aspaklarya... Elisheva..." Miriam says. "Each of you has had a gift that might seem like both a blessing and a curse. Elisheva, you have been unable to remember your life. Aspaklarya, you have been unable to forget. If you both are willing, we can help you give your gifts to each other."

We both look up. I look into the angel's eyes. Aspaklarya looks into Miriam's. Slowly, we both nod.

Aspaklarya and I pull back slightly from each other. The sound of a single note fills the room, emanating from the angel, though it is not the sound of a voice. Miriam, always the first of the singers, always the one who seemed able to cause water and stone themselves to sing, joins with him. Aspaklarya joins and sings that magical note, her voice powerful and pure. I open my mouth and am amazed to hear the note emerging from it, soft, unsteady, but gradually growing in strength, in certainty.

Our souls meet and I see flashes of what I know are memories, but of Aspaklarya's life, not mine. Born amidst rags and dirt in Judah, so many earthly lifetimes ago, she survives, struggles for food, has at least one good childhood friend, then is torn away from her world and enslaved. I see years spent in a shabby tent in a location that she does not know, spent as a tool and victim of so many soldiers that she no longer cares to tell them apart, then, when she is found to be with child, thrown out to live in rags and dirt again, feeding on scraps. I see images of travel, of savagery, as she and all others of her people march through months of cold to a camp on the banks of a fetid canal.

Then a moment of hope, of the possibility of comfort, before she sees her hope as foolishness, her savior as a madman, and runs screaming, away, anywhere, away from the hell that is all that her life has known. She runs for days, until the sabbath, until she reaches a river consumed by fire, a wall of flame that rises to the sky, that falls from the sky. She reaches the banks, screams a psalm to God, "I entrust my spirit into your hands!". Then she leaps into the water, leaps into the flame and falls, falls, endlessly, falls without harm... and awakens in a meadow in the gentle rain. Our sisters, waiting there, find her, bring her here, nurse her to health, help her find a place, a role, until she finds love, their love, my love, the love of this invisible God in whom we love to believe.

The long note ends and I find myself back in this room, this embrace, my breathing heavy and my voice raw from the unexpected singing.

"It is done," Miriam says. We all gradually drop our hands and step back, standing as a rough square in the silence. "The mind, the soul, do not heal in an instant. This is only the beginning of how you will learn to change.

"Aspaklarya, you still remember, and will not forget it all immediately. But over time, your memories will become less vivid, more tolerable, as they do for the rest of us, until they eventually drop away. You will not forget all that you have learned, but you will discover how to proceed with a life in which you can use your learning. You are an embodiment of all the stories that you have heard, that you have lived, have told, have known. And with these stories, you will come to bless the world.

"Elisheva, your memories will return as you grow able to manage them. While soon you will forget even this moment, it will return, along with the rest of your life. And you will live to understand, to accept, to love who you were, who you are, and who you can be. You will remain here, since the magic of this place requires that one soul remain present within it so that others can leave. But when your time will come, your soul will finally depart from here. Your destiny is different from that of the rest of us. The angel will guide you out of history and into the greater soul of the world."

Again we stand in silence. Then Miriam turns again to Aspaklarya. "It is time for you to go. Your sisters await, off in a place in which people do not yet live, lifetimes away in a world near the star of Istahar. There you will heal and learn, then return to this land. The stories will need you."

Aspaklarya takes a step backward, then turns away and walks, guided by the sound of the water, to the entrance to the ritual bath. She turns back toward me, and our eyes meet. I can tell that she is seeing me, vaguely, dimly, as one might glimpse an object at the bottom of a windswept, clouded lake, for the first time, for the last time.

Then she steps out of view. But I can see in my mind, as clearly as if I see it with my eyes, her walking to the pile of robes, removing her own, folding it and placing it with them, then walking down the ramp into the water, her long red hair floating behind her as the water covers her legs, her waist, her breasts, her shoulders, her eyes, until she is fully immersed. At that moment, I hear water then air rush to fill a space that suddenly holds nothing, and I know that she is gone.

I look away from the entrance to the bath, and see that Miriam has moved closer to the angel. Once again, the angel again holds her hands in his, then they step apart and she turns again to me. "When I leave," she says, "most of this place will cease to be. Follow the angel now to a space that has been protected, in which you can live until it is time for your soul to leave." She looks around and sighs. "I shall miss this place. But I must return to my brothers, to the desert, since the stories insist that it is there that I die. I will not be back in the desert long, before I, too, am gathered back into the soul of God."

I reach forward and, impulsively, embrace her, kissing her on the cheek. Then I feel the angel's cool hand on my shoulder. Guided by his touch, I step away, turn away. We walk out of the room through another doorway, down a hallway that I have never seen before, and into this room in which I now stand. I do not hear Miriam leave, do not sense the disappearance of the place in which I have lived. But when I look back toward the doorway through which I entered this space, I see only a solid, seamless wall.

This is the room in which I now live, alone: the soft stone bed, the drawers within it containing my continually replenished clothes and food, this stream along the wall at which I now stand, pulling the cord that raises the cup of water to me.

As I now take the cup of water in my hands, I feel the memory of the angel's hand on my shoulder as if it were his real touch. But it is not memory: his hand is again on my shoulder, his body casting a shadow on the wall and the water.

Startled, I turn around, dropping the cup. My angel has indeed returned. I reach out to steady myself, and rest first my hand then my head against his solid chest.

But his presence does not seem quite the same, and this room does not seem the same. With this latest episode of memory, I am aware of how small this space has grown.

I walk along the wall, along the stream, to the corner where I now know a doorway had once been. I push my hand against the wall then turn to face the angel again, a question in my eyes.

Without walking, the angel is now by my side. He lifts his hands to my face, his palms covering my eyes.

The darkness hovers before my eyes. Then an image forms, becoming brighter, growing texture. It is rock, a wall of rock, the wall that hides the entrance to the cave that was the most frequent portal through which people came into our space.

As if I am walking, then flying backwards, rising from the ground, propelled by angel's wings, I see the hills that contain the cave and the meadow before it, then more of the landscape, losing detail as it gains in scope. I see the river that runs to the east of the meadow, see more of the hills, villages, cities. Jerusalem appears, at once unbuilt, constructed, flourishing, in flames, destroyed, desolate, then rebuilt again, in cycles like the rings of an aged tree. Then I see the ocean to the west, the desert to the east, the three rivers meeting at a plain, a city (unbuilt, flourishing, destroyed, revived) where the life of all people began.

We rise higher, then higher still, into the heavens, so high that I expect to enter the realm of the angels themselves. The plane of the land starts to curve until it seems like it is painted on a ball. Then the ball recedes, and it is surrounded by blackness, separated by only a thin blanket of blue and white from the darkness of the face of the deep. Beyond it, I see the moon, large, brilliant, grey, more clearly than I have ever seen it before. The points of the stars are spread across all that I see, more numerous indeed than the sands of the desert.

On the sphere of the land, eruptions of gold burst forth from points scattered across its visible face. My sisters are emerging from the hidden place in which we live, returning to the world of common places and times. The eruptions move out, forming tendrils of golden fire, spreading around the world, forming first a hatchwork then a haze of gold as my sisters and their stories grow to be experienced everywhere.

The tendrils explode, moving in all possible ways, not only high and low and in the paths of the holy winds, but in other unknown directions. I am viewing the world not only through mirrors of space but of time, seeing all places, all times, as one. In that moment of realization, I see that the tendrils spell out the ultimate, unpronounceable name of God. I am seeing the prophesied day at the end of time, the day which is all days, on which God is all that there is, and his name is the name of all reality.

Then the vision fades back into darkness. I am again in the room, my face in the angel's hands.

He moves his hands away and I collapse, falling forward. He catches me with one arm, lifts me effortlessly, moves his other hand below me so that his arm catches the back of my thighs, and swings it upward. I lie on the platforms of his hands as if I am floating in mid-air.

He carries me back to my stone bed and lays me down so softly that I feel no jolt, no sense of the moment when my skin meets stone, just a knowledge that my body is now supported by the surface of the bed.

The angel steps away then returns. His hands, cupped, hover above me.

Shifting a finger slightly, he lets a drop of water fall onto my lips. I open my mouth and drink from a stream of water that he lets flow from his hands.

His hands move away, and again I see his face above me, not quite smiling, not quite sad.

Angel, why have you shown me this? What have you shown me?

The angel says nothing. I understand and accept his silence.

With one dry hand, he brushes hair from my eyes. He rests the other hand against my cheek. This time, he does not cover my eyes. I see him, and in this moment, that is all that I want to see.

Speak to me, he says. Who are you? Where are you now?

And again I feel that I am falling, away from where I am, down into the voice of another, surrounded by visions of gold, rivers of gold, plains of gold, visions not of wealth, nor of earthly beauty, but visions of the spread of truth, of the whispered word of our God.

THE BOOK OF RETURNING
ספר האזובֶת

SHADRACH

אשׁדך

Shadrach was a Judean man living in Babylon. Nebuchadnezzar, the king of Babylon, sent out a call for

> "...young men without any physical defect, handsome, showing aptitude for every kind of learning, well informed, quick to understand, and qualified to serve in the king's palace."
>
> *(Daniel 1:4)*

Shadrach was one of four men selected, along with Meshach, Abednego, and Daniel.

Nebuchadnezzar built an enormous golden idol on the plain of Dura. The whole court gathered at the idol and were ordered to worship it. The Judean men refused. The king told them that they would be thrown into the furnace inside the idol if they did not comply, but they still refused, saying that God would rescue them.

(According to legend, they consulted with Ezekiel, who said that they would fail, but they proceeded anyway. God then told Ezekiel that they would indeed survive, but, much like with Abraham's sacrifice of Isaac, that it was important for them to proceed even if they hadn't been promised a miracle.)

The furnace was heated to a temperature "seven times hotter than mortals' fire," and the men were thrown in. But when the king looked in, he saw the three men walking around, unbound and unharmed, accompanied by a mysterious fourth man. (And it's curious that, while the previous chapter talk about Daniel and the three as a group, Daniel isn't mentioned in this story at all.)

The king praised the God of Israel and promoted the men to be high officials in Babylon.

Shadrach speaks as he falls toward the fire.

Seven times hotter than mortals' fire. And thus the roaring metal melts, collapses, drowns. Seven times hotter than mortals' fire. And thus our human flesh should be turning to ashes, to gases, to a burst of absence where lives had been.

We should be afraid but are not afraid, we three who are falling into the furnace at this giant golden idol's core. As we walked here, proud in our resistance, arm in arm, up the long, high ramp to the idol's mouth, we sang out King David's song, the one that Daniel had taught us. Where we should have seen this barren plain of dust, we saw green pastures; where we should have felt this inhuman heat, we felt cool breezes, the breath of spring across the still waters of rivers that we had never seen. As our captors tied us up, we looked into their eyes and whispered: "May the Lord give you peace." As they pulled the hoods over our eyes, we returned to King David's song, repeating over and over "*Lo ira ra*. I will fear no evil. I will fear no evil."

And now our captors have pushed us down, one by one, into the mouth of the idol, and we are falling. We should be dying, should be burning, should long ago have hit bottom, in the belly of this idol who is only ten times the height of a man. But we do not feel the fire, do not collide. We are falling, more and more slowly, until we are suspended, without weight, in an upward rush of cooling air.

Our bindings, our hoods are untying, unfolding from us, expanding, becoming not shrouds but flowering cocoons. The tongues of flame flicker around us, moving as slowly as the branches of willows in gentle breezes. Below us is a meadow. Something like a man is standing at its center, hands and face aglow, waving and beckoning us to come down to him. We drop softly to the ground beside him, landing like butterflies, like leaves.

As we look at him, face to face, we realize that this is no apparition, no angel of death. It is our friend, our teacher, Daniel. I wonder, then do not wonder, that I had not been surprised by his absence when we had stood up to our captors and refused to bow to the idol, that I had never realized that he was not human but rather a visitor from the Lord, that I am not surprised that he now appears like this to us.

Daniel is smiling and speaking to us. Though his lips do not move, we hear his voice within our minds. "You have been brave and did not fear, and you have been protected. Stand with me, and we will see the fire speak."

Around us we hear a liquid ringing, a roaring of metal as it succumbs to the fire. Seven times hotter than mortals' fire, this fire that the king's magicians believe that they have set, but that could come from nowhere but the Lord, is hotter than the idol's gold can stand. We are dropping, slowly, steadily. The idol's knees, softening, bend, dropping to the ground. Then it bends at the elbows, at the waist, turning and dropping, until it falls and prostrates itself on the plain of dust, facing east, its eyes to the rising sun. (We cannot feel it bend and fall, though we can see it: our pearl of protection, our meadow, surrounds us, suspended, slowly turning, so that our feet always point toward the ground.)

The eyes of the idol open, revealing orbs of blue-green fire that the magicians had not made. The metal of its forehead melts, rearranges, hardens, to spell in clear Hebrew letters the unspeakable name of the Lord. And its throat, its lips, melt, rearrange, form into changing, resonant vibrating channels. The heat of the fire summons wind from its depths to rush from its mouth. A voice greater than that of a thousand trumpets yet clearer, more beautiful, than the laughter of a child roars from its lips, singing out, echoing from the mountains that surround our plain. "Listen, Israel," it sings out, "the Lord your God is the one god!"

The people on the plain are dropping to the ground, prostrating themselves like the idol, bowing not to the idol but to the one god that it has revealed. And now there is silence, as the echoes fade, as most of the people listen within themselves and hear the words of the idol resonate within their hearts. Most, but not all—some stubborn people, wicked people, people whose hearts are not open to hear, break the silence with bitter laughter, mocking the words of the voice of the fire.

Now there is a new roaring, as the fire returns to its gyrations of sound. One last stream of flame emerges from the idol's mouth like the tongue of a serpent. It passes over those who lie prostrate, but touches each of the mocking people more quickly than they themselves can move, ignites them, turns them to flame, to ashes, to dust.

And the idol is again melting, its back opening to the sky, the gold of its body flowing across the plain like lava, like dense water rushing through a wadi after sudden rain, opening and darting around the people on the ground, leaving them on islands of earth surrounded by the flowing gold.

Amid this glistening golden ocean, a path before us cools, solidifies, hardens. At the end of the path, the king—yes, Nebuchadnezzar himself—is lying on the ground, immobilized by fear and awe. We walk forward, the three of us and Daniel, until we reach him.

Daniel is reaching down toward him, taking his hand, and guiding him upward until he stands among us. He embraces the king. The king embraces each of us, then turns and calls out to his satraps, his prefects, his governors, and his advisors: "Praise be to the God of Shadrach, Meshach and Abednego, who has sent his angel and rescued the servants who trusted in him!" Though he has seen Daniel before, he has not recognized him in his angel's garb with his face aglow.

Now the silence is returning, save for the whisper of the cooling breeze that drifts across and blesses the plain. The molten gold is disappearing, evaporating and sinking swiftly into the ground. Now no sign remains of the idol, nor of the fire, nor of the people who died. The only sign of what has happened remains echoing in our hearts.

The king waves his hand, and the music begins, the horn, the flute, the zither, the lyre, the harp and all other sounds repeating, resounding, embellishing and improvising on the melody with which the idol had proclaimed the glory of our Lord. Slowly, the king, his company, the three of us (and where is Daniel? Had we seen Daniel today?) walk on, across the plain of dust, back to the castles in which we will redefine our lives.

For comments and discussion about the tale of Shadrach
and to hear the audio version, please visit
http://www.thebookofvoices.com/Shadrach

BELSHAZZAR

בלשאצר

Belshazzar reigned over Babylon a few years after the death of Nebuchadnezzar.

Belshazzar held a famous feast in his palace. It went quite well, until, as the Bible says,

> Suddenly the fingers of a human hand appeared and wrote on the plaster of the wall, near the lamp stand in the royal palace. The king watched the hand as it wrote...
>
> *(Daniel 5:5)*

The hand wrote the words "*M'ney, m'ney, t'keyl, ufarsin.*" The words seemed to refer to coins, but no one knew what they meant.

Belshazzar called for an interpreter. Daniel appeared and interpreted the words. They meant that Belshazzar's reign and his kingdom were about to end. Belshazzar died that night, and Darius the Mede took over the kingdom.

Belshazzar speaks as he waits for Daniel to arrive.

Here, now, I am waiting; in this gaping, gasping silence, in the midst of this blaring party, waiting; in this air suffused with incense, with the scents of meat and sweat, waiting; waiting for this supposed prophet, for this man who is said to speak of dreams, in dreams, to dreams; waiting, praying that he will soon arrive, that he will never arrive.

The Persians, the Medes, are at the gates of this city. Tomorrow they will enter, and my reign will end. Something has happened to me, to us, to this nation, to this empire. We are no longer who we were. Those whom we swore to protect have cast us away, as if the empires for which they have left us will be better, as if the other empires would be any different.

297

We are all here in this palace, this maze of buildings that seem to stretch on forever, here in the great hall, fires lit, music playing, dancers in motion across the floor, in this one last party, celebrating all that we have known, all that will end tomorrow.

But I can only vaguely hear, smell, see the world that surrounds me. My thoughts, my senses have been suspended, caught in a web of what must be madness, balanced on the points of a triangle of words, three words, incessantly repeating, the names of three coins (one repeated twice), maddening, mundane, elusive. I know what each means on its own, but what they mean together I cannot say. And these words circle, shift, repeat, echoing within me, until I sense only a howling, humming ordered chaos, an intricately textured smear to which all other words and thoughts must bow.

Now the words have broken free. Looking up from my goblet a moment ago, a lifetime ago, I saw what I thought was a final hallucination. A ghostly hand appeared, four times larger than any human hand, glowing like burning ebony, like gold, writing, slowly, carefully, to my horror, these words upon my wall, in letters of fire against the royal blue tapestries, these three simple words that have enslaved me, naming these coins for a purpose that I cannot understand: m'ney, m'ney, t'keyl and farsin.

At first I had thought that they had appeared only to me. But then another person pointed to the wall and gaped, and another, then two, three, many more, all those at our table, all those who could see the wall from where they sat. Some applauded, seeing it as magic, some were frightened, some amused. Those who saw it asked each other why the words were there and what they could mean. Nobody knew.

Then they looked to me and saw that I, too, was staring blankly at the words. They knew that I had not summoned them as a trick, as entertainment, knew that I was disturbed by them, knew that I needed them gone. My advisors came to me, all my enchanters, my Chaldeans, my astrologers, my wise men. None of them had done this. None could say why the words were there.

And then, at last, my beloved queen returned from the ladies' chamber, saw the writing, saw my fear, saw the advisors gathered there. She placed a hand on my hand, looked into my eyes, then turned to the advisors. "Be gone," she said to them. "Return to the celebration. Act as if nothing is wrong. Nothing is wrong. And summon Daniel, the man of Judah, who interprets secrets and brings meaning to dreams."

They returned to the party, to the music, to the wine, all but one who stepped away to go to the far end of the palace, to bring us Daniel. We have left to wait, waiting as the music plays, waiting as the fire of the letters shifts and flickers but does not die, as I close my eyes and fight against being swallowed by the words, though with each moment my will to fight them fades.

But now, abruptly, the noise in my mind has stopped, has cleared. It is replaced by the reverberation of a single name, my own name, Belshazzar. It has been so long since anyone, even my queen, has called me anything other than "My King" that it takes me a brief moment to recognize it. I think, "I am Belshazzar," then, automatically, "I am king. I am here."

"You are here, but you are lost," the voice within my mind says, "lost within your kingdom, lost within yourself, lost within a song."

"A song?" I wonder.

"The words within your mind, the words upon the wall," it says. "Listen closely to them."

I listen to them, repeat them within my mind. I still do not understand.

"Listen to the words. Repeat the words. The words have a melody," it says.

"*M'ney, m'ney, t'keyl* and *farsin*," I think to myself. Then again, "*m'ney, m'ney, t'keyl* and *farsin*." And suddenly I realize that my inner voice is not speaking the words but singing them.

"Listen more deeply," says the voice within me. "Whose voice is singing?"

The words, the melody circles within, through, around me. The melody rises in pitch, lightens, becomes bright. And I know it is not my voice, but the voice of a little girl. "Yes," the speaking voice says to me, "and where had you heard this song?"

I listen, focus, and my palace, my world drop away. I am outdoors in the early morning. I am young. I am leading my army into battle. The enemy waits, just over a hill, not knowing that we are about to attack. I wave my army forward, and they raise their swords and rush toward the top of the hill.

I am first to the peak, and I realize that I hear a child's voice. Just over the ridge, a little girl is wandering among the flowers, not picking them, just looking at them, smelling them, then moving to the next. And she is singing as she walks:

"A m'ney, a m'ney, a t'keyl and some farsin
These are the coins that my father gave me

A m'ney, a m'ney, a t'keyl and some farsin
To buy a locket with a picture
of the boy I will marry.

A m'ney, a m'ney, a t'keyl and some farsin
I throw the coins in the waiting river
A m'ney, a m'ney, a t'keyl and some farsin
The ripples spell the name
of the boy I will marry..."

Then the sound of the girl is lost as my army rushes past me, obscuring her from view. I turn to signal them, to stop them, to protect the child—but I hesitate, and the critical instant is lost, as the momentum of our army carries them over the hill and into battle. The enemy, hearing us, rushes forward, their front line meeting ours. The moment, the song, the girl disappear in a sudden frenzy of iron, of bronze, of blood.

And in the madness of battle, I forget the girl, forget the song, until—"Yes," says the voice within my mind, "until now."

"Why now?" I ask. "Why have I remembered this?"

"This moment, like all moments, is the product of all the previous moments of your life, all the streams of choices within your history that you could have changed, could have stopped. You hesitated, did not speak up for the girl, and she was lost. And now, you have hesitated, have failed to support your kingdom as you should. You have not lived up to your responsibility, and your reign is at an end."

"The girl... " I ask. "Did she survive?"

"No," says the voice, without anger. "But she died suddenly, without knowing that it was happening, without fear, too swiftly to feel the pain."

"And the kingdom... will it survive?"

"You know the answer to that. It has come to its end."

"Can you change this?" I ask.

"It will not change. History has made its choice. But not all is sealed."

I listen in my own soul for any hope, for any sense of peace. There is none to be found. "If you can affect these things at all, can you make my passing, the passing of my kingdom, less savage than it might be?"

"And why should I do that?"

"Out of..." I pause. "Out of compassion?"

"Do you deserve compassion? Have you acted from compassion in your own life?"

I peer down a corridor of memory. "No, not that I can recall. No. I have never acted from compassion. I am not worthy of compassion."

There is a long silence, then the seeming sound of a gentle smile. "That you realize that you have not been worthy of compassion is the first step in becoming worthy. If you are willing, there is this that we can change: At the end of the night's festivities, you and your queen will return to your quarters to sleep. There, in your sleep, you each will die: you, so that you will not see the end of your kingdom, and your queen, so that she will be spared what the enemy would do to her should they find her alive without you. You will die peacefully, without knowledge, without fear or pain. At dawn, your servants will find your bodies, and the palace will go into mourning. When the enemy arrives, they will find a kingdom without a king. Those that remain will surrender. The king of the Medes, an honorable man, will let them live, will give them amnesty, will work to absorb your kingdom into his so that the people can live well under his reign."

I say nothing, but feel my soul gliding from shock to terror to acceptance to understanding to peace.

"And though you will die," the voice says, "your soul, like the soul of all that die, all that live, will live again, absorbed into the loam of the soul of all and spun out again, in different combinations with the souls of others. And in your next existence, the greater part of your soul will be merged with the greater part of the soul of the little girl, the girl with the flowers and the songs, the girl that you now mourn. Thus each part of your soul, and the universal soul of humankind, may teach the other and itself about strength, about joy, about comfort, about compassion, about song."

There is a long silence within myself. I listen, and hear that the words have returned, but not in the torrents that blocked out the world, but in the melody of a child's voice that blesses it. The sound of the life outside myself, of my people, of my party return.

I open my eyes, and I see that Daniel, the prophet, is standing before me, his eyes opening gradually as we emerge from our shared dream. We look at each other and nod.

And now he is speaking aloud, his voice the same as the voice within my head. He is speaking of the wrongs that I have done, and is declaring a meaning to the words on the wall: cryptic, stretching their meaning, not telling others of the pain within my memory, of where the words were born, of what they mean.

The party is continuing. The people far from my table do not know that anything strange has occurred. Those around me are listening intently to the prophet, wanting to believe that they understand what he is saying.

But I am only vaguely listening to the prophet, to the music, to the people around me. I am holding the hand of my queen, resting my head on her shoulder. I am quietly humming a child's song, a melody that draws a path between my history and my hope, the pain of my past and my future peace, the wrongs that I have done and the sacrifice that I will make to set things right, the memories of sorrow and the dreams of imminent joy.

For comments and discussion about the tale of Belshazzar and to hear the audio version, please visit http://www.thebookofvoices.com/Belshazzar

Darius

𐎭𐎠𐎼𐎹𐎺𐎢𐏁

Darius the Mede was the ruler of a vast empire that included Babylonia and Judea, not long after Belshazzar. (The Darius who took
over from Belshazzar was someone else.)

Early in his reign, some seventy years after the First Temple was
destroyed, Darius ordered that the Temple in Jerusalem was to be
rebuilt, using funds from the royal treasury. The government was
to return the gold and silver items that had been taken from the
First Temple.

The Bible quotes his decree:

> "May God, who has caused his Name to dwell there, overthrow
> any king or people who lifts a hand to change this decree or to
> destroy this temple in Jerusalem.
> I Darius have decreed it. Let it be carried out with diligence."
> *(Ezra 6:12)*

Darius's history was recorded in the Behistun Inscription, inscribed in three languages in an enormous cliff in what is now
Iran. The text tells of his life and early victories, ruling by the grace
of Ahura Mazda, a god who brought order to the universe.

While Darius maintained and expanded his empire throughout his career, his army was defeated by the army of Athens in the
Battle of Marathon.

Darius speaks at the end of his life, just after that battle.

I am empty of words. All the words that a life might be allotted left
me long ago, many spent in a swift torrent of decisions, decrees, and

303

regulations, others set in stone on that cliff in Behistun, where few travel and few read the words that I once had thought immortal.

Now almost as many years of my life have passed since I had had those words inscribed as had passed before I wrote them. I have ruled for more than four times as many years as I had by then.

Those words spoke of so many victories. By grace of my god, I was invincible then. All who rose up against me were vanquished. I brought order and righteousness as all the nations that surrounded me came under my control. I wrote of those who surrendered to me and of those who would not, who I kept barely alive and displayed at the gates of my cities.

But now the future does not seem so bright, nor victory so sure. When I close my eyes I am frightened by the faces of those that we tortured, staring out at me without ears, noses, tongues, each with his one remaining eye, as if offering rebuke, as if laughing without sound at what has become of this land.

And the whispers returning to me from Marathon, where our ships had sailed to vanquish the Athenians, speak of failure and destruction. Our mainland is intact, and our borders have held, but too few ships will return. Our runners tell us that theirs claim victory. Let them claim it. Let them have their joy, since someone must. We will return, and we will have our victory again. For now, I am tired, and have seen too much of war to fear collapse or to yearn for celebration. I know that none of us is victorious forever. Even that which is set in stone must someday crumble and decay.

I am tired. I am old. I must die sometime, and I pray that my god grants me a death that is proper, while we still have our claim to power. Let me not find myself staring out from a face like those that haunt my fears. Let history record that I died in a moment of peace, and remember me as a good and righteous ruler, one who brought order to this once-chaotic land.

Let at least some speak favorably of me: the odd historian, those who discuss and admire well-crafted systems of law and of commerce, and perhaps those people in that city of Jerusalem who thrive on dreams and tell their stories so well. Their temple, built, destroyed, is now, by my order, to be built again (though my nightmares show that temple, like so many others standing proudly now, being destroyed again and perhaps, in visions far less clear, recovered yet again; my mind's ear rings with future echoes of glass continually broken, of shards that glisten, obscuring joy, and drawing hearts and blood away to memories of tears). Let the systems that they too have built continue. Let their memory of me be kind.

Maybe, when as many nights have passed again as there have been since my god created our world, someone may see an echo of my inscription cast in words written in light. Let them say that King Darius increased the amount of order in the world. That will be enough.

For comments and discussion about the tale of Darius
and to hear the audio version, please visit
http://www.thebookofvoices.com/Darius

HAGGAI

חַגַּי

Haggai was a prophet in Judah, speaking in the second year of the reign of Darius.

The Bible tells us nothing about him. For most people, it tells us at least a father's name, but we don't even get that. What we do know is that he was single-mindedly focused on the building of the Second Temple. He brought several messages to Zerubbabel, the governor of Judah, and to the High Priest.

In the Bible, Haggai says:

> This is what the Lord Almighty says: 'Give careful thought to your ways. Go up into the mountains and bring down timber and build my house, so that I may take pleasure in it and be honored... Who of you is left who saw this house in its former glory? How does it look to you now? Does it not seem to you like nothing? But now be strong... and work. For I am with you...'
> *(Haggai 1:8, 2:3-4)*

Haggai speaks early one morning, as he lies on the ground.

I fade slowly into consciousness, awakened by the sound of panting, the scent of stale breath, and a rough wetness moving against my face. My eyes blink open after several tries and look into the eyes of a small dog, mottled grey with a white stripe on its nose. I sneeze, and the dog yelps, stops licking my face, and backs away a few hands' breadths before he returns and starts licking again.

I try to stand and discover that I can't. A heavy weight lies on top of my head, back, and one leg. I reach back with one hand and feel rough wood, and suddenly remember where I am and how I got here. I am just inside the borders of Jerusalem, lying in the dirt, pinned face down under a beam that I had been dragging in the middle of the night toward the site of the temple.

I hear a high-pitched voice in the distance call, "Caleb! Caleb, where are you?" The dog yelps, its bark pitched even higher than that voice, piercing and almost painful this close to my ears. Small feet, running, approach to my left. From the sound of it, they seem bare, without sandals, though I can't turn my head to the left to see them. Equally small hands reach down, coming into view, and pick up the dog, who yelps again.

The feet walk around me and stand in front of my face. "Hello," the voice says.

"Hello," I reply.

"Why are you lying on the ground?" it asks.

I attempt to shrug, but the beam on my back keeps me from moving. "I fell," I say. "The beam fell on top of me. I cannot get it off my back."

"Why do you have a beam?"

"I was carrying it up to the top of the hill."

"Why?"

"I'm rebuilding the temple."

"The temple? What's that?"

"It's a building. People go there to worship the Lord."

The voice says nothing. Perhaps the child has nodded. The feet step closer to me.

"Can you help move the beam off of me?" I ask.

I feel the child push on the beam. "Too heavy," he says.

"Can you find someone to help move the beam off me?"

There's a silence, then, "Maybe Shimshon or Tzvi can help. They're big."

"Could you go get them?" I ask.

The voice, again, says nothing. I hope that the child has nodded again. The feet turn and run away from me. As they get farther away, more of the boy comes into view. He is young, maybe six years old, in a simple short robe of a vague brown that contrasts with his curly black hair.

A long time passes, as do several more pairs of feet. No one else stops or says anything. Another dog runs past, farther away. A salamander wanders quite close by, but doesn't seem to notice me. I move my arms, place my palms on the ground, and try to push upward. When I get a few fingers' breadths off the ground, the beam slips very slightly, banging into the back of my head. I collapse, raising a small cloud of dust. Again, I sneeze.

The boy returns with two larger boys, though seeing them, I doubt whether they'll be much help: the one to the first boy's left is quite tall, but limps; the one to the right, though shorter than each of the others, appears to weigh as much as the two of them combined.

They come up to me, close enough that all I can see is the three pairs of feet. The pair to the right (the fat boy, I think, if they haven't changed places as they have approached) tap impatiently. "Who are you?" says the voice from that side.

"My name is Haggai. Can you help me?"

"What can you give us?" he asks.

I pause, thinking. I really don't have anything. "An opportunity," I reply. "You will be remembered as one of the first people to help rebuild the temple."

"Why would I want that?" he says.

"I—it's just a good thing, a chance to do something good."

"Let's look in his pockets," says the voice from the other side.

"How, you idiot?" asks the one with all the questions. "He's lying on top of them. Let's go."

"I will not just leave him lying here!" says the one in the center, the one who brought the other two here. "Can you just try to lift the beam? Or are you too weak to lift it?"

"I am not!" The boy on the right moves closer and pushes on the beam. It rocks slightly, then falls back into position, once again hitting me in the head.

"So?" says the boy to the left.

"The balance is wrong, obviously," says the boy on the right. "You have to learn how to do these things." He walks to the end of the beam, just past the top of my head. The other two join him, out of my sight. "Now: you put your hands under this end, here. And you put your hands under there, where I had them just now. I'll go around here."

Two feet appear again in front of me. I feel hands under the beam, sliding against my back on either side of it. "Now lift on my count: four... three... two... Caleb!"

I suddenly feel paws on my head and a slurping noise. The dog apparently has returned, and decided to jump up and lick the face of one of the boys.

"One?" asks another boy, and two sets of hands lift the beam.

"Not—ow!" I sense several things in the same instant: The feet of the boy in front of me fly up and out of my view. A cloud of dust replaces them, causing me, again, to sneeze. The beam lifts off me slightly and slides to my left, landing on my shoulder and bouncing further over, off of me and onto the ground. One of the boys (I sense, gratefully, that it's the thin one) lands on my back. The boy at my head cheers. The dog yelps, again far too high and loud and far too close to my ear.

"What's going on here?" A deep voice approaches from behind me, accompanied by the slapping of sandal soles against the dirt.

The boy lying on top of me scrambles to his feet. "Nothing, father."

The man stops to my left. "If you are involved, Shimshon, it is never just 'nothing'. Who are you?" he says, apparently to me.

Pressing my right palm against the dirt (I feel two sharp pebbles jabbing into it), I roll over onto my back and look up at the man. He is shorter, stockier than the instant image that my mind had formed from hearing his voice, but still formidable. "My name is Haggai, the son of—"

"Yes, yes, Haggai the supposed prophet. Well, get up."

I bend my knees, roll onto my calves, and try to stand, but can't quite get my balance, after the night spent under the weight of the beam. I start to crumble, my hands flying out to grab the air. The man catches me under my arms and holds me up until I manage to stand on my own.

"What are you doing out here with this beam?" he asks. "Have you been here all night?"

"Most of the night. I was trying to bring it over to the temple site. I'm rebuilding the temple."

"By dragging a single beam over?"

I shrug. "One has to start somewhere."

He laughs. "I suppose one does. And what will you do with the beam when you get there?"

"I think it lies along the southern edge. It may be too long, but I can try to find a saw and cut it to size if it is."

"Do you have plans for how to build it? Or do you think that the Lord will let you know bit by bit?"

I reach into my pocket and pull out a small scroll. It unrolls unevenly, after having been flattened under my weight. "Actually, he told Ezekiel some time ago."

The man takes the scroll from me, turns so that it catches the sunlight, and peers at it. "There's a lot of information here, but it needs to be more complete. I can tell that this 'man who shone like copper' that he quotes was not an architect. Now, is this south wall that you are building for the gate, the court, or the temple itself?"

"It's for... one of those."

He looks up at me, then back down at the scroll. "Words will not be enough. I need to draw plans."

"Yes," I reply. "Thank you."

"Do you have any experience in construction?" he asks.

I shrug. "None at all. I figure that the Lord will help me when I need it."

He smiles. "Well, I guess I've turned into some sort of messenger of the Lord. Look, do you really mean to do this? And will you commit to sticking with the job until it's done?"

"Yes, I do and I will."

"That is a start, then," he says. "Do you have any funding?"

"I hope that the Lord will provide."

He sighs. "A community project, then. Well, my wife is good at pulling that kind of thing together. And I'm an architect. My team has just finished with Zerubbabel's summer home, so we have some time to get this happening."

"Yes," I say again. "Thank you."

"We can go up to my office and take a serious look at this. And we should get you some breakfast. But first we have to get this beam out of the road. Think you can handle that end?"

I bend down and lift it slightly. "This end, yes."

He steps over to the other end. "Then I'll grab this one, on my mark." He pauses, then yells, "Shimshon! Tzvi! Yerachmiel! Stop playing with the dog! Get over here and help us!"

The three boys, who have wandered off to sit under a nearby tree, stand and come toward us. "Stay, Caleb!" shouts the youngest. The dog yelps again (his voice not as painful, now that it is not right next to my ear) and stays.

"Now stand over here—no, on the other side of the beam, that's right—and we'll all lift and move it over to that stone. On my mark: four... three... two... one... Now!"

We all lift the beam and carry it as far to our left as the beam is tall. "Now, gently! Lay it down."

We lower it to the ground. The man pulls a bit of limestone from his pocket and makes a mark on the beam. "There," he says. "People will know that it's mine and won't take it."

As we stand, I get a closer look at the man's face. "Haven't I seen you before, down at the temple site, when I was trying to get people to work on the rebuilding?"

"Oh, yes," he replies. "I've been there many times."

"So why are you helping now, when you chose not to help then?"

"Because then, all you were doing was yelling," he says. "Yes, I heard you there, babbling endlessly, talking, shouting, threatening us with the Lord's wrath, telling parables that, frankly, no one could understand. But now..." He puts the limestone back in his pocket, pulls his hand out, and gestures down at the beam. "Now you are actually doing something. It is a ridiculous move—this beam is the wrong kind of wood, by the way, for the part that I think you are trying to build—but it's action, rather than words. And if you are willing to keep working on this project rather than just yelling about it, we can start to get something done."

He looks down as his sons. "Boys! I think you all have chores waiting. And please try to keep Caleb out of trouble. And you..." He looks up and slaps me on the shoulder (the right one, fortunately, not the one on which his son let the beam fall). "You need breakfast, then we'll try to make some sense out of these plans. We have a lot of work to do."

For comments and discussion about the tale of Haggai
and to hear the audio version, please visit
http://www.thebookofvoices.com/Haggai

ASHERAH

אשרה

> Asherah was worshipped by many as a goddess alongside God in the Biblical era, until the people who believed in only one god caused her worship to disappear. Memories of her remain in the Biblical text mostly as derogatory references. Belief in her eventually shifted into belief in more abstracted female figures, such as Wisdom. As the Bible says,
>
> "Does not wisdom call out? Does not understanding raise her voice? At the highest point along the way, where the paths meet, she takes her stand."
>
> *(Proverbs 8:1-2)*
>
> Asherah speaks just before the dedication of the Second Temple.

I come into being in the gentle rain. I step forth from the embrace of the Tree of Life, guided by this pair of angels, one female, one male.

"We have waited for you," they say.

"Have you waited long?"

In unison, they shrug. "All time is the same here. But anticipation preceded you."

I look around. "So this is Eden."

"That is what the people call it. Had you never been here before?"

I look through my memories of past and future times. "My stories begin after the people left the garden. None of the stories remember my having been in it. Why have you called me here?"

They gesture to the space behind me. I turn. There, not far away, sits a woman, human, ancient in years as measured by people. She is huddled, sitting on the ground, leaning against the base of the Tree of the Knowledge of Good and Evil. Her knees are drawn up toward her, her hands resting on them. She looks steadily toward me, a stone-like visage not of defiance but of certainty.

"A person in the garden?" I ask. "Are we at the end of days?"

"No," they say. "Some get to visit, but only a few, and only for a short time. This one is here by permission of the archangels above us. She, and especially her sacred sisters, prayed for her to be allowed to come here. And they especially prayed that she might meet you."

I walk toward the woman and offer her my hand. "Asherah?" she asks.

"Yes, I have been called Asherah," I reply.

"You look–"

"Exactly as you imagined?"

"Yes. But how?"

"I exist outside of space," I say, "outside of material form. I have no body, most of the time. When someone needs to see me, a temporary body forms, built from the story that the person has told herself of how I must appear."

"This would lead to problems," she says, "if two people were to see you. If one would see you as tall and the other as short, and both were to embrace –" She stops herself and laughs. "Forgive me. I am too practical. I'm worrying about measures and paradoxes in the presence of a goddess."

I laugh with her. "I enjoy hearing you think like this. I have never figured out how it works, myself. I do not remember the creation of the world, but assume that God, and whoever else might have been with him, worked out the rules of science, magic, and all that lies between them, at the start."

"The world would be an easier place if he would just tell us what the rules are."

I nod. "There is so much that people do not know. I have appeared, at times, to help them learn. But God has never been particularly interested in making things easy for you. He challenges you to work your way through the world. That is his way as your Father."

"And you, as our Mother?" she asks.

"I bring you what you need to survive the learning. I catch you when you fall, heal your wounds, and support you in your path."

"But now…" she says, then pauses. "So few… only I know you now."

"When is 'now'? From what time have you come here?"

"I have lived a long time with my sisters, where conventional time does not work as it does outside. As far as saying when this is in the history of our people, I can say that we have lived for a long time in the land of our Fathers. We were once driven from this land, and the Temple — the place where most worshiped the Father God, but where we once had a tree, a space, sacred to you — was destroyed. But now, after a long enough time has passed that almost all who remembered that Temple are gone, we have returned, and the men are raising a new Temple in its place."

"The men?" I ask. "Are there no women involved?"

The woman sighs and looks down. "In my day, in the time that I was queen, so many lifetimes ago, we had powerful women, the finest architects of whom one could dream. Now, they are gone. As people say, those who have the power over others get to write the stories. And the men have taken the power and told the official stories for generations. So women are seen as less than men, destined only to serve them."

I look into the stories in my memory. There are so many — tales of people calling on me, praying to me, of my helping them, nurturing them, strengthening them. But the stories become thinner over time, until after a while time seems to break.

"I see no stories of that age," I say. "Where are they? Where am I in them?"

"Few speak of you anymore, and fewer know your name. The men, when they wrote the stories down, removed all mentions of your worship other than as folly or a curse to be removed. Houses no longer contain the figurines by which we remembered you. Your presence, your memory, your stories — all are gone."

I sigh and sit down next to her, resting my back against the broad trunk of the tree. "And all my physical children are gone, long gone, since God's vengeful flood wiped out the last of the children of Cain."

"How can we survive?" the woman cries out. "How can we carry on without your memory? Do your stories ever return?"

I close my eyes and look deep into myself, into the stories of past and future that make up my own memory. "Yes, there are stories of people who remember me. They come from your future, as far into the future as humanity has memories of the past. Gradually, my history is revealed. People once again find my figures and my stories, and decode the ways in which the men hid my existence in the texts that they came to call sacred. And they come together, some in your land, some in cities on the far side of the land on the far side of the ocean. They speak and sing of me in a great, ever-changing text, written on light, which all can read almost instantly, wherever they are, on your world and beyond."

"And you become the equal of the Father God?" she asks. "And all worship you together?"

"Not all," I reply. "But many. And it does seem that I survive in other ways."

"How?"

"Stories are not the only ways for us to carry meaning. While I lose my name for some thousands of years, I take on others. I seem to grow into metaphor."

The woman looks deeply at me but says nothing.

"Do you hear people among you speak of Wisdom?" I ask her. "What do they say?"

"They say that she is among us, that she speaks to us," she says.

"And who is this Wisdom?" I ask.

"Is it you?" she cries.

"It is, or it can be, if that is how you wish to see her. And what of the Sabbath?"

"They say that she is a queen who visits us and blesses us each week. Is she also you?"

"She is, if you believe her to be. And don't the people speak of the Presence of God as if separate from God himself, as female, the one who aids and comforts humanity?"

"This also is you?" she says.

"It is, or it can be. Who I am is whoever I am in your hearts, until the stories and the memories return."

She sits, again silent. She looks at me, looks down, then looks up again. "But what is there that we can see, now that the figures are gone? You are the light that shines deep within our hearts, but must the light be hidden from our eyes?"

It is my turn to look away and pause. "There is another fire, another light," I say. "The stories say that a fire burned forever at the original Temple, at the Outer Altar where all could see it. What became of that fire when the Temple fell?"

"We have that fire." The voices came from the angels. "But like the original Ark of the Covenant, it will remain here until the end of days, to be returned when all souls become one."

"This is God's will?" the woman asks.

"This is what we know to happen," they reply. "It is not within our power to change it."

"Then I will become that fire for you," I say to the woman. "When people see the Eternal Flame, they will see the presence of God, and knowing of that presence, of the one who bridges the worlds between the mundane and that which cannot be known, they will know me."

"You will become flame?" she says. "I would not see you destroy yourself for us!"

I smile and rest my hand on her shoulder. "This body is not my body. It is made of stories and exists only in your mind, in this place where metaphors become real. I will not be destroyed, but will spread out like smoke in gentle wind into the greater stories that people will tell."

I rise and, stepping over to the two great trees, pick up fallen branches, one from the Tree of Life and, careful not to dislodge its fruit, one from the Tree of the Knowledge of Good and Evil. I stand between the trees and stroke the branches against each other until they begin to smolder.

"Wait!" The woman has stood and called out to me. When she hears her voice, she is suddenly ashamed. "I'm sorry. I didn't mean to sound so –"

"So much like a queen calling to servants? I understand. After all, you were a queen for such a long time."

"I –" She falters. "I have known of you for such a long time," she says, "and for so many lifetimes, I have longed to meet you, longed for your embrace. And now you are leaving again, and…"

I open my arms, one smoldering branch in each hand. The angels each take a branch from me, moving in perfect unison. "Come to me," I say.

The woman moves slowly to me, as if she were a child approaching the mother than she had feared that she would never meet. When she reaches me, I wrap my arms around her as her arms embrace me.

We stand for a long time, here where time has no meaning. The body that I wear senses the gradations in color of her hair and of her robe, the sound of her soft breath, the scent and texture of her flowing white hair, and her taste as I kiss her on her brow.

"I will remember you," she says. "And Mother, dearest Asherah, please remember me in the stories that you know, the stories that you become. Let the stories know that I, your servant Maacah, did everything to honor you, gave up everything to be true to you, and longed to be with you all her life."

"I will remember," I say, "and we will come together again at the end of time. And you will be the one to carry my memory. When I become flame, please carry the fire back to the World of Appearances, so that, once again, I might live at the holy Temple."

"I swear it," she says.

I kiss her one more time, then she and I end our embrace. Each of us takes a step back. The angels, moving together, return the branches to my outstretched hands.

I touch the branches to each other. Sparks burst out from each and become flame. I raise them into the air then bring them close to me. My hands come together in front of this body's heart.

The body begins to glow, to emit light, emit heat. It burns, not like wood but like the fire within a gemstone. It becomes a pillar of light, then contracts. The fire catches the branches as they lie on the ground, and they become a slow, steady flame.

I feel myself drifting away, dissipating, back into the stories, back into the hearts of those who, whether or not they know the name that Cain gave me, feel my presence across time. I feel the stories leap across the years, the lifetimes, toward the time that they reemerge, written in fire, written in light, as the world and its people move closer to the joys that await us at the end of time.

For comments and discussion about the tale of Asherah
and to hear the audio version, please visit
http://www.thebookofvoices.com/Asherah

JUSHAB-HESED

𝕳𝕾𝕯 𝕵𝕾𝕳

Jushab-Hesed was the son of Zerubbabel, the governor of Judah to whom Haggai spoke his prophecies. Zerubbabel governed during the building and dedication of the Second Temple.

The Bible only mentions Jushab-Hesed once, in a genealogy:

> The sons of Zerubbabel: Meshullam and Hananiah. Shelomith was their sister. There were also five others: Hashubah, Ohel, Berekiah, Hasadiah and Jushab-Hesed.
>
> *(1 Chronicles 3:19-20)*

Jushab-Hesed speaks as a small child at the dedication of the Second Temple.

My father is big. His shoulders are strong. Sitting on them, I can see people everywhere, cheering, singing, crying, looking at us, and looking up into the sky. I can't count how many people there are. I asked my father if he thought there were a hundred people here. He laughed. He said that there were hundreds of hundreds.

There was a big building here, back when my father's father's father lived here. He says that it was bigger than any building that I have ever seen. He says that we will be building a new one, even bigger, even better. He says that God will live there. But I know that God lives everywhere. Hi, God.

This place was a mess when we got here, full of trash and broken stones. Everybody got to help out with cleaning it up. People who could carry heavy things carried them. Other people carried smaller things. Some people made lists. I helped take little things from the people who made the lists. There were piles for everything. I put things in the right piles.

Some people took the big old stones and made them into a table in the middle here. Animals are lying on it. I saw people walking the animals up to the table, but then my father put me down to stand next to him for a while, and all I could see was other people's legs. When he picked me up again, the animals were lying there, not moving. Some of the stone table that used to be grey is red now.

A lot of people are singing. Many of them are in a big circle around the stone table and the people working there. Other people are singing along, but they don't sing as well. I don't understand what they are singing. I think it has to do with what the people at the table are doing.

But now everyone is getting quiet. A very old woman is coming out of the crowd, walking to the stone table. She is carrying a small box. I think it is made of stone, but it is glowing. She is opening the lid. Fire shoots up from it. A beam of fire is rising from the box, up into the sky. It looks like the stone pillars that were in front of the big buildings where my old home was, but it is made of fire, and it looks like it is going up forever.

I am leaning back, farther and farther, to try to see the top. I'm not afraid of falling. My father is holding my feet tight against his chest, and somebody else has pressed a big hand up against my back, holding me up. I lean forward to look at the table again, and the big hand lifts me back into place.

The old woman is gone. The box of fire is resting on the table. The big man nearest the table is looking up and saying something to the sky in his loud, deep voice. The pillar of fire is rising out of the box, with a brilliant circle of light at the bottom of it. It hovers as far above the table as my father is tall. The circle is spinning and getting wider, spreading out until it is bigger than the table. The circle is spinning, faster and faster, and coming down. It is covering the whole stone table and all the animals on it. There is a loud noise like the ocean, and a smell like cooking meat.

And now the circle is rising, getting smaller, riding up the pillar of fire into the sky. Then the pillar moves over and slowly comes down, back into the open box. It's still burning there, as small as a candle but a hundred times as bright. People are singing again. The animals are gone.

I bend down and ask my father, "Where did the animals go?"

"They went to be with God," he says.

"Like my grandfather?"

"No," he says, then, "Well, yes. No. Well, it's different for animals. But sort of the same. Yes, they are all with God."

"I miss my grandfather," I say.

He pats me on my leg. "Yes. I miss him, too."

My grandfather walked with us most of the way here from Babylonia. It was a long walk. I don't know how long it was, but it was the rainy season when we left and it was dry when we arrived. Most of us walked. There were some horses and other animals, but only the lookouts rode them. And there were some carts and carriages. The old and sick people and the littlest children rode in them. People brought things from their homes in them, too.

We walked almost every day, but some days we didn't. My father told me that we were stopping every seventh day to rest on the sabbath.

My grandfather was very old and tired, even before we left. My father asked him to stay in Babylonia until we were ready here. He insisted on walking with us. But he got older and more tired everyday.

Then one day, we were walking in the hot sun, my grandfather and me, holding hands and walking slowly while my father looked at things up ahead. Suddenly, my grandfather made an odd noise, stumbled, and fell over. I fell with him, but I didn't get hurt because I'm littler and didn't have as far to fall.

Everyone around us stopped. My grandfather put his hand over his heart and made a face. It must have really hurt.

Some big men gently helped my grandfather over to the shade of a tree and laid him down. I stayed with him while they went to get my father. I lay down next to him, with my head on his chest.

He whispered my name. "Jushab-Hesed," he said, "I have walked as far as I can. I can't continue with you."

"Where are you going to go?" I said.

"To be with God. I hope I am going to be with God. I was hoping to see Jerusalem while I lived. You will have to walk on, to see Jerusalem. Maybe somehow I will get to see it through your eyes." He was quiet for a while. He just breathed, but his breathing got less even, like parchment shaken in the wind.

Then he spoke again. "Jushab-Hesed... your name... You know it means that you will return kindness. You have to grow up to be a good man. Be good, be kind to people, even if..." He stopped. Then his eyes opened wide and fluttered shut. I heard him say, as quietly as I've ever heard anyone say anything, "Listen, Israel, the Lord our God is the one Lord..." Then he let out a long breath and was quiet.

I lay there with him for a long time. My father came running over with my bigger brothers and sisters. My biggest sister, Shelomith, picked me up and carried me away.

I never saw my grandfather again. I guess he's with God. And my father has always seemed a little sadder since then.

But I'm not sad now. I'm looking around, and everyone is singing and cheering. And I listen inside myself, and I think I can feel my grandfather looking out through my eyes. "See, Grandfather?" I say aloud. "We're in Jerusalem! This is Jerusalem!"

I look down at my father's face. He is a bit sad, but he is smiling, looking back up at me. "Yes," he says. "We have made it. This is really Jerusalem." He leans his head back, and his hair tickles my belly. Then he hugs my legs even tighter. We both look ahead of us, to the middle of the space, to the stone table and the box of fire. And I know that my grandfather is everywhere, that kindness is everywhere, that God is everywhere. Hi, God.

For comments and discussion about
the tale of Jushab-Hesed
and to hear the audio version, please visit
http://www.thebookofvoices.com/JushabHesed

GOD

( )

> God is... too vast, complex, and paradoxical for me to explain here.
> Go with what you know.
>
> God speaks, across all time, to all of us.

First, for a timeless moment, there was nothing. Then, sometime within that moment, I began. I cannot tell whether I immediately knew that I existed, or whether I gradually became aware that I was there. But at some point I began, and time began, and this world began, and I found my spirit drifting over the face of darkness within darkness. And while the darkness had its beauty, I knew that it could be better. I let there be light. And it was good.

But with the light, I saw that there was nothing else in this universe, that there was nothing to see. When I separated the mortal world from heaven, it was better (though I had no use for a heaven yet); when I separated the dry land from the water, it was better still. And as I distinguished living, moving things from those that less visibly lived, and as I made their forms ever larger, then ever more complex, it became, with each step, better.

But though what I created was perfect, there was a stillness, an automatic feel to the world that I knew could be improved.

I looked throughout the earth, and I looked throughout heaven, but the only minds, the only souls that I found were echoes of my own, as if I were caught in a hall of twisting mirrors, where reflections distorted, split off, and developed names of their own.

So I created you, the humans (along with your kin that you have not met, on other worlds beyond your own), inseparably merging the souls that had spun off from mine in heaven with the bodies that were evolving on the earth.

From the first moment, you made surprising demands of me, argued with me, and disobeyed. It was good. It brought me new life and new challenges, and taught me new ways to behave.

When the first of you ate from the forbidden tree, demanding a knowledge of good and evil from which I had been shielding you, I lashed out in immediate fury, smashed the boundaries of the garden that I had made for you, and expelled you onto the rest of the earth.

Outside the garden, death came upon you as it came upon all other living creatures. Those who realized that they themselves would eventually die were surprised and saddened. This in turn surprised me, since it had not happened with other living things. I meant death as a way of returning, of reintegrating, as your souls would be reabsorbed into the global soul, reconnecting, blending again with the souls of others. With the birth of each new person, I would then send forth another portion of that astral dough, that global soul, another mixture of what once were individuals, to merge with physical form and become other intelligent life, here or on the other worlds. That you feared death saddened me, and I learned that I would have to treat death carefully in working with you.

Then, generations later, your disobedience grew unmanageable. I tried to speak to you, but no one would listen. I sent down my angels, my messengers, but they, too, fell under the sway of the errant humans, those who thought only of themselves and not of how they supported and were supported by the world. The corruption spread across your land. Angered again, I lashed out again, determined to recall the souls of all the people of the earth. I swore, also, to wipe out the other life, starting over with the fewest living things that could bring good life back to the world. So I set aside one family of humans and pairs of each of the other species, then unleashed the waters above to blend again with the waters below, then to evaporate and return.

But when I saw the devastation that I had caused, I swore that I would never again assault the earth and all its living creatures to punish what a single one of its species had done. The earth would abide, with its rhythms and its seasons, and the innocent creatures would thrive.

And then, once again, a city grew evil, and I swore to destroy all within.

But I was surprised again when one of you spoke directly to me and challenged me to spare the city if I could find a certain number of good people within it. When I agreed, he asked for mercy on the behalf of fewer and fewer people. When even these few were not found, I did indeed destroy the city, but I remembered that this person had argued with me, not from arrogance and belligerence but from concern for doing what was right. And that was good.

When I challenged him to give up that which was most dear to him, to sacrifice his son, as a favor to me, he agreed without question. Seeing that he would obey, I told him that this need not happen, that despite what people thought that a god would require, I would never demand a pointless human sacrifice. He responded not with anger, either at the demand or at its revocation, but with love, showing a mercy toward me that I had never seen before. And I learned from this mercy, and tried to extend it toward others as we progressed.

Years later, when a man, alone on a mountain, asked me for simple words as to what his people should do, I thought for an infinite moment, then wrote a few rules down on slabs of rock for him. In turn, I asked him what he saw when he caught a flash of what I am, and what the people's image of me would be. He told me, in few words, that the god he envisioned would be compassionate, gracious, slow to anger, with abundant goodness and truth, extending kindness for generations, forgiving iniquity and transgression and sin while not clearing the guilty.

But he also warned that he saw my stubbornness, my anger, my vengefulness, that I would not stop at punishing the guilty, but would strike out against their children and grandchildren. And I tried to learn from him, to live up to the image that he described of what I should be, and to recognize my aspects that lashed out against those who did not acknowledge me.

For in those first days, when I was learning how to maintain this world, when I smashed the garden and sent its people out into this world of danger and death, when the goodness of the universe became trapped and encased in the shards of the borders of heaven from which only the love and actions of people could melt and release them, I shattered too. My reflections, my scrambled fragments of myself separated from me and flew out into world, each believing that it was the real god.

People saw those fragments and believed in them, and blocked out my voice, refusing to see that these fragments were incomplete fictions, that I was the true god, that their sacrifices were confused, that they were blocking the return of the needed unity to the world. I grew angry at them, as I tried to reach them and could not be heard, as my own voice and the voices of those that I sent to speak to them were drowned out by the distortions of their accidental gods.

And, yes, I grew angry again and again, and destroyed their people, their children, their cities, and their lands, sometimes even blocking the hearts of some who might have come to me so that I could have my vengeance upon them. As these people grew fewer, fewer of those who remained believed in each of the fragmentary gods. Over generations, as the last believer in each of the fragments died, that fragment came back to me and was reabsorbed into my own divinity, as the souls of the humans who died were absorbed into the greater global soul. I learned from what they had seen, and what had been in the hearts of the humans who had believed in them. And, in the beauty and terror that I saw, and what it showed me of my own short-comings and the repercussions of my wrath and of how, in working with people, I could be more effective and more gentle, the learning was good.

As I look across time, I see what I am and what you are, and what I can be and what you can be. What I see is good. But it will be even better. And when I am not the god that I could be, I call on you to call on me, confront me with how I have behaved, and teach me what I have wanted to teach you.

Yes, I see everything, and yes, I know every fact in the world, and yes, I can do anything that I want.

But in building this universe, working with you, talking, arguing, and wrestling with you, I am learning, ever more clearly, what I want and what I should want.

And as I help you learn to be better people, I thank you for helping me learn to be a better God.

For comments and discussion about the tale of God and to hear the audio version, please visit http://www.thebookofvoices.com/God

ELISHEVA (EPILOGUE)
אלישׁבע

And now I am alone, alone except for my silent angel, who comes and goes in ways that I cannot understand. How long have I been alone? My sense of time has fractured, scrambled. I can no longer remember the sequence of events, other than by reconstructing patterns, believing that one thing must have caused another and therefore must have preceded it.

It has been so long since I spoke with my own voice, so many years, longer than the lives of many that I have known. I was so young then, just barely no longer a girl. Now I am old, my hair white, my steps slowed, my body no longer informing me of the cycles of time.

And now, after all these years, the voices of my life are returning. Perhaps this means that death is preparing to visit me, that soon I will forget to return from sleep, that after one dream ends the next will never come. I cannot say if I am prepared for this. Perhaps, when it comes, no one is prepared. Perhaps, when it comes, each of us finds that she is ready.

These memories are returning with the help of this angel, he who sits here, silent, questioning, as his presence confronts and caresses my soul. I know now that I have been blessed with the fading of forgetting, a blessing of pain as my protective cowl of not-knowing is swept away, exposing me to the harsh light of history and time. My own memories are finally returning to fill the places where the memories of others once had dwelled.

When my mind strays, I can find myself there, in the life of my memories, in those years lost long ago. It was a small life, in a small village, but it was all the life that I should have needed. I had family, parents, brothers, though their faces are now unclear, as if I no longer have memories of their faces but only memories of having had memories. I do recall my father's scent as he held me, the striking red of my mother's hair, contrasting with the distant green of the hills of Judea as my head rested on her shoulder. And there were sounds: dogs, water running in a stream, animals and blades in my father's slaughterhouse, coarse laughter from where the men gathered, song and far more fluid laughter from where the women came together.

My mind falls back into my memories and I again am there, small, agile, innocent. The families make their crafts, tend their crops, their herds. The children huddle with the families or run freely in the town, comfortable, certain, as their parents are certain, that each person in the village will look out for each child as if it is her own.

And the soldiers... Yes, the soldiers, walking the village or standing guard, some with swords, some with horses, some speaking our language, some speaking the language of Rome or of whatever common homeland two or more of them might share. They are strong, strange, powerful and frightening. They are beautiful.

Where the soldiers live was once a school. The teachers are gone. I don't know where they have gone. I only know that the stories that the grown-ups tell of where the missing people have gone differ from person to person.

The soldiers who are not on patrol (there is always someone on patrol) remain at the house, sleeping, drinking, laughing, exercising. Out in the yard, behind the house, they remove their clothes, then stretch, run, stress their muscles against the walls and ground, lift heavy objects, and wrestle. The grown-ups try to keep us from seeing them there, but we still sneak off and try to watch from what we believe is a hidden place.

When I can listen past the terror, the guilt, their images still can make me smile. Most of the memories are vague, unfocused, but details stand out, sharp as the edges of the stones in this room:

A soldier's hand presses against the wall near where I hide. I can see the veins standing out with the pressure of exercise, the dirt under the nails, the scar that leads along the back of his hand, interrupting the fine hair, from the joint of his thumb to past his wrist.

Two wrestle on flat ground: one is almost prone on his stomach, his upper arms bulging as he tries to keep from collapsing completely. The other lies across his back. His nearer arm tries to knock the lower soldier's arms away from the ground so that he will fall. His other arm wraps around the side that is farther from me, emerging from underneath to grasp the nearer edge of the lower soldier's flat belly. Its fingers almost align with the ridges of the other's tensed muscles. Trails of sweat erase the dust of the ground from each soldier's pale skin.

Another lies on his back on a stone bench, his legs toward me, lifting an iron bar with added weights high into the air. His feet are planted firmly on the ground to each side. The setting sun shines through the hollowed circle of the weight bar, his chest, and his arms, His muscled chest blocks his face from my view, though I can picture the grimace that the soldiers wear when they lift the weights. His sex nestles between his thighs, inert for the moment, different from the few that I have seen of the village men and boys. (At another time—after? before? – when I ask my mother why it is different, she tells me that it is because he is not one of us, that he is not holy. At the time, I don't understand how holiness makes that different, or how that difference makes men holy.)

And I remember knowing that over time, the fear of the soldiers has been growing. Grown-ups, and sometimes whole families, disappear from the village, and I hear that soldiers have taken them. The grown-ups try to shelter me, to keep the fear from me, but I sense that all are afraid.

My brother frequently comes and goes from the village, silently, always moving by night. He brings word of events outside the village, words that I overhear, much as they try to hide them from me. He speaks in whispers, in mystery, speaks of greater fear outside the village, of destruction in the cities, in Jerusalem. But I am told never to repeat what he says, never to tell anyone that he is here, never to tell anyone where he is going. Sometimes he brings other men with him. Sometimes they are wounded. My mother cares for them in secret, touches their wounds with herbs and gives them teas and blessings to help them heal. We return them to strength. They give us strength. But we never speak of them outside the house, never let others know that they are here.

So I wander through the village, silent in both innocence and knowledge. Sometimes I speak to the people of the town. Sometimes I speak to the soldiers, shyly, cautiously. There is one in particular, one soldier to whom I speak, stranger, gentler, even more beautiful than the others. His skin is pale, lighter than my father's, more golden than my mother's. His hair is a different shade of gold, like the hay that we feed to our animals, finer along his arms and legs as they are left bare by his uniform.

When I see him in my memory (faded as it is, though sharp now with many images that I wish would have dimmed), the settings, the images rush together, forming a tapestry. I can only bring together, once again, memories of memories of his face.

He would always stand away from the direct sunlight, not concealed by shadows but protected by them. When I first summoned the courage to speak to him, I asked him if he feared the sun.

He laughed. "No," he said, "but I respect its power. The sun shines with less power in the land where my ancestors were born, and my people have this unfortunate fair skin. If I stand in the sun for too long, I burn."

"Do you burst into flames?" I asked.

"No," he said, "but my skin feels as if it has. It turns bright red and becomes quite painful."

"But I have heard that your people, the soldiers, do not feel pain."

He laughed again, this time more ruefully. "No, we do feel pain, though we try not to let it rule over us. As with the sun, we approach it not with fear, but with respect."

I sat for a while, there on the large stone at the entrance to the market, watching my soldier as he watched the people setting up their wares.

I was surprised when he spoke again. "May I tell you a story?" he asked. I nodded.

"Once, long ago, in that time from which only stories remain, my people had a beautiful princess. Her skin was so white that milk seemed dark when compared to it. Her hair was so fine, so bright, and so pale that it looked both like glass and like gold. Her eyes were the clear blue of a lake without waves, of a sky without clouds.

"But as beautiful as she was, the princess was also quite disagreeable and quite stubborn. Whenever anyone told her anything, she would behave as if the opposite were true—unless, of course, she realized that people were trying to fool her by lying to her, by telling her the exact opposite of the truth.

"Ever since she had been old enough to understand words, she had been told that she could never stand out in the sunshine, that the sun would burn her. Her family, and the people in the castle who tended to her family, kept her indoors all day, and only let her walk outside after the sun had set.

"One night, however, the first night of autumn, the night before her twelfth birthday, she decided that she would no longer be kept out of the sun. She went to sleep early and awakened early, with the first glimmer-ings of false dawn.

"She put on her warmest coat and boots, and crept out of the back door of the castle. Moving like a silent cat in the darkness, she made her way to a hidden cove above the eastern shore.

"As the sun first peaked over the horizon, it saw her waiting there. 'You must leave,' the sun god called out to her. 'You will burn when I rise.'

"'I do not fear you,' she replied.

"The sun tried to hold back. But even the power of the sun god could not stop the wheel of fate that forces the sun to rise.

"The sun god called upon the god of storms to cause shade to fall on the princess. The god of storms gathered what clouds he could to stand be-tween the princess and the sun. But the power of the sun was too strong, and the clouds burned away.

"The sun god and the god of storms called upon the spirits of the north-ern wind. The spirits gathered and tried to blow the princess back into the shadows. But the princess held onto a great oak tree. The strength of her grip was as mighty as the strength of her will, and the wind could not blow her away.

"The sun god, the god of storms, and the spirits of the northern wind called upon the goddess of the moon for aid. She leaped across the sky, became full, and eclipsed the sun. But the world started to dissolve into chaos: the tides were confused, unplanned magic erupted in the light of the eclipse's edge, and all the women in the world began to go mad. Soon the wheel of fate overcame even the goddess of the moon.

"'Go home,' they all cried. The sun god, the god of storms, the spirits of the northern wind, and the goddess of the moon all pleaded with the princess. 'I do not fear you!' she said.

"The god of storms, the spirits of the northern wind, and the goddess of the moon all returned, reluctantly, to their place in the heavens. The sun shone fully upon the princess. 'You do not have to fear me,' he said. 'But you do have to respect me.'

"The sun god looked away as his rays struck the princess. First her hair, then her cloak, then her skin began to smolder, then burst into flame.

"The flames awakened the spirit of the oak tree. It reached down with its branches and enveloped the princess. It absorbed the flames and directed them into its own leaves, which dried and became the colors of fire.

"But the last of the flames reached deep into the soul of the princess, and, in an instant, turned her body to ash. The spirits of the eastern wind gently blew upon the ashes and scattered them along the shore. These became the seeds of the morning flowers, which open each day to greet the dawn, die in the afternoon, and are reborn again each morning.

"And ever since then, every year, at the beginning of autumn, the leaves of the oak tree turn the color of flame, mourning and celebrating the life of the stubborn little princess."

My soldier smiled and looked down at me. "That is the story," he said.

"It is beautiful," I said, "but sad."

"Such are the stories of my people. Beautiful, but sad. Can you tell me one of the stories of your people?"

I closed my eyes and thought for a while. "Once," I said, "back before my grandmother's grandmother's grandmother was born, there were many more Jews in Judea. We were members of thirteen tribes, but all members of a single family, brought together by powerful kings.

"But the people of Judea did evil things, and we were banished from the land. All the people had to take a long journey to a place called Babylon. When they arrived in Babylon, however, they discovered that only a few tribes had gotten there. Ten tribes were missing.

"For years, nobody knew where the ten tribes were. But one day a wanderer came back with a story of where they had gone.

"Far to the east of Babylon, there is a river named Sambatyon. The ten tribes crossed the river, into a land that resembles the garden of Eden. Nobody goes hungry there, nobody cries, and when people die, they die gently, saying goodbye to their family and friends.

"No one can cross the river now. When all ten tribes had reached the magic land, an angel blessed the river. Six days of the week, the river churns with rocks. They spin and fly into the air, smashing together, killing anyone who tries to cross. On the Sabbath, the river turns to still fire, and anyone who tries to cross is burned alive.

"But someday, an anointed leader will guide the lost tribes back here, back home. Then we will all live here like they do there. There won't be any more soldiers." I looked up at him. "You would get to go home."

"Yes," he said. "I would like that. Though the weather is better here."

"Except for the bright sun," I said.

"Even with the bright sun."

After that, we spoke frequently. He would stand there in the shade near the entrance to the market. I would sit on the rock. We would tell each other the stories of our peoples.

I can no longer remember how much time passed. Was it months? Years? I recall telling him stories in the heat of summer and during the winter rains. I feel like I knew him for what seemed, as compared to my then-short life, to have been a long time.

But then, one hot, awful evening, I heard the sound of soldiers, and of a person screaming. The sound grew closer, more fierce. A group of soldiers came over a nearby hill, dragging a screaming man, whipping him as they went.

Must I tell you this? Angel, must I remember? Is it for this that I get to speak with my own voice, only to remember, to repeat my pain? May I go back to the stories, return to speaking in the voices of the stories? Will this be the last story that I remember, that I tell before I die? Let me, please, tell you another story, any other story.

Of course, the angel is silent. All I hear in my mind is his insistence: Speak to me.

I am trying to remember the other stories, all the other stories of all the other voices, the other lives that have flowed through me. But they are gone. They have gone silent. The only voice that I hear within me is my own.

Angel, the men neared. The screaming man was covered in blood, staggering, trying to keep his feet from dragging against the rocks on the road. One was twisted unnaturally at the knee. The other had lost its sandal.

And then the man looked up, and I saw the face of my brother. "Ethan!" I called.

He turned his head toward me and screamed, "Elisheva!"

My soldier looked sharply toward me. "Do you know him?" he said.

"He is my brother!"

Suddenly, he clamped his left hand over my mouth so that I could say nothing more. With his strong right arm, he lifted me by the waist into the air.

"Be silent!" he whispered. "I will protect you." He strode to the barracks, opened the door to a small room, stepped down and released me.

I tried to duck around him and go back outside. He took one step over and blocked the doorway. "You cannot go out," he said. "Your life is in danger."

"But my brother—"

"We can do nothing to save your brother. But you may be able to survive. Remain quiet. I will return." He stepped out the door, began to slam it, then, stopping the motion, made it close quietly.

I sat silently, shaking, watching the shaft of sunlight that came into the room from the small window in the door, watching it creep through the room as the day wore on. Twice, from the village, from the direction of my home, I heard further screams, once a man and once a woman, each starting suddenly, then, just as suddenly, ending.

The room held little: the stool on which I sat; a wooden platform with a mat for sleeping; a small table, on it a few scrolls in a language that I could not recognize, a straight razor, a mirror, and some dolls that must have been idols of his gods. I held the dolls and talked to them. I tried not to think of my brother.

When the day ended, when the light of the sun through the window had been replaced by the light of the moon, my soldier returned. He looked in through the window first, signaling me to again be silent, then unlatched the door, stepped in and closed it.

"My brother," I whispered, "is he—"

"No. Yes," he said. "Your brother is gone. A brave man. But gone."

"My family!" I said more loudly. "I must go to my family!"

"No," he said. "You can never return to —"

I leaped up, ran around him, and tried to open the door. My soldier grabbed me, lifted me in the air, held me close to him so that I could not run, my feet far off the ground, my chest to his chest, my cheek to his rough cheek.

From that height, I could see out the window. I could feel myself understand what I was seeing piece by piece, like a steady stream of cold facts: I see bright light. I see fire. It is a house. A house is burning. That house is where my house should be. My house is on fire. My house is burning.

"My house!" I cried out. "My parents!"

"Be silent!" he said. "You cannot —"

And then comes memory without sound, without feeling, a moment without thought, a moment of simple motion. He turned—we turned—and

I saw the table come within view, within reach. Without my telling it to do so, my left hand reached down, reached the razor that rested by the mirror, grasped the handle of the razor—Angel, can we stop this memory? I do not want to remember this, all this that I had forgotten so well—

I pounded on his shoulder with my right hand. He looked down, away from my left hand.

And in one swift motion, without fear, without thought, I brought the razor up and slashed his throat, smoothly, cleanly, as I had so often seen my father do to the animals that he slaughtered.

My soldier showed no expression, made no sound. He stood for an instant, wavering. Then he dropped me and, bending at the knees, fell forward, to the ground, landing on me, crushing me, the weight of his chest pressing down on me, the blood spurting and streaming from his throat onto my body, onto my face, into my eyes, blinding me, drowning me.

I pushed up, pushed against him, but did not have the strength to lift him. Then I reached over with my right hand and pushed against his shoulder. There was no motion for an instant. But then, gradually, he slid off of me, slowly, heavily, his body, my body, made slick by the blood, his head striking heavily against the ground, splashing more of the blood against me.

I rose. I must have run from him. The memory of sound returns, but I am missing moments, and the moments start to lose their order. I am pressing against the door. I am standing outside the room. I feel the heat coming from in front of me. I run toward the heat. I am shouting, screaming, crying without words. My feet slide against the ground, still slick with the blood in which they have stepped. I brush my hands against my eyes, trying to clear the blood from them, only adding the blood from my hands to the blood on my eyes. I continue to run. I stumble against roots and stones on the ground. I run closer, almost reaching the flames.

Then I am lifted into the air, held by someone, someone that I do not know, someone who whispers words in my ear that make me calm, that make me relax. I feel the terror leave. My arms wrap around the person's shoulders, rest against the strength and unexpected softness of the person's back. Do I feel dense clothing? Do I feel flowing hair? Do I feel wings?

And then I feel nothing.

Time must have passed; how much time I cannot tell. But after that time, I do know that I am with friends. I am with teachers. I am safe. I am here where I will spend the rest of my life, here in this school beyond the caves, here where so many women (and some few men) have come since before the times of the great judges. Here we study, we learn, we are healed and learn to heal. Those who are blessed with appropriate gifts become prophets. The rest of us become teachers, healers, singers of song. Some stay in the caves. Some go out into the world to try to bring healing to it.

We have a name, as a group, but we rarely use it. As I try to reach for the name, I find that it, too, now is missing. Some outside the school call us "The Women," or sometimes "The Daughters of Jerusalem," or "The Daughters of Jephthah." We let them call us whatever they wish. We know when they call for us, whatever the name.

My memories of the years when I grew into a woman are sparse. Most days were like any other days, and the memory of their order remains unclear.

But I do know that I was silent. When I would open my mouth to speak, I could not form words. Words connected to memory, and memory connected to pain. When I reached for words, all that I could find were images and memories of fire and blood and pain. My voice would emerge in wordless cries, slashing through the silence like fire, like knives. Even when I would try to sing, even without words, my voice would clash with and destroy the others' harmonies, stunning them into silences that echoes my own.

But then a day came—or perhaps a night, since deep in the school we cannot distinguish day from night—when we were sitting in a class. A teacher was reading from a book of the chronicles of creation. She told of the end of the garden of Eden, of the day that we were banished into this world of pain.

The book told the story of God and the story of Adam, the story of what God said to Adam, the story of how Adam had placed all the blame for the eating of the fruit from the tree of knowledge of Good and Evil on our mother Eve. The story spoke in the voice of God and spoke in the voice of Adam.

Then one of my classmates called out, "What of Eve? Why do we not hear stories of Eve? Where is her voice?"

I stood suddenly, threw my head back, looked upward, opened my mouth and let loose a wordless howl. Our teachers and attendants rushed toward me, certain that I would have one of my explosions, that I would scream and thrash until I could be calmed.

Then, just as suddenly, I looked forward, looked at my teacher, past my teacher. "Where has the beauty gone?" I called out. "Where is my garden? All I see around me are storms and dirt. Where rivers of life once were, I now see only death, death becoming torrents of mud. My world is turning to dust, to pouring rain, to shreds, to parodies of life. All I desire is my husband, and he has been stolen from me. All joy is stolen from my heart." I looked upward again and howled.

My teacher rose and walked quietly toward me. "Elisheva?" she asked gently. "Can you hear me, Elisheva?"

"There is no Elisheva!" I cried out.

"Speak to me," my teacher calmly said. "Who are you? Where are you now?"

"I am in a place that is no place," I said. "I am—How can I say who I am? Who I am has been stolen. But my husband has given me a name. He says that my name is Eve."

My teacher nodded, then gestured to the others. "All will be well," she said. "Please sit. Sit and listen."

She reached out to touch my shoulder. I pulled away from her touch. "Eve," she said, "please speak to me. Where are you now?"

"I am standing on high ground. Around me, the red earth is seeping away in the pouring rain, turning to torrents, to torrents that carry life away, torrents that stream across the earth like rivers of blood.

"I am standing here, and my past is disappearing. The garden is retreating, and I can scarcely recall what green looked like. I cannot tell what came before and came after. In the garden all was one long day, a day of rest. Now time is moving. I cannot reach the garden. Between us stands an angel, an angel of fire, an angel with a flaming sword.

"I look around me. I see what is here now. I see what will be. I will have a life of pain. I will have children, and they will be born in pain, and they will bring me pain. They will take what new life I can bring to this world of death and throw it away. One will kill the other then disappear from my life. Then another will be born to bring more generations of pain."

My teacher may have said something more to me, but I did not hear.

"Where is my husband?" I called. "Where is my friend? I desire my husband, though he betrayed me. I miss my friend the snake, whose life I destroyed, whom I betrayed. All this world is lost, all turned to death. I have brought death to the world, have brought evil. Though the snake has been cast to the ground, I am lower still. I am beneath the reach of goodness. I crawl beneath the worm."

I looked down, placed my head in my hands and wept. I may have said more, or Eve may have said more through me. I cannot recall. After that moment of clarity, of transition, my sense of remembered time once again fails. But I do have the faintest memory of the sense of an angel's presence, the breath of an angel's whisper, the brush of an angel's wings as time fell away from me.

I know that many feared me, though that fear eventually turned to respect. I had no voice of my own, little sense of myself. But I would sit with the others and listen to the teaching of stories. Sometimes, without warning, I would erupt with unexpected voices, with the voices of people in the stories.

I could not recall whom I had been, what I had said. But others among us would remember the stories, would write them down. I would look at them, and know that the voices came from me, though they were never mine. Over time, enough time for me to grow from young to very old, they collected the stories, building a book of voices for those who might follow, for those who might want to read and to hear them anew.

All my sisters are gone now. Our people have been banished from Judea to harsher lives, to lands with harsher names. My sisters have gone with them, out into the wider world, into that moment and into other times, to comfort and to heal, to advise, to challenge, and to teach. They shine as lenses, as mirrors, focusing truth, focusing love upon, within, through the world just as my own mirror, my beloved Aspaklarya, focused and brought forth the stories, the history, and finally the memory that defied me, defined me, defiled my sense of my soul, then at last has deified my sense of who we were, who we are, and who we all can be, as reflections of aspects of the infinite images of the unity of our souls, the unity of God.

No one will ever find our school again, not until such time as our world is healed, when the anointed leader will bring our people home, from this world of the mundane, from those blessed lands beyond Sambatyon, from beyond the walls of death and the veils of time. The mouth of the cave is sealed, our school invisible to the eyes of the world.

Now I alone remain, alone except for this angel, who sits here in infinite patience. Having listened to me speak with the voices of our history, of our stories, he has now drawn from me my own story, my own voice. I have no more words within me. I sense that it is time to go.

Lying here in silence, I feel my space disappearing from around me. The impenetrable walls that surround this room, the wondrous vaulted ceiling that had shown us not the sky but where everything is in the sky, all are turning to gauze, to mist. I cannot see beyond them. What they were and where they were is becoming steadily less clear. The floor, once carved with blessings and names of power, is shimmering, translucent. Lights and colors play beyond the nameable, the visible, as if this space is now detaching from the world.

I lie here on the soft stone table, waiting, alone but not alone. My angel rises from his seat, the feathers of his wings fluttering, whispering, in the wind, in the absence of wind. He leans over me, placing one hand on my forehead, one hand on my heart. I say to him the only words that remain: "Speak to me. Who are you? Where are you now?"

He looks into my eyes. His lips move, as if to form words, but then stop. He bends down, closer to me, touching his lips to mine in a kiss that seems to take an instant, to take an eternity.

I know who you are now, my angel, my Daniel, messenger of God, you who guide and protect us, you who move outside of time, saving us and blessing us. And I know who I am, who I have been, who I will be, in the past that lies before me, in the futures that I have endured.

In the moment that I know him, I know that he is gone. But we will meet again.

And I know, again, that I am not alone. To my left, I sense an animal's scent, an animal's heat. I turn my head and see a ram, beautiful, majestic, its perfect horns emerging from its mighty head. If played as trumpets, each would give a tone that would shake the foundations of the world.

The ram nuzzles its head against me then fixes me in its gentle gaze. Its eyes are infinitely deep, infinitely solemn, infinitely forgiving, the eyes of my mother, of my teacher, of my angel, of my soldier. I touch my left hand to the top of its head, and move it along the curve of its horns.

The horns have letters on them, words, raised in relief. It is the text of the final confession, the last words we say before death.

My hand moves along the horns, reading the words, speaking the words that my breath, my lips can no longer speak. My fingers whisper of acceptance, of confession, prayers for myself, for all those whom I have loved.

The moments of my current life pass before me one last time, not in a line, in any order of occurrence, but as clouds of connections, arranged, focused, on the instants that touched my heart, on the moments of change. My soul looks deep into the cloud, arrives at its center.

There I see my village, my soldier. I see myself allowing myself to be taken away, failing to die when my family died, surviving only because I had betrayed my family, my people, because I had seen an enemy as a friend. And on the other side of that moment, I see myself turning and betraying that friend, repaying his mercy by killing him, his blood staining my body, forever staining my soul.

I hover in that moment, that moment of definition, of betrayal, that moment that seemed to seal the meaning of who I was, who I was to be.

But then I hear a voice emerging, not heard with my ears but with my heart, the voice of eternity, the voice of the ram: "All these moments have passed before you. Yes, that moment was one of them. And your life, as with all the lives whose voices have spoken from you, feels as if it is focused only on one single moment.

"But no one moment defines a life. God weighs each whole life by the sum of all its actions. God will weigh this life, from the gentle joy that you brought to the world as a child, through that one moment of pain and your labors of healing from that pain, into the light that you have brought to your sisters, to the world, by bringing voices to the people of your history, to the people of the stories. We must hope, must trust, must believe that you have increased the beauty in the world. Have faith that your life will be seen to have been good."

The voice again grows silent. The words that my fingers read come to an end. I touch the head of the ram one more time, then bring my arm to rest by my side.

The ram backs away into the vagueness of the mist that is contracting around me. He backs out of sight, pauses, then charges forward, running towards me with the hoof beats of a thousand armies. He bows his head, coming closer. He smashes into the stone table on which I lie.

The table disappears, dissolves. And I am falling, deep into the mist, into the infinite softness, into visions beyond visions, sounds beyond sounds, the scents of a thousand sacrifices, the taste of the sweetest morsels ever blessed. My senses unite, explode. I feel nothing. I feel everything. I am falling. I am falling. I am falling.

Time is ending. Time is shattering. Time is beginning. I am surrounded by all that I have loved, all that I have lost. All are one, alone. The room, the world, fill with darkness, light. I fall back past angels, past angels' bones, into deserts, into floods, into storms, into gentle rains, into stories, into gardens, into all people, all people becoming two people, becoming one person, becoming beasts, birds, fish, the creatures of the sea, the sea itself, the waters below the land, the waters above, the heavens, the lights of the heavens, the moon, the sun, the land, the grass, the fruit, the trees, life, breath, into the words themselves, the words of naming, the words of creation, morning, evening, night, day, darkness, light, let there be, let there be, let there be, let there be this angel, this angel who has always been there, this angel who has never been there, this face, this face, this face of the waters, this face of the deep, this face of God, this breath of God, this breath that breathed me forth into life, that will breathe me back from life, that dissolves my soul, that shatters my soul, that breathes me into the unformed and void, where all of us, all of me, all of you are one and our name is one, into this nothing, this everything, to which we will return, from which we all will return, return, return, return, return.

TRANSLATOR'S POSTSCRIPT

Justin and Emily:

Here ends the Book of Voices, as the angel gave it to me in San Francisco, and as I have translated it here over the past ten years.

Reading this text in its proper order for the first time, as a book on paper rather than a less-linear set of memories, I see sections that inspire joy alongside sections that inspire doubt. I see that, here and there, what the voices tell us diverges from what the Bible says. Is the Bible (written, after all, by divinely inspired humans, often centuries after the events) wrong? If not, were the voices wrong? Was Elisheva merely insane, dreaming up voices saying what she believed to be true about their lives? Or (and I cannot dismiss this possibility) am I the one who is insane? Were the angel and the words of the voices figments of my own imaginings? Has my desire to know my past and my mother's past caused my subconscious to extrude this collection of apparent memories to explain itself to itself?

I'm not worried about which of these possibilities is true. Read these testimonies as you will, as fact, fiction, fabrications, or ravings. What is important is that they are now out in the world, on paper and in other forms, for people to judge, enjoy, or dismiss as they will.

I can accept what it tells me of myself: I was born in Judea. My mother carried me, still a newborn, to the banks of the rivers of Babylon. When, soon afterward, she ran through the wall of fire and broke through the walls of time, we were cast into the present day. In between those moments, no time at all passed in my life,

341

but decades passed in hers, as she lived and healed with the Sisters of Sarah. I was still an infant when we were reunited here.

My mother spoke the languages of those days, when she spoke at all, which correlates with that. So do her names, the Hebrew "Drorit" and the Aramaic "Aspaklarya," and the last name that we apparently took on when we arrived here: the Hebrew word "Atid," or "Future."

Knowing all this changes surprisingly little in my life. I am the same person that I always have been. I remember nothing of Judea and Babylon, since I was so young. Given that those times were apparently so hellish, that is for the best. My conscious life has been spent here in America, where I have been living for the past fifty-odd years at the usual pace. I have learned what I needed to learn, forgotten what I needed to forget, and fallen in and out of love — though in these past years with your father, I have found a love that I believe will last.

Justin and Emily: I came into your life when you were still very young, so it seems to you that I have always been here. I would love for you to always be here with me. I know that you are headed off to distant colleges, off into your own lives.

I hope that you will keep your eyes, your ears, your hearts open to whatever and whomever you encounter. And if an odd woman or man comes to you in need of help, with offers of help, or with unusual news, stay open to the possibility that a world from outside of time may be reaching out to you. He or she may be Elijah, or Daniel, or your own specific angel. Or she may be an emissary from the Sisters of Sarah, stepping out again into the modern world to spread the magic of what you may or may not choose to believe is the word of God

Fondly,

Ariel

AFTERWORD

אחרית דבר

AFTERWORD

In the time that we both lived in the Incarnation Priory, an ad-hoc interfaith intentional household in Berkeley, California, Tom Bickley said that I had "a charism for community." (I had to look the word up. It means a gift of grace or a distinct calling.) I pursued this calling through my work in creating and writing for egalitarian performance ensembles, my job turning people on to books and music at a San Francisco bookstore, the weekly dinners that I would cook at the priory, and through my writing.

I write from this desire for community. I rarely write or compose anything unless I have a clear sense of specific people who will read, hear, or perform it. I post most of what I write online in hopes that people would read, respond to, and discuss the posts.

By early 2007, I had been writing a blog at josephzitt.com for more than five years, and was looking for a new angle from which to write. While I enjoy the blog format, I had grown tired of writing about my own experiences and myself.

In January, 2007, the Toms River Multigenerational Orchestra asked me to compose a work for speaker and string orchestra based on the story of Moses. (I'll admit that I had an inside track on this unpaid commission, since the conductor is my mother.) After I worried for a week about what to write, the first few lines of a monologue came to me: "I am standing in the desert. I am standing in the desert, and a bush is burning before me. A bush is burning, and it is not consumed..." I sat down and wrote the rest of the monologue almost as quickly as I could type. Over the next few weeks, I wrote the music. The orchestra premiered the work, as planned, just before Passover.

Still, while I had tired of writing about myself, I wanted to write about emotional matters that I experienced and observed in my own life. In wondering how to do that, I remembered a story that I had heard about the author Theodore Sturgeon (as recounted by Samuel R. Delany in his introduction to Sturgeon's collection Microcosmic God). Sturgeon was upset about the political situation in the McCarthy era, but wasn't able to write anything directly about it for fear of it turning into a simple diatribe. His editor, Horace Gold, suggested a story line that seemed entirely irrelevant — but said that if he wrote that, he would safely express exactly what he thought about McCarthy.

So I decided that I would do a series of linked posts from the points of view of other people. But who would the people be?

Growing up, I had a strong Jewish education. Both my parents both taught Hebrew school, and I attended a Jewish day school through seventh grade, at which we studied the usual secular subjects in the mornings and Hebrew language and religious studies in the afternoons. I recognized the Bible as the best source of suggestions for characters that I either knew well or that I could research easily. I had a good library of Biblical legends from Jewish and other perspectives, as well as access to a wide collection of folk and scholarly resources both through libraries and online. And, if no nifty stories were to appear, I could take the fiction writer's prerogative and just make stories up.

Using the Moses monologue as a model (though it is formatted as verse, and all the other pieces except that of Asaph are formatted as prose), I chose to write a series of brief pieces from the viewpoints of different characters in the Hebrew Bible. No characters would be repeated. Each would speak one monologue, in the first person and in present tense.

Rather than making a list of people about whom I wanted to write, I decided to let chance operations choose them.

To begin each piece, I consulted a random number table, then went to the appropriate line in the Bible. The first character whose name appeared in or after that line, and about whom I hadn't already written, became the subject of the new piece. (I say "character" rather than "person" since, to my surprise, the random numbers selected God as a speaker early in the process.) I waited until I had finished each piece before discovering the subject of the next, so that I could focus on the current piece without worrying about what was to come.

The writing of the pieces fell into a surprisingly consistent rhythm. Late each Friday night or early Saturday morning, I posted a completed piece then discovered the subject of the next. I first read about the subject in the Biblical text itself, then checked Wikipedia (an unreliable source for finding anything definite, but a good pointer to better information). On Sunday and Monday, I looked into other sources, checking both the printed books to which I had access (at the bookstore at which I worked, at the Incarnation Priory at which I lived, and in both the Berkeley Public Library and, occasionally, the library of the Graduate Theological Union just up the hill from the Priory) and the incredible archive of academic literature in the online JSTOR database. By each Monday afternoon, I worried that I had no idea what I was going to write. But an idea would hit me on Tuesday morning, and on Tuesday afternoon I would write the first few sentences. The pieces came together more clearly on Wednesday and Thursday, as I wrote down more of the text and did more focused research. I wrote the rest of most pieces on Friday, usually at one of several coffee shops in Berkeley. Then I posted the completed piece, and the cycle began again.

I composed the first 38 pieces following this weekly process, taking a few weeks off over the course of the year to deal with other matters. (When taking a hiatus, I always posted a notice to the site to announce when the next piece would appear.) They were written and posted in this order:

2007:

March 31:	Moab
April 7:	Aaron
April 14:	Sichon
April 21:	Abraham
April 25:	Jonah
May 3:	Hazael
May 12:	Shadrach
May 18:	Judah
May 25:	God
June 1:	Darius
June 8:	Hezekiah
June 16:	Samuel
June 22:	Jehoiakim
June 30:	Elijah

July 6:	David
July 14:	Jacob
July 21:	Jeremiah
July 27:	Isaac
August 4:	Ahab
August 10:	Zimri
September 1:	Gideon
September 8:	Zadok
September 15:	Haggai
September 29:	Pharaoh Hophra
October 6:	Jushab-Hesed
October 13:	Belshazzar
October 19:	Ezekiel
October 27:	Nathan
November 3:	Solomon
November 10:	Asaph
November 17:	Zedekiah
November 23:	The Shulammite
December 1:	Joseph

2008:

January 5:	Asa
January 12:	Benjamin
January 19:	Jehu
January 26:	Jeroboam
February 2:	Pharaoh (of the Exodus)

At that point, I decided to switch strategies. The immediate trigger was that the chance operations selected Jezebel, and I felt that I had nothing to write for her, having written about her in the pieces on Ahab and Jehu. (I later decided that this had been a cop-out; with more thought, I was able to come up with more for her to say, and may return to her in later projects.)

I had also realized that several key people would never appear using my method, since, for example, the Wife of Cain and the Daughter of Jephthah never are given names. As story threads unexpectedly formed, the shape of the work become visible, and I saw that I needed to write pieces to fill in certain points of the history. Needing someone at the time of the great flood, for example, I wrote about Japheth; needing someone at the destruction of the First Temple, I wrote about Seraiah.

I also decided, after some uncertainty, to include the piece about Moses in the book, so his was the first of the latter set to be posted.

2008:

February 8:	Moses
February 16:	The Wife of Cain
February 29:	Japheth
March 22:	Jephthah's Daughter
March 29:	Seraiah
April 26:	Adam
October 15:	Lot

2009:

March 28:	Terach
April 10:	Serach

A fictional context for how we came to be reading these stories gradually came into view. I knew fairly quickly that they were channeled by someone named Elisheva in the first century A.D. (At first, Elisheva was to have been a potter, and I named her for a brilliant ceramics artist I had met in Berkeley named Elizabeth.) As the workings of the hidden school of prophets came into view, a context for her character developed. Toward the end of the project, I posted initial versions of Elisheva's prologue and epilogue, then, as I wrote the interludes (which were not posted online) filled in the needed pieces on Sarah and on Miriam. It was only in writing Sarah's monologue that I discovered that the school was named the Sisters of Sarah.

2009:

May 10:	Elisheva (Prologue)
May 14:	Elisheva (Epilogue)
July 17:	Sarah

2010:

January 9:	Miriam

Having Elisheva channel the stories helped deal with a central quandary in creating the text. Historical research has shown pretty conclusively that many of the stories in the Bible probably didn't happen exactly as they were told there. I had to decide whether to stick more closely to the traditional stories or to probable history. My rule of thumb became to use the stories as Elisheva might have believed them to have happened. But aspects of history, as well as of the power and fragility of storytelling, poked through, as in the story of the Wife of Cain (brought into being by the stories' need for her) and in the story of Joseph (who senses alternate versions of his life in parallel to the one that he consciously lives).

After the first edition was published, I got good feedback from people reading the book. Most wanted more context for the stories. A friend who had quite a good religious background still felt as if she had to do research in the Bible before reading them to avoid getting lost..

Recognizing that further work was needed, I created the introductions for the stories. In the course of doing so, the character of the translator, Ariel, came into being, with a backstory (told in the Transalator's Preface and Afterword) that established a reason for the added information to exist.

I also wrote several more stories, filling out some gaps in the cycle and bringing in other important voices. I published the first drafts of each on the blog site when they were done:

2011:
    March 5:   Jonathan

2012:
    October 13:   Achinoam

2013:
    January 13:   Obadiah
    May 18:   Asherah

Here are some books that I found useful or enlightening as I've been writing this project.

Albertz, Rainer. *A History of Israelite Religion in the Old Testament Period.* The Old Testament library. Louisville, KY: Westminster/John Knox Press, 1994

Bloch, Ariel A., and Chana Bloch. *The Song of Songs: A New Translation with an Introduction and Commentary.* New York: Random House, 1995.

Delany, Samuel R. *About Writing: Seven Essays, Four Letters, and Five Interviews.* Middletown, CT: Wesleyan University Press, 2005.

Friedman, Richard Elliott. *Who Wrote the Bible?* Englewood Cliffs, NJ: Prentice Hall, 1987.

Greenspahn, Frederick E. *The Hebrew Bible: New Insights and Scholarship.* Jewish studies in the 21st century. New York: New York University Press, 2008.

Heschel, Abraham Joshua. *The Prophets*. New York: Perennial, 2001.

Jewish Publication Society. *Tanakh = [Tanakh] : a New Translation of the Holy Scriptures According to the Traditional Hebrew Text*. Philadelphia: Jewish Publication Society, 1985.

Kugel, James L. *How to Read the Bible: A Guide to Scripture, Then and Now*. New York: Free Press, 2007.

Mabry, John R. *The Monster God: Coming to Terms With the Dark Side of Divinity*. Winchester, U.K.; Washington: O Books, 2008

Moyers, Bill D. *Genesis: A Living Conversation*. New York: Doubleday, 1996.

Oliveros, Pauline. *Deep Listening: A Composer's Sound Practice*. New York: iUniverse, Inc, 2005.

Rosenberg, David, and Harold Bloom. *The Book of J*. New York: Grove Weidenfeld, 1990.

Trible, Phyllis. *Texts of Terror: Literary-Feminist Readings of Biblical Narratives. Overtures to Biblical theology, 13*. Philadelphia: Fortress Press, 1984.

Zornberg, Avivah Gottlieb. *Genesis: The Beginning of Desire*. Philadelphia: Jewish Publication Society, 1995.

The Book of Voices is not quite a novel, but not quite just a short-story collection. In science fiction circles, A. E. Van Vogt referred to his similarly structured books as "fix-ups." Ray Bradbury called his *Martian Chronicles* a "half-cousin to a novel." Ursula K. Le Guin eloquently wrote (in the introduction to *The Birthday of the World*) of her stories of the Ekumen as a "story suite": " a book of stories linked by place, characters, theme, and movement, so as to form not a novel but a whole."

As I grew up, the ideas and forms of science fiction had at least as much of an impact on my inner landscapes my religious studies. I took for granted the idea that you could always ask one more question, or peek around the corner of accepted reality to wonder what was really going on. This book was heavily influenced by what are now considered classic works of science fiction, including Robert A. Heinlein's "Future History" series, the *Robots* and *Foundation* series by Isaac Asimov, Le Guin's stories of the Ekumen, Michael Moorcock's *Behold the Man*, Robert Silverberg's *Dying Inside*, just about everything by Samuel R. Delany, and the wide range of vistas imagined in the *Dangerous Visions* anthologies edited by Harlan Ellison. I have also influenced by the fan fiction that I have encountered in various media and genres, which showed me how new stories could be inserted into and wrapped around existing facts and stories, enriching the web of tales.

This book would not have been possible without the enthusiasm, erudition, and advice of friends and readers. These include

- From the community connected to the Incarnation Priory: Tom Bickley, Nancy Beckman, Mary Fuller, and Brothers Tom Schultz, Lary Pearce, and Rafael Campbell Dixon of the Order of the Holy Cross;
- From the community of Grace North Church: Fr. Richard Mapplebeckpalmer, Beth St. John, Bill Denham, and my publisher, John Mabry of The Apocryphile Press;
- From the community of staff and customers of Borders Store #57: Valerie Nance, Pam Ruane, Chelsey Stewart, Mary Anne Stein, and Yolanda Eberly;
- From the community of readers and people who commented on the developing text and other aspects of creating the book: Jane Redmont, John Cowan, Steven Hart, Claudia Crowley, Joyce Brabner, and Shoshannah Forbes;
- From the teachers who turned me on to some of the depths and exciting possibilities within Jewish texts and myths over the decades: Jacob Travis, Reverend Naftali Ungar, and, most especially, Rabbi Isaac Furman;
- and Katherine Setar and Brad Fischer, and the rest of the Cornelius Cardew Choir, who helped keep me alive and closer to sanity in difficult times than I otherwise might have been.

I look forward to a community forming that includes and expands on The Book of Voices. The stories of the Bible are available to everybody. I hope that people are inspired to look into the texts, myths, and stories, to look within the stories within themselves, to find the resonances between them, and to bring new stories to life.

Thank you for reading and becoming involved in the world of The Book of Voices.

Joseph Zitt
jzitt@josephzitt.com
August 2010, revised July 2013

ABOUT THE AUTHOR

Joseph Zitt has written about musical improvisation, Jewish mysticism, customer service, and what happens around a church at midnight, in books including *Shekhinah: the Presence* and *The Rounds* (both from The Apocryphile Press), *19th Nervous Breakdown: Making Human Connections in the Landscape of Commerce,* and *Surprise Me with Beauty: the Music of Human Systems.* He has created performances and music in a wide range of media, many of which can be downloaded from his Web site, www.josephzitt.com. After careers as a technical writer, programmer, and bookseller, he is studying Media Arts near Cleveland, Ohio.